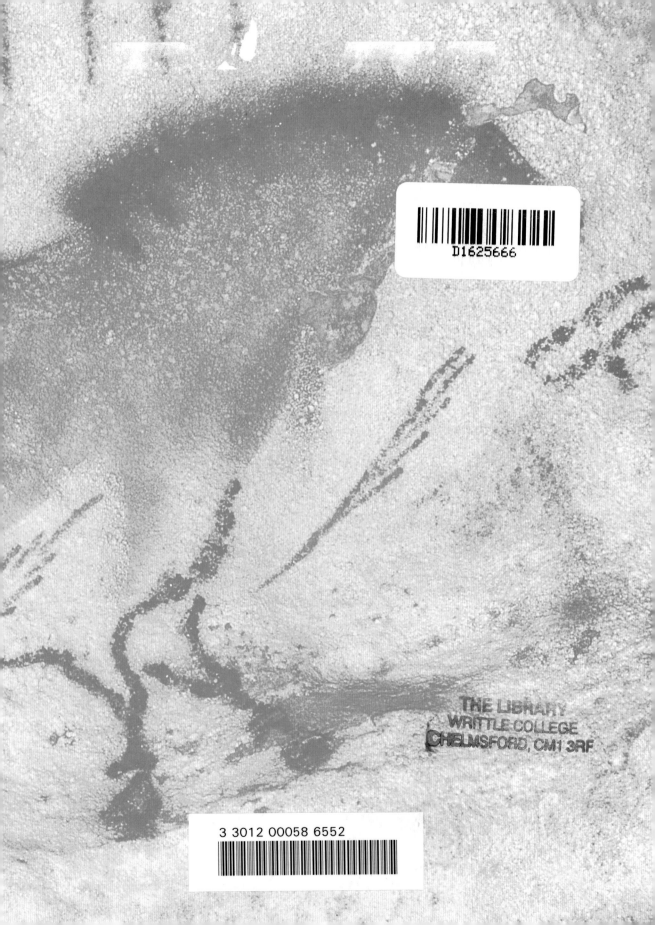

A HISTORY
OF THE
HORSE

A HISTORY OF THE HORSE

VOLUME I

The Iberian Horse from Ice Age to Antiquity

PAULO GAVIÃO GONZAGA

J. A. ALLEN

ISBN 0 85131 867 3

J. A. Allen
Clerkenwell House
Clerkenwell Green
London EC1R 0HT

J. A. Allen is an imprint of Robert Hale Limited

British Library Cataloguing in Publication Data
A catalogue record for this book is available from the British Library

Edited by Elizabeth O'Beirne-Ranelagh
Design and Typesetting by Paul Saunders
Maps and diagrams by Rodney Paull
Drawings on pages 27, 29, 30, 31 by Maggie Raynor

Colour separation by Tenon & Polert Colour Scanning Limited, Hong Kong
Printed by New Era Printing Company Ltd.

To my wife Estherzinha

CONTENTS

LIST OF ILLUSTRATIONS

FOREWORD

PAULO GAVIÃO GONZAGA is the largest breeder of Lusitano horses in the world today, with more than 300 mares on his Brazilian stud. He is not only the largest breeder, but also one of the best, with mares from some of the top Portuguese studs: Veiga, Andrade, Coimbra, Núncio, the National Stud and my own breeding. Naturally interested in the origins of the Lusitano horse, he has undertaken extensive research into its roots, collecting an immense amount of information concerning the birth of equitation.

This work examines the subject of the Iberian horse's origins in a new light, correcting and explaining with full, historically-based arguments an issue which has often been misunderstood. For a long time we have been impressed by the obvious similarities between the following types of horse:

- the ancient Turkoman and Persian horse;
- the old sculptures in terra-cotta made by the Chinese;
- the horses still existing in North Afghanistan;
- the Libyan and Moroccan Barb;
- the Iberian horse engraved and painted in prehistoric times and still seen today in Portugal.

In this fascinating book these enigmas are thoroughly and clearly discussed. The author explains the existence of two types of light 'hot-blooded' horse around the Black Sea, the Caspian Sea and the Mediter-ranean. One is the ancestor of the modern Arabian Horse; the other is the ancestor of the Turkoman, Berber and Iberian Horse. Both gave rise to the English Thoroughbred and have contributed to all the modern Warm Blood riding horses.

This book also contests the old theories which suggest that the light 'quality' horse came to Iberia via Africa. It shows the presence 'since the most distant pre-historic times' of such a horse in Iberia and its very early domestication. 'Equitation may have been born in Portugal and spread from here to the rest of Europe.'

Plato, the fifth century BC Greek philospher, wrote about the existence of an ancient civilization, predating Egypt's splendour, beyond the Pillars of Hercules (Strait of Gibraltar), the legendary Atlantis. He describes the tradition in which the kings pursued wild bulls, driving them to the centre of the city where they were killed and sacrificed to the gods. In Portugal, bullfighting on horseback followed by immobilizing the wild bull by hand is a clear survival of Plato's testimony. It confirms the very ancient use of the horse in Iberia with a high level of equitation.

At the end of the last ice age, in the Upper Palaeolithic, the largest density of megalithic monuments (and also the oldest ones) was found in Atlantic Iberia. This megalithic culture expanded to the north of Europe after that time, producing the last stone monuments in Britanny, Germany and Great Britain (Stonehenge). The megalithic dolmens and menhirs anticipated the pyramids and obelisks of later Mesopotamian and Egyptian civilizations. The stone *alabard*, found in Iberia, is proof of the use of cavalry ever since the Stone Age.

In the Iron Age, we find engravings and paintings on funerary ceramic ware in Iberia, showing warriors riding light horses with convex profiles, and using long, light, wooden spears with an equal iron weight at both ends. These were held at the point of balance in the middle of the spear, allowing rapid offensive and defensive movements. This was the consequence of a long period of evolution in equitation, using a high quality horse, that allowed the rider to stop and start at lightning speed and turn with cat-like agility. As a result of this evolution, the horse developed a courageous personality, but is always gentle and willing to follow the subtlest hints from its rider, thus creating the Greek myth of the centaur.

Arsênio Raposo Cordeiro

President of the International Lusitano Breed Council

ACKNOWLEDGEMENTS

THE FINAL AND MOST gratifying job in bringing the writing of a book to its ultimate end is the acknowledgement of all the cooperation, help and stimulus received from so many friends during its preparation.

My deepest gratitude goes to Arsênio Raposo Cordeiro, who was always available for consultation and graciously opened all his archives, books and photographs to me, providing all kinds of information and contacts necessary for the completion of this work. Arsênio, together with the Andrades, Dr Ruy and Eng°. Fernando Sommer, form a trio of the most respected authorities on the Iberian horse. It is virtually impossible to write anything about the Lusitano, ancient or modern, without using their work. I want to thank Arsênio Cordeiro and Sra Maria de Sommer d'Andrade for authorizing the reproduction of so many illustrations that form the basic structure of my work. I must also acknowledge the precious assistance given to me by Dr João Costa Ferreira, director of Coudelaria de Alter, who supplied so many of the photographs used here. Other sources are acknowledged at the end of this book.

Needless to say, all thoughts, ideas and theories advanced here are entirely my own responsibility.

A very special and important mention must be made to express my most sincere and enormous indebtedness to Elizabeth O'Beirne-Ranelagh. Those who have gone through the intoxicating experience of writing in a foreign language – even that most friendly of languages, English – know how difficult and frustrating it can be to try to express oneself properly in other than one's mother tongue, the agony of not being able to find the correct words and the nightmare of being constantly afraid of making grammatical and other stylistic mistakes. I was relieved of this torment by the most competent text revision done by Elizabeth. Without her, this book would never have seen the light of day. I must also express my gratitude to my publishers, J. A. Allen, in the person of Caroline Burt who accepted the risk of publishing this work and participated in the effort of putting it all together, and to Paul Saunders, who so competently designed the layout of this book.

To all these and many other friends not mentioned here I can only say Muito Obrigado!

Paulo Gavião Gonzaga

Chapter One

INTRODUCTION

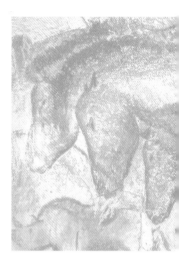

THIS BOOK PAINTS IN BROAD brush strokes the overall picture of the history of the horse in Eurasia and North Africa. It attempts to answer a number of questions and hopes to correct some wrong assumptions, the majority of which are born from hasty generalizations and distort the true story of the Iberian horse, a story virtually unknown even amongst aficionados of equine history. These questions cannot be properly addressed, nor a convincing case presented, without knowledge – even if superficial – of the prehistory of Europe and in particular of the Iberian Peninsula, the easel on which this multi-layered painting was created over millions of years.

Much of the specialized literature dedicated to European prehistory refers to specific studies with limited remits, either encompassing restricted geographical zones or focussing from a cultural, ecological or socio-economic point of view only on certain areas.

The overwhelming majority of published work on ancient equine history is for obvious reasons based on the Middle Eastern experience. This is the source of what we know about ancient civilizations which – after the nomadic horsemen – were the first organized societies to use the horse and the first communities to leave written accounts about the role played by horses in their lives. From these sources we learn something about the nomadic horsemen from the steppes, the main suppliers of domesticated animals. No contemporaneous documents exist from Europe north or west of Greece. This dearth of information about the western world has led to the serious risk of errors arising from undue generalizations: the

1.1 Horses and bulls painted in black. From the 'Rotunda' cave at Lascaux, France, c. 15,000 BC.

unacceptable extension of facts, tendencies or phenomena, verified in one region, to others near or far, where in fact such events did not take place at all, or came about with less intensity and at a later time. Unfortunately, there is a paucity of literature on Iberian archaeology, compared with the abundant studies on the rest of Eurasia. Probably for that reason, the generalization trap has caught a great number of authors, with such errors appearing in many texts on Iberian prehistory; for example, the Peninsula is included in ecological, historical or cultural cycles that occurred contemporaneously north of the Pyrenees, but whose impact was small or irrelevant in Portugal or Spain. On the other hand, cultural and economic changes that began in other parts of Eurasia but had important consequences in Iberia are often underestimated or totally forgotten.

Geographically speaking, the Iberian Peninsula is an appendage of Europe, connected but at the same time separated from the continent by the Cantabrian and the Pyrenean mountain ranges. These mountains isolate it from the environmental conditions prevailing on the rest of the continent, creating a completely different ecology and a climate more favourable to the long-term survival of fauna and flora during the ice ages. For this and other reasons, the behaviour of the biota there has always differed from the rest of Europe.

Ancestral horses, from evolution to 6000 BC

It is known for certain that the genus *Equus* evolved in North America, arriving in Eurasia during the Final Pliocene, between 2 and 5 million years ago. How many separate families of wild horse arose here is still a controversial question, and the object of endless and heated debates amongst specialists. The most widespread theory is Ebhardt's,[1] which distinguishes four primitive origins. This school of thought is known as 'pluri-phyletic', or of multiple origins, as opposed to the 'mono-phyletics' who accept only a single wild ancestor for all modern equines. Ebhardt's classification considers four 'Types' (I to IV) of ancestral horse: I – the northern pony (*Equus ferus*), II – the great northern horse (*Equus woldrichii*), III - the Eurasian horse (*Equus germanicus*), and IV – the Asian horse (*Equus lybicus*) (see Chapter 2).

A more modern theory, proposed by Uerpmann,[2] classifies Eurasian wild horses into four geographically separated sub-species: (1) *Equus ferus ferus,* the steppe horse; (2) *Equus ferus sylvestris,* the northern European forest horse; (3) *Equus ferus lusitanicus,* the Iberian horse and (4) *Equus ferus scynthicus,* the horse from the Black Sea. This diverging classification, if accepted, would explain not only the abundance of equines in Iberia, but would also support the thesis that equitation – the art of horse riding – was born in the Peninsula and spread from there to the rest of Europe.

The discussion of whether or not the Iberian Horse is an ancestral type is, however, irrelevant to this book, its conclusions being valid whatever his origin (Fig. 1.2). What is affirmed here is that horses have lived continuously in the Iberian Peninsula since the Pleistocene (2 million years ago), and the evidence for this is conclusive.

The existence of two broad types of horse, one heavy and another refined, is a constant from the Palaeolithic to historical times in all Eurasia (Fig. 1.3). It is possible to consider Ebhardt's types I and II as coarse animals and types III and IV as forming a more delicate, refined class (Fig.1.4).

No archaeological evidence is older than the depiction of wild horses in the cave and rock art of Iberia (Fig. 1.5). These wild horses would certainly have crossed with others, such as the horse from Solutré that roamed in the south of France, and other indigenous ones living in southern Iberia. It

1.2 The Spanish horse, as depicted by Baron Eisenberg, the seventeenth-century equestrian author, in his book *L'Art de monter à cheval ou Description du ménage moderne dans sa perfection*. See opposite page for translation of his description.

LE CHEVAL D'ESPAGNE.   1

L'EXPERIENCE a suffisamment fait connoître, que le CHEVAL D'ESPAGNE est sans contredit de tous les Chevaux du monde le plus parfait pour le Manége, non seulement par rapport à sa taille, qui est très-belle, mais aussi en ce qu'il est dispos, vigoureux & docile; de sorte que tout ce qu'on lui enseigne avec raison & patience, il le comprend & l'exécute avec la derniere justesse. Quant à sa beauté, on peut voir dans la figure vis-à-vis, qu'il a la Tête légere, mince, décharnée & sans ganaches; les Oreilles petites & bien placées; les Yeux grands & vifs; les Naseaux ouverts pour respirer & s'ébrouer aisément; l'Encolure souple & bien rélevée; la Criniere fine & étroite; le Poitrail assez large, & les Epaules libres; les Jambes de devant très-bien faites, c'est-à-dire le bras charnu, le genouil large & le canon droit, où l'on voit les nerfs nets & détachez, le boulet large, le paturon rond & court, ce qu'on appelle bien-jointe, & le pied, ou le sabot, assez pourvû de corne. Son corsage est le plus beau qu'on puisse voir, & son dos semble fait exprès pour y mettre la selle, parce que le garot est haut, & les épaules peu chargées. Il a les Reins bons & la Croupe très-bien formée; la Queuë belle & garnie, & attachée de telle sorte, qu'en maniant, il la porte toûjours en panache, ce qui lui donne un grand air: les Hanches si souples, qu'il s'assied dessus, les Cuisses fournies & proportionnées à la rondeur de la Croupe; les Jarrets bons & faits pour les pouvoir plier & se soutenir, comme aussi généralement le reste des jambes de derriere. En un mot, il semble que la Nature l'ait fait exprès pour le Manége: & véritablement il n'y en a point qui le surpassent en cœur, en magnanimité, ni en feu.

A

is interesting to note that the types represented in the Altamira caves in northern Spain (the *garrano* or pony type) and the ones depicted in the Escoural cave in southern Portugal (more like the Lusitano we know today) indicate different natural evolutions and consequently also different crossings.

It is possible to distinguish five important migrations of prehistoric horses:

(1) The first is the migration that took place at the end of the last Ice Age, about 10,000 years ago during the Mesolithic, when wild horses were forced to move eastwards by the forests that recolonized the pasturelands of southwestern and central Europe. This is the only true migration, with whole populations of horses abandoning their habitats to move to new ones in eastern Europe and western Asia. It is possible that, as part of this exodus, some of these horses moved south, joining the indigenous horses which survived in the Iberian Peninsula during the Ice Ages. The inclusion of Iberia in the Mesolithic extinctions of European horses is an example of the dangers mentioned above of making generalizations apply to all areas.

(2) The second migration, during the Neolithic, was part of the so-called 'Asia Minor ('Neolithic', 'Agriculture' or 'Traction') Package' that took place in the opposite direction, from east to west, with the diffusion of agriculture (4500–2500 BC). It lasted longer, was less concentrated than the first movement, and did not have the same impact everywhere. In the more remote regions, such as Iberia, there was vigorous indigenous

1.3 *Translation* 'Experience has made it well known that, without doubt, the Spanish Horse is the best horse in the world for equitation, not only because of his shape, which is very beautiful, but also because of his disposition, vigorous and docile; such that everything he is taught with intelligence and patience he understands and executes perfectly. As to beauty, it can be seen from the picture that he has a light head, lean, dry and without a pronounced lower jaw; small and well-set ears; big, expressive eyes; open nostrils for easy breathing and snorting; a supple neck held high; a fine, sparse mane; a rather wide chest and free shoulders; front legs very well made, in other words fleshy forearms, wide knees and straight cannons with clean, detached tendons; wide fetlocks, round, short pasterns, known as well-jointed, and the feet, or hooves, with good horn. His coat is the most beautiful that can be seen, and his back seems expressly made for a saddle, because his withers are high and shoulders light. He has good loins and a very well-shaped croup; a beautiful and full tail set on in such a way that he always carries it with panache, giving him an impressive air: his haunches are so flexible that he sits upon them, his thighs strong and in proportion with the roundness of the croup; his hocks good and made to bend and support him, and the same in general of the rest of the hind leg. In a single word, it seems that Nature made him expressly for equitation: and in truth there is none that surpasses him in heart, magnanimity or spirit.'

1.3 Chart of man's development in Europe to AD 1000.

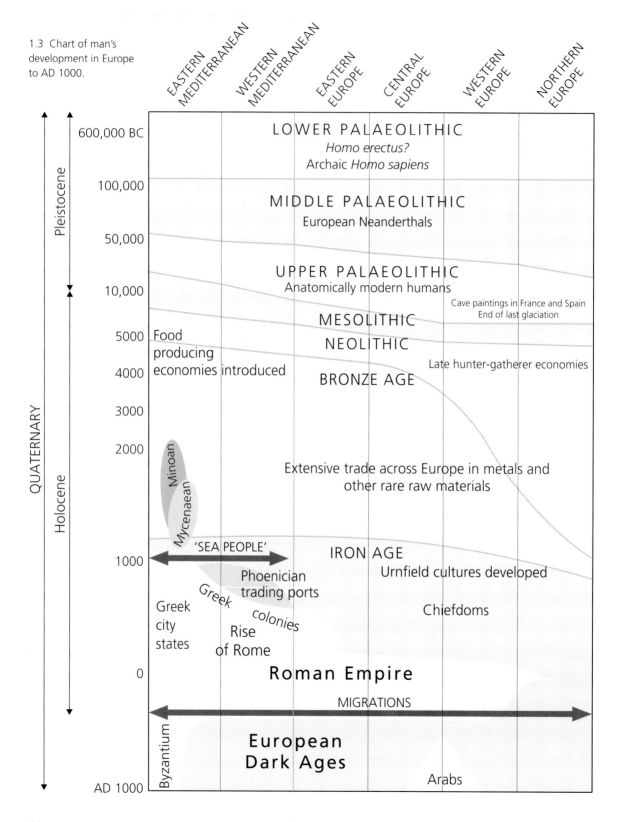

EASTERN MEDITERRANEAN | WESTERN MEDITERRANEAN | EASTERN EUROPE | CENTRAL EUROPE | WESTERN EUROPE | NORTHERN EUROPE

QUATERNARY

Pleistocene

Holocene

600,000 BC

LOWER PALAEOLITHIC
Homo erectus?
Archaic *Homo sapiens*

100,000

MIDDLE PALAEOLITHIC
European Neanderthals

50,000

UPPER PALAEOLITHIC
Anatomically modern humans

10,000

Cave paintings in France and Spain
End of last glaciation

MESOLITHIC

5000   Food producing economies introduced

NEOLITHIC

4000

Late hunter-gatherer economies

BRONZE AGE

3000

2000

Minoan
Mycenaean

Extensive trade across Europe in metals and other rare raw materials

'SEA PEOPLE'

1000

IRON AGE
Urnfield cultures developed

Greek
Phoenician trading ports
colonies

Greek city states
Rise of Rome

Chiefdoms

0

Roman Empire

MIGRATIONS

Byzantium

European Dark Ages

Arabs

AD 1000

resistance to the values and techniques of the new agriculture, with only selected components of the package of innovations being absorbed by the local population. In armed conflicts involving cavalry and chariots (the latter being conspicuously absent in western Europe), resistance could only succeed if the locals already had some basic knowledge of domesticated horses and so could oppose the invaders that deployed them. These arguments help to dispel the idea that equitation arrived in Iberia with Neolithic agriculturalists and reinforce the opinion that equitation was either locally developed or already introduced by agents other than this first agriculturalist group.

(3) Around 3000 BC, the so-called 'Battle-Axe' peoples, Indo-Europeans from southern Russia, invaded eastern Europe, the Pontic-Caspian region and Asia Minor. They are considered by some authors as the agents responsible for the diffusion of equitation and 'horses of quality' across all these regions. The intimate association between the Indo-Europeans and the horse is very impressive, making it the emblematic animal of these peoples. Linguistic studies definitively prove through the root *ekwos* the deep penetration of the domesticated horse into the lives of all the peoples who spoke Indo-European languages, in other words the 'large geographical arch' that reaches from the Atlantic to India.[3]

(4) Later on, circa 2500 BC, came the 'Bell-Beaker' phenomenon. It is believed that these peoples started from Portugal and, following the Atlantic coast, reached the British Isles and Germany; and that from there, they went up the Rhine as far as the valley of the Danube. On their way north they were responsible for the spread of equitation, well established in Iberia, as well as of the 'horses of quality' on which they rode. On their return, in the so-called 'Reflux', they may have brought back to Iberia new riding techniques and horses of eastern origin, as well as crosses between the two strains.

(5) Finally, horses and chariots were introduced by Indo-Europeans into Asia Minor during the third millennium and, from there, taken to Egypt by the conquering Hyksos in 1750 BC. Cavalry first appeared as a war weapon around 1200 BC when the so-called 'Sea Peoples' destroyed the ancient Minoan and Mycenean civilizations as well as those of Asia Minor. These sea raiders took horses to Libya, from where they intended to invade Egypt, only to be beaten by Ramses III. How far west these 'Sea

1.4 Quality horse (bottom) and heavy horse (right and top)
from the cave at Trois Frères, Ariège, France, c. 12,000 BC.

Peoples' went is still unknown; however, ceramics and other artefacts of Asiatic origin, dating from this same period, were found in Iberia, leading many authors to consider that these peoples might also have introduced agriculture and the ridden horse into the Peninsula, many centuries before the Greek and Phoenician colonization.

Keeping in mind the amount of transhumance in prehistoric times caused by human actions or by glaciers, it is obvious, with all these primitive horse types living in the same or neighbouring areas at the same time, that cross-breeding amongst them would have been frequent. This led not only to the formation of other derived types but also to morphological variations within each group, according to the climatic conditions of the breeding areas and the degree of contact with other primitive groups. Consequently, there is no sharp division differentiating these groups as isolated breeds, but rather a gradation, with the extremes exhibiting pure characteristics of a particular ancestral type and an intermediate mass composed of animals with characteristics inherited from more than one primitive ancestral type. This is the only possible explanation for the similarities evident between, for example, the Turkoman and the Iberian horse, both indigenous strains of 'horses of quality' that were formed at the opposite extremes of the vast tract of land separating Iberia from Central Asia.

Except in the case of the first migration, there were no large movements of whole populations of horses, but only of groups of domesticated animals of varying numbers; probably more numerous when coming by the land routes than when arriving by sea. Estimations of the number of migrating animals and the influence they had upon the indigenous equine populations are pure guesswork. It is possible, however, to put forward some hypotheses: (1) considering the many destinations and the obstacles en route, it is safe to assume that invading herds were not extensive compared to the local populations; (2) horses are not predators and when rival groups meet, the worst that can happen is that stallions fight, resulting in the stronger one taking over the leadership of the group with the expulsion or death of the defeated contender. If the invading stallion wins, new blood will be injected into the indigenous population and, although at first the mares of his original group will produce some stock of pure blood, after a couple of generations indiscriminate crossing would end all distinctions, with the much larger local herd assimilating and dominating the foreign blood.

1.5 Côa Valley, Portugal, c. 30,000 BC. Rock art depicting three horses, possibly one a stallion covering a mare.

This was the case with all the migrations into the Iberian Peninsula: a large number of horses may have come in each time, but always met with a much larger local population. Not only were the foreign strains absorbed but also the indigenous herds offered a generous supply of new animals to the arriving horsemen, who thus exported Iberian blood to other countries.

Contrary to what was until recently the accepted understanding, horses were initially domesticated for meat, later for riding and finally for traction, and not in the reverse order – traction followed by equitation. The predominant opinion is that all these phases of domestication were initiated on the borders of the Black Sea. The introduction of these innovations into Europe, when and by whom, is still debatable. We have accepted the theory of a 'demic [demotic] diffusion' from the east, together with agriculture, i.e. peoples and their cultures invading new areas. The invention of the sail in the Aegean was contemporary with that diffusion, giving broader horizons to navigation in the Mediterranean. The transportation of horses aboard ship had been practised since around 1200 BC, and the introduction of sailing boats may have created new maritime routes, facilitating the spread of equitation all over the coasts of western and southern Europe.

There is much discussion about the possible route of *Equus* from North America to Iberia. They reached Asia via land bridges from America, and may then either have traversed Europe and crossed the Pyrenees, or entered Africa from the east and crossed the Strait of Gibralter. It does not make sense to suppose that horses may, at any time, have swum across the Strait of Gibraltar, which separated Europe from Africa even at the glacial maximum. In the following chapters we strongly refute this suggested route and present substantial evidence in support of the theory that horses went from Iberia to North Africa as domesticated animals during the Neolithic. There is absolutely no evidence attesting to the existence of horses in North Africa before the Hyksos' invasion in the second millennium BC. The peoples of the Maghrib and the Sahara have been subjected to intense Iberian cultural influence at least since the 'Bell-Beaker' period (see Chapter 6); we can assume that ridden horses were included in cultural exchanges. Much later, horses from Egypt and Libya joined that equine population and, from cross-breeding, the Berber or Barb horse was formed (Fig.1.6). All this explains the similarities between the Iberian and the Barb, no doubt strengthened during the Punic and Roman presences in Iberia.

The techniques of traction and equitation were responsible for a social, economic and political upheaval whose consequences are still felt today.

1.6 The Barb horse, as depicted by Baron Eisenberg in his *L'Art de monter à cheval* (1759), together with description.

LE CHEVAL BARBE.   2

APRES le Cheval d'Espagne, vient le BARBE, qui est aussi très-propre pour le Manége, quoique généralement plus petit, n'ayant ni tant de force, ni tant de brillant dans son air, ni tant de liberté dans les épaules. Avec tout cela il ne manque pas de ressources, ayant de bonnes hanches, & une grande gentillesse dans sa maniere de manier, particuliere-ment sur la Volte; son Terre-à-terre est un des plus beaux de tous les Chevaux du monde, & par la souplesse de ses han-ches, il donne beaucoup de plaisir au Cavalier en le travaillant, parce qu'il est extrêmement docile & de bonne mémoire. Ainsi il est facile à dresser, pourvû que ce soit avec douceur & discrétion, & des aides fines; mais point du tout par la ri-gueur, ou par de longues leçons, qui rebutent sa bonne volonté, ou étouffent son humeur, la meilleure en effet de tous les Chevaux du monde.

1.6 *Translation* 'After the Spanish Horse, comes the Barb, which is also very good for equitation, although usually smaller, not as strong, lacking the same brilliance in his bearing, and not so free in his shoulders. Even so, he does not lack quality, having good thighs and a great gracefulness at work, especially in his turns; his *Terre-à-terre* is one of the most beautiful amongst all horses in the world, and the suppleness of his haunches gives a lot of pleasure to his rider during its execution, because his is extremely docile and has a good memory. Therefore he is easy to train, as long as it is done with kindness and discretion, and with delicate aids; but never with harshness, or long lessons, which wear out his good will, or stifle his disposition, which is in fact the best among all horses in the world.'

Transport and communications were greatly improved by the ridden horse as well as by maritime and fluvial navigation, increasing the mobility of human groups and extending commercial transactions. Imbedded in these changes was what was to become the most important activity of the following millennia: war, the process that has shaped the world into its political, economic, cultural and religious divisions from the historical period up to the present day. The horse was undoubtedly the main agent of this process.

Transportation, agriculture, war and the apparatus of power engendered the genetic selection methods that resulted in the breeding of larger, stronger horses, better fitted to the new demands of war and utility. These improved animals, no matter where they appeared, represented a technological advance, a military superiority which in most instances signified for their owners victory on the battlefield and domination over others. In the process genetically improved animals were disseminated so that a new uniformity was rapidly achieved, only to be destabilized again by the next improving invasion, and so on in a chain of events that allowed these innovations to be transmitted rapidly over a wide area.

The experience acquired in Central Asia over many centuries of driving and riding resulted in the establishment of a number of famous horse-breeding centres, such as Bactria, Ferghana, China and Turkomania (Fig. 1.7), countries that produced some of the most renowned 'quality horses' of antiquity. Bactrian horses were taken to Libya by the Cretans who founded Cyrene in 630 BC; this Greek colony became one of the most important breeding centres of the first millennium, supplying Greece, Asia Minor and Africa with 'quality horses'. Commercial relations between Cyrene and Iberia existed at that time.

A further misapprehension plaguing most equine literature is the assumption that the role of the chariot in the ancient civilizations of the Aegean, Asia Minor and Egypt was similar in other epochs and places. The use of the chariot in war at this time was confined to the Middle East. The more sophisticated city-states that succeeded the Middle Eastern civilizations and appeared in Europe were born after the 'Great Catastrophe' (see Chapter 6) and the final days of chariotry, which was replaced by cavalry as the main arbiter of battle. In other words, the war horse was not adopted by Iron Age societies until his use had become, so to speak, more democratic, with cavalry troops replacing the chariot which had been a vehicle of privilege reserved for the exclusive use of the aristocracy and elite of the

1.7 The Turkish horse, as depicted and described by Baron Eisenberg in *L'Art de monter à cheval* (1759).

LE CHEVAL TURC.   6

J'AI vû beaucoup de Chevaux Turcs qui étoient très-beaux & très-grands , principalement ceux qui viennent de Babylone, où le Grand Seigneur a des Haras qui ont été très-bien faits. Ces Chevaux font vifs & fringans , ils trottent avec vigueur; leur galop eft affez brillant, & leur partir très-prompt; ils font courageux & même intrépides dans l'occafion : c'eft dommage feulement qu'on ne peut pas les avoir jeunes , comme les autres Chevaux , pour leur placer la tête de bonne-heure ; car tous ceux qui font montez par des Turcs battent à la main , & font de terribles grimaces de la bouche ; parce que les Mords dont fe fervent les Turcs, font mal faits , & les rendent durs & défagréables à la main. Cependant j'en ai vû quelques-uns, montez par d'habiles gens, qui étoient fort bien bridez, & qui portoient la tête auffi ferme, & avoient l'appui auffi agréable qu'aucun Cheval d'Efpagne. La faute n'eft donc pas de leur côté , mais de ceux qui ne fçavent pas les brider.

1.7 *Translation* 'I have seen many Turkish Horses which were very big and beautiful, mainly those from Babylon, where the Grand Seigneurs had very good studs. These horses are lively and mettlesome, with a strong trot; their gallop is brilliant, and they take off very quickly; they are courageous and even fearless on occasion: it is just a shame that they cannot be obtained young, like other horses, so as to train them to carry their heads correctly; because all those ridden by Turks pull against the hand and make terrible movements with the mouth; because the bits which the Turks use are badly made and make them hard and disagreeable to the hand. Nonetheless I have seen some, ridden by capable horsemen, which bridle well and carry the head quite still, and take a contact as well as any Spanish horse. The fault is not theirs, but those who do not know how to bridle them.

old Oriental civilizations. The Iron Age environment was socially, culturally, economically and militarily very different. Different too were the processes developed to breed and train the new lighter, more refined cavalry horses and supply them to their new masters.

The much larger territory occupied by horse users in the Iron Age – from China to Iberia – combined with the increase in the numbers of horses was also an agent for change. It is important to keep in mind the similarities and differences that existed at the two extremes of the horse world of the Iron Age: Iberia and the Mongolian steppes, a vast tract of land interrupted by the territory of the Pontic-Caspian 'quality horse'. These areas had in common a relatively underdeveloped culture, good horses, and the knowledge of equitation and cavalry tactics, factors that made them fierce enemies for all who met them in war. They also developed efficient 'quality' (Pontic and Iberian) or coarse (Mongolian) horse-breeding programmes and supplied both animals and mercenaries to other richer, more powerful countries and empires. The differences between them were the physical environment itself: flat, cold, dry, semi-desert steppes in the east, where only very tough men and horses could survive, compared with the mountainous, fertile, gentle, warmer, more humid climate allowing better feeding and living conditions in the central (Pontic) area and in the west. The geopolitical differences were also great: the steppes were open country, continuously subject to frequent invasions and the domino effect of one people displacing their neighbours who in turn invaded others, and so on in endless succession, whereas the Iberian Peninsula was a *finis terra* protected all around by mountains and sea. While the steppe tribes often had to leave their countries in search of food, or were pushed out by other tribes moving in on them with the same motive, the Iberian peoples never had to leave their homeland, always rich in water and food. If attacked by neighbours or other enemies, victors and losers would continue to live side by side in a new power hierarchy.

The result of all this was that horsemen from the steppes developed a culture of raid, an appetite for pillage and a horse that could serve them all

1.8 A typical Assyrian light chariot with six-spoked wheels, drawn by three richly caparisoned horses and carrying three warriors. King Ashurnasirpal on campaign (Assyrian wall art from Nimrud, the north-west palace, 9th century BC).

1.9 A set of Iberian funerary vases decorated with horses' heads, dating from the Iron Age and revealing the horse cult of the local population.

through their hardships: a tough, resilient, reliable and trusty companion that they never abandoned. Besides serving his master as mount or draught animal, the horse was a source of nourishment, furnishing milk and meat, and his hide and hairs provided raw material for tents and harnesses. In fact, when meeting the elegant saddle horses of the Pontic-Caspian region, the Huns and other nomads rarely exchanged their ugly beasts for these more refined but less hardy mounts, because with no permanent home they were always on the move, and had to be prepared for sudden retreat to wild landscapes where the finer horses would not survive.

In Iberia, on the contrary, cavalries and men had roots. They did not have to travel great distances over unfriendly, harsh landscapes, but could live and fight around their homelands. Cavalry tactics, unaffected by any previous chariot warfare experience, were developed to win bouts of individual combat, horseman against horseman, or horseman against infantry in direct fighting or harassment. The objective was to conquer or defend country or positions, not pillage or raid without territorial ambitions. For this the horse had to be fast, flexible, courageous and easy to ride.

Notwithstanding these differences, however, in both cases the warrior's life was entirely dependent on his horse's abilities to take him into the *mêlée* and to extricate him safely and rapidly from battle. The tactics of both cavalries were also very similar, consisting of a surprise attack followed by a hasty retreat, encouraging the enemy's pursuit only to turn around and attack or ambush him after he had, in hot pursuit, gone far enough from his camp or companions. The weapons, however, were different: steppe horsemen used the composite bow whereas the Iberian warrior rode with javelin, swords and spear. Dressage, as it was known in the classical world, was probably born from these military exercises.

However, the most significant difference between the Iberian and other horses was created by the selection over thousands of years of horses fit for *gineta* combat, the typical Lusitanian war tactic (see Chapter 8). As Ruy d'Andrade very properly observes:

> The Iberian warrior with his Iberian horse created the *gineta* and the *gineta* in turn formed the Iberian horse – not, as many people think, the Moors, the Arabs or sapient equitation. Sapient are they, our horses, since the beginning and we, the Iberians who since the origin of equitation formed ourselves thus.[4]

1.10 Head of a quality Iberian horse, detail of the decoration on one of the Iron Age funerary vases shown in Fig. 1.9.

Historical period, from 2000 BC

The picture described above was to be profoundly altered during the historical period. Wars, raids and invasions became the dominant activity of Roman times, and the horse the most powerful weapon. Large cavalry contingents of all nationalities were transported all over the Empire and on to its boundaries, increasing cross-breeding and diminishing once again the differences between the horse types.

Most of what we know about the historical period in Iberia is from the Classics, literary texts of supreme poetic beauty but often lacking in scientific or factual accuracy. They are, however, the only written source of information, some of it extremely valuable, notwithstanding some mythological or artistic licence. More reliable can be the coins, sculptures and other artefacts which can be correctly dated by modern scientific methods.

By the end of the second millennium BC, the Urnfield culture, probably introduced by the Scythians, a horse-people who invaded the Danube valley, was born in Europe. In the eighth century BC, the Hallstatt culture, derived from the Urnfield culture and believed to be the cradle of the Celts, appeared in Germany. These fighting horsemen did not have territorial ambitions, but made raid and pillage their main objective. Defeating other peoples and invading their countries, the Celts were important agents in the dissemination of many new cultural values, particularly martial arts and equitation. From the Celts the Gauls and other Barbarians were descended, terrible enemies and future auxiliaries of the Romans.

In southern Iberia, also around the eighth century, the Tartessian culture took over from the Cynesians, or Cynetes. Herodotus writes about the Cynesians, a people living at the western end of Europe. The name of this culture, according to some authors, came from the Greek *gymnétes* which means mounted warrior. From the Tartessians came the Iberian culture, which extended from southern Iberia to France, and from the contacts of the Iberians with the northern Celts were born the Celtiberians of the Meseta and the Lusitanos of Portugal – both horse cultures. This was the picture that the Greeks, Phoenicians, Carthaginians and later Romans faced in the Iberian Peninsula. The first three of these founded many commercial outposts both in the Mediterranean and on the Atlantic coasts and were responsible for the 'orientalizing' period of Iberia. All these cultures from Iberia were typified by mounted warriors, who fought with great efficiency on horseback, having supplied mercenary cavalries to Romans and Carthaginians during the Punic Wars. It is also certain that the Phoenicians and Carthaginians transported horses from Iberia to Africa and Asia, and introduced prestige chariots from Asia into Spain.

In other words, there was a very active circulation of horses connecting the more important breeding areas, such as the Pontic-Caspian, North Africa and Iberia, with each other and with intermediate neighbouring areas such as Gaul, Italy, Macedonia and Greece. Although each movement involved a limited number of animals – perhaps a few thousand – thus not having much effect individually, their repetition over the millennia may have ended up by introducing noticeable blood relationships between the breeds.

The themes outlined in this chapter will be discussed in detail in the following pages, other than the historical period which is the subject of the second volume of this work. First, however, we will examine more closely the evolution of the horse and the different types that existed in Europe.

1.11 Carthaginian gold coin, 350-320 BC, probably representing a Berber horse from North Africa.

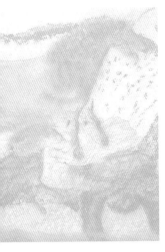

Chapter Two

HORSES – ANCESTRAL, WILD AND DOMESTICATED: AN OVERVIEW

THE EVOLUTION OF THE HORSE

It is not the objective of this work to explore the history and origins of the genus *Equus* and its various intermediate forms and species until the modern horse made its appearance in the Miocene, around 15 million years ago. There follows only a brief summary of that long and dramatic evolution so as to provide a framework for discussing the ancestral and wild horses of the past (Fig. 2.1).

The *Perissodactyla* (odd-toed ungulates) came from the early Eocene, 55 million years ago: the first representative of the family was the little *Hyracotherium*. In the middle Eocene, some 46 million years ago, came the genera *Orohippus* and *Eohippus*. In the Oligocene, about 38 million years ago, the subfamily *Anchitherium* evolved. During the Miocene, around 24 million years ago, the environment changed, with large areas reverting to grassland. The equids that opted to live on these grasslands had to evolve very rapidly to adapt to the new environment. It was in this epoch that the subfamily *Hipparioninae,* still three-toed, spread from North America into Eurasia (Fig. 2.2).

Horses, asses and zebras probably evolved along separate lines in the Miocene (15 million years ago), and *circa* 5 million years ago zebras were widespread throughout Europe, where they continued to evolve until some 100,000 years ago. Two different species of primitive zebra can be identified: *Equus stenonis* and *Equus robustus*.

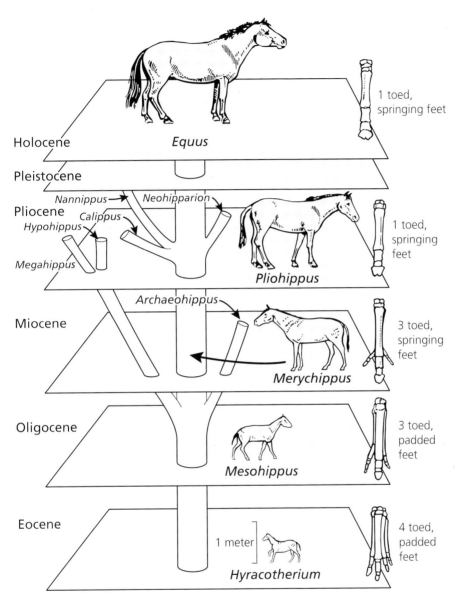

Holocene — *Equus* — 1 toed, springing feet

Pleistocene

Pliocene — Nannippus → Neohipparion, Calippus, Hypohippus, Megahippus — *Pliohippus* — 1 toed, springing feet

Miocene — Archaeohippus — *Merychippus* — 3 toed, springing feet

Oligocene — *Mesohippus* — 3 toed, padded feet

Eocene — 1 meter — *Hyracotherium* — 4 toed, padded feet

2.1 The evolution of the horse. Horses generally increased in size until the Pleistocene, and the number of toes on each foot decreased from four on the Hyracotherium to one on the modern horse.

The four subgenera of the genus *Equus*, which diversified during the Pleistocene, have a number of important differences. Horses (*Equus*) have chestnuts on all four legs, while asses (*Asinus*) and zebras (*Hippotigris* and *Dolichohippus*) only have them on the forelimbs. Horses have long hairy tails, while in the ass and zebra tail hairs are short. Body colour pattern is another difference: horses do not have a very light-coloured underside; they have dark flanks and, normally, no stripes. Asses and zebras have lighter undersides and zebras are always striped. Some wild horses may have kept some of the ancient characteristics of the genus and, as we will see when discussing the Sorraia, some domesticated and feral horses retain body stripes, or have chestnuts on the forelegs only.

2.2. The lineage of the horse family. During the Quaternary, Equus migrated from the Americas, where it became extinct, and continued to evolve in Eurasia.

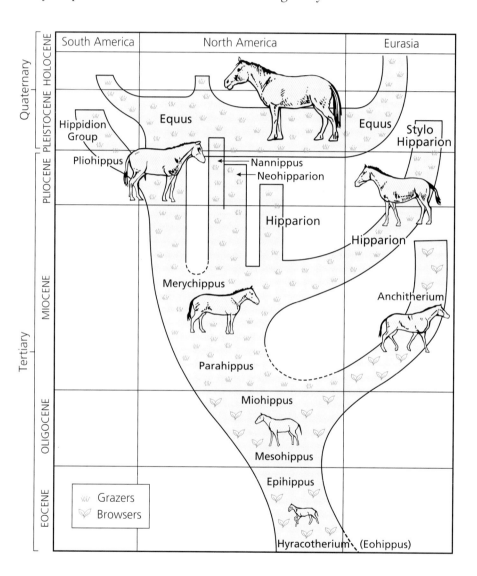

One of the first fully developed horses to live in Eurasia (700,000 BC) was *Equus mosbachensis,* which initially was wrongly supposed to be descended from *Equus robustus.* Horses in fact derived from the subgenus *Hippotigris,* and the first representatives of the subgenus *Equus* were also striped. According to many hippologists, the primitive characteristics that may still be common to some modern equids are the tufted tail and the presence of chestnuts on the forelimbs only. The modern horse with a fully haired tail and chestnuts on all four legs is the most advanced member of the family Equidae.

The very controversial and fascinating subject of identifying the true ancestral horse has been the focus of endless discussions and no consensus will be reached until such time as DNA tests, new fossil findings and/or other investigative techniques give us the incontrovertible, scientific conclusion that will finally eliminate all the current inaccurate and biased speculative opinions. As the hippologist George Gaylord Simpson perceptively said, most classifications of horse type reflect only the enthusiasm of their authors for a certain breed or theory, horse types being 'built out of ideas and not from reality'.

Notwithstanding all these limitations, it is an instructive and agreeable mental exercise for horse lovers to explore the minefield surrounding zoological and historical investigation, not only for the few precious bits of information provided but also for the wealth of detail revealed about the different approaches and techniques utilized in the past by many famous hippologists.

Because there is a lot of confusion with the terminology used to designate horse species of the past, it is important to establish the correct nomenclature before going further with this theme. We must define the terms and wording that will be used, and their correct meaning, to avoid even more confusion and misunderstanding.

To begin with, we have the term **'ancestral'** horse. By 'ancestral' we mean the species that lived in remote prehistoric times, or in other words, the first known representatives in Eurasia of the genus *Equus,* from the Miocene. From these horses are descended all the 'wild' horses of prehistoric and subsequent periods.

'Wild' horses are all the species that roamed free in the wild before domestication, all of them now extinct, except for a few Przewalski horses kept in zoos, if these can be considered truly wild.

'Feral' horses are the domesticated animals that reverted to wild status, for example the Mustangs. Obviously they are descended from 'wild' horses which in turn are descended from 'ancestral' types.

ANCESTRAL HORSES

One of the first authorities to study the origin of the horse was the French zoologist André Sanson (1826–1902). He classified fossil horses into two groups: short-headed and long-headed, according to the form of the skull. The main groups were then subdivided into four sub-groups each, corresponding to eight different species (four in each group) which he considered to be the ancestral types from which all modern domestic horses are descended.

The long-headed group consisted only of heavy horses. The short-headed group was composed of one heavy species and three lighter ones, which Sanson called the Irish, the African (including the Iberian and the Berber) and the Asiatic (the Arabian and all other European riding horses).

By the end of the nineteenth century, J. C. Ewart, studying the Celtic pony (*Equus caballus celticus*), similar to Sanson's Irish group, found that there were many discrepancies between the various types, such as short-haired tail root, small chestnuts on the front legs, and other aberrations not present in other types of horse. He classified horses into three distinct groups, each one with a supposed different ancestor, namely: *Equus przewalskii,* the steppe horse having as ancestor the type now known as the Przewalski horse; *Equus solutreensiis,* or the forest horse, having the Solutré horse as the ancestor (see p. 3), and finally *Equus celticus,* or the plateau variety, which had the Celtic pony as the ancestor.

At the same date, William Ridgeway, a great enthusiast of the Arabian horse, wrote that this breed is probably the only one that lacks chestnuts on the hindlegs, besides having a dished face, a completely different skull and body structure, and other very particular characteristics, suggesting that it may be another 'type'.

At the beginning of the twentieth century, another zoologist, Otto Antonius, studying Gmelin's eighteenth-century work on the Tarpan, considered this Russian wild horse as a true ancestral 'type', naming it *Equus gmelinii,* although this particular species was already known as *Equus ferus,* so that today we have the rather confusing situation of two accepted names for the same horse. Antonius' classification distinguished three types: *Equus orientalis,* whose wild ancestor was the Tarpan (*Equus gmelinii*); *Equus ferus* (different from the above), the wild ancestor being the Przewalski horse; and *Equus robustus,* having as wild ancestor the big, strong, horse of Western Europe. Another zoologist, Hilzheimer, gave the three groups the names of Tarpan, Celtic pony and 'cold-blooded' horses.

In the 1970s, the German zoologist G. Nobis came up with a systematic classification that considered all horses from Eurasia as belonging to one single species, with animals of variable sizes. This wild horse, according to Nobis, appeared by the end of the Pleistocene, survived the Ice Age and lived through the Neolithic. Still according to Nobis, the small ones lived at the extremes of the Eurasian horse country, i.e. in Western Europe and in Central Asia; the medium-sized ones, which formed the majority of the population, lived scattered throughout the vast area in between. Nobis justified the variation in sizes as caused by the different environments and called the species *Equus ferus* (as opposed to *Equus caballus,* the domesticated horse); he also called the Mongolian subspecies *Equus ferus przewalskii* and the Russian Tarpan, another subspecies, *Equus ferus gmelinii*. This idea was taken up by Bökönyi, as described below.

The next person to propose a different taxonomy was the Swede, B. Lundholm, who after careful investigation of prehistoric horse skulls from northern Europe proposed a systematic classification of ancestral horses into two different groups: the first, called the eastern group, was formed by horses that had the third molar tooth bigger than the second; the other group, called the western group, had the two molars the same size.

The Przewalski horse and the Tarpan were classified in the 'eastern group'. In the 'western group', Lundholm distinguished two types: one large horse from Germany, which he called *Equus germanicus,* and a small horse from southern Germany that he called *Microhippus*. His next step was to compare Swedish horses with these types. In this process he found that the older prehistoric horses, although smaller animals, belonged to the *E. germanicus* type. The more recent domesticated horses, on the other hand, he found to belong to the *Microhippus* type. However, some Swiss Bronze Age and Central Asian horses, as well as most of those from Eastern Europe, were found to be of the Tarpan type. According to Colin Groves:

> This was the first evidence, from hard fossil data, that there were several types of wild horse in Eurasia in the past, and that different types gave rise to domestic types in situ. What is more, the evidence suggests that some of these varying types might have been not just races of one species, but actual different species: for their ranges overlapped.[1]

Another classification which still persists in equestrian circles divides the domestic horse into two groups: the occidental (cold-blood) and the oriental (warm-blood), and considers them as derived from different wild ancestors.

In modern times, authors have split into two main groups or schools of thought, one (the monophyletic school), like many of the above-mentioned authors, considers all wild horses to be descended from one single ancestor, and the second (the diphyletic or pluriphyletic school) considers wild horses to have more than one ancestor. Darwin was the first to formulate the monophyletic theory. Lundholm and Ebhardt both defended the diphyletic theory.

Ebhardt's horse types

The German horse-breeder Hermann Ebhardt[2] proposed a classification for the ancestral horse based primarily on social behaviour rather than on physical characteristics. He watched herds (including stallions, mares and youngstock) of many different breeds in captivity, analysing how they behaved when roaming free at pasture and their reaction when approached by man. From this series of observations he concluded that there must have existed four ancestral horse types or species. The next step was to associate behaviour with morphological characteristics and to try to deduce what the ancestors of each group of horses would have looked like. Finally, he turned to fossil evidence to verify whether there was a match to his reconstructed types. Interestingly enough, the results were positive, with a strong correlation between the respective types and fossils. Ebhardt considered those that did not correspond so exactly to be crosses or hybrids. The four ancestral types that emerged from this process constitute a highly acceptable systematic classification that is still very much in use today.

TYPE I

In Ebhardt's classification, Type I is the northern pony. The basic rather confusing name given for the species is *Equus ferus*. It corresponds to Lundholm's eastern group, having the third molar longer than the second. It lived on the Atlantic seashore and in the mountains of Western Europe, but also reached Eastern Europe and the Pontic steppes (Fig. 2.3).

Characteristics

All authors that use this four-type classification agree that Type I stood at about 12.2 hands (127 cm) at the end of the Ice Age, although the first specimens from the earlier interglacial were about 16 hands (160.5 cm). Type I horses had black manes and tails, black lower legs, and a dark bay (brown) water-resistant coat protecting them from the cold and the humid climate prevalent in their main habitat. Type I may have included individuals with either upright or long manes and some with forelocks.

Type I had a broad forehead, long head and narrow muzzle, large nostrils, big round eyes, a convex or straight profile and small ears. The teeth were high crowned with thick enamel, appropriate for the kind of food in their main habitat.

They had a heavy, medium to short, upright ewe neck, strong wide body, with the rump higher than the withers, wide chest, short, somewhat concave back, and a wide and sloping rump with low-set tail. Short legs, with short broad cannon bones, short pasterns and strong, round hooves gave them the sure-footedness necessary in the area where they lived.

2.3 Theories of possible types of ancestral horse: Ebhardt's Type I.

Social behaviour

The descendants of Type I ponies live in compact herds, kept together by a stallion. Young males stay at the periphery of the herd, and leave it when sufficiently mature, at 4–5 years. There is a rank order among the mares, based on age, and on whether they have foals or not. The herd moves forward together, leaving behind it a uniformly grazed pasture. Their reaction to man is one of flight, galloping against the wind and then slowing down to a trot or pace, until stopping and turning back to look and investigate.

It was originally an open-country horse that adapted to mountainous terrain, marshy lands and tundra and steppe areas.

Modern descendants

According to Colin Groves, the northern ponies divided early on into three groups which evolved along similar lines: 'three ecotypes as they may be called: one on the tundra, one in the open forests, one on the steppe'.[3] The latter two groups can be traced back to the last interglacial period, between 120,000 and 80,000 years ago, and their subsequent evolution can also be traced. The steppe group of northern ponies were medium-sized animals with large teeth and long noses. Groves places the Tarpan and the

Przewalski horse in the steppe group. The forest group lived in the open, mixed forest or parkland region of Eastern Europe; the tundra group is represented in Europe by the late Ice Age horses from Solutré. According to another opinion:

> this early horse gradually evolved into two types: the Celtic pony and the primitive heavy horse of the European forests. The Celtic lived along harsh coastal regions where there was little food. These conditions resulted in his development as a small short-legged animal. The heavy draft horse, on the other hand, thrived in lush forests, where he grew to massive proportions but retained many of his earlier characteristics: short legs (relative to body size), a large barrel and a heavy coat.[4]

There is no doubt that Type I has contributed to the stock of the Konik, Exmoor and Icelandic ponies, the Hanoverian horse and the Dülmeners. In Iberia it is represented by the *garrano* from Portugal or the *jaca* from Spain; the *garrano* certainly contributed to the Sorraia, the Lusitano and the Spanish horse. Regarding the Przewalski horse, the prevalent opinion today classifies him as Type II rather than Type I, but this is unclear.

The situation concerning the Tarpan is also unclear. As the Konik derived from him, some authors, like Grove, consider him as a pure Type I, whereas the majority of modern authors consider the Tarpan to be a cross between Types I and III, with maybe some contribution from Type IV.

2.4 The modern *garrano* (Portugal) or *jaca* (Spain), typical of the Type I horse which has existed in Iberia since the end of the Pleistocene.

TYPE II

Ebhardt's Type II, the great horse from the north, is sometimes called *Equus woldrichii* (Fig. 2.5). It belongs in Lundholm's second eastern group, although its remains have been found in some sites in Eastern Europe from the last Ice Age. It was basically a tundra species. Original interglacial Type II horses were huge, standing 16.3–17.3 hands (170–80 cm); those from the last Ice Age were smaller, averaging 16.3 hands (170 cm) and in early post-glacial times they were 14.2–15 hands (148-54 cm).

2.5 Theories of possible types of ancestral horse: Ebhardt's Type II.

Characteristics

Type II was extremely large but, like Type I, decreased in size with time. Its habitat was the Mongolian steppes and China. It had a yellow-dun coat, lighter on the belly and inside the legs, which were black on the lower parts. The thick coat protected it from the cold temperatures and frosts. It had a dark stiff mane and tail, with no forelock, a black dorsal stripe and sometimes zebra stripes on the legs.

It had a big heavy head, a rather short nose, a narrow, flat forehead, a large, wide muzzle with a beard, and large nostrils like Type I. It had small teeth, small ears and a convex profile. The wide, strong, long body was divided from the low, heavy, short neck by straight shoulders. The rump was higher than the withers. Strong, relatively short legs, short flat cannon bones and short pasterns ended in large, round wide hooves and feathered fetlocks.

Social behaviour

The descendants of Type II horses have a looser herd structure than Type I. When moving forward grazing, the herd spreads out instead of staying together like Type I, leaving behind pockets of cropped grass instead of the uniformly grazed pasture left by Type I herds.

The animals get closer together at man's approach, looking back at the stranger with high outstretched necks – probably an aggressive posture from primeval eras – and then turn around, jumping in the air and running away against the wind, with the stallion following behind the mares.

Modern descendants

Ebhardt says this type did not have much influence on the domestic horse. This opinion is not shared by many other hippologists who believe that some Russian breeds are derived from it, as well as the horses used by the Germanic tribes and the large type of Icelandic horse, the Highland Garron, the Devon packhorse and some others that may derive from crosses between Types II and I. Some authors consider that the Przewalski horse derives from Type II ancestors.

TYPE III

Type III horse was called *Germanicus* by Lundholm, and belongs to his western group, as the third and second molars are the same size. It may be a descendant of the Mosbach horse, the most ancient and primitive horse fossil of Europe. It was tall, averaging 15.2 hands (158 cm) by the end of the second glaciation and 14 hands (142 cm) at the end of the Ice Age. Its habitat was Europe but it migrated into Asia at the end of the Ice Age, where it lived in the southern Caspian area, Turkestan and Iran (Fig. 2.6).

2.6 Theories of possible types of ancestral horse: Ebhardt's Type III.

Characteristics

Type III had a long head with a small narrow forehead and convex profile, a fine delicate muzzle, straight jaw, small teeth, long ears and eyes placed higher on the head, a long neck and clean throatlatch.

The prominent withers, higher then the rump, reached far on to a medium to long back, long inclined shoulders, narrow chest and body, and sloping croup. Long legs, cannon bones and pasterns ended in oval, medium-sized hoofs with no feathering. These characteristics made him capable of moving with collection, placing the hind legs under the body mass and the nose vertically, the ideal requirements for a good riding horse. Probably the dark mane, with intermingled light-coloured hairs at the bottom, was long and lay on the neck, although some sub-types may have had upright manes. The coat was dun or grullo (mouse dun) with a darker face. Type III always had a dorsal black line, and zebra stripes on the legs and very often also on the shoulders.

Social behaviour

Judging from modern descendants, the herd was mostly female, with the stallion visiting it during the mating season. Young horses lived together in small herds. It was probably sedentary, occupying year-round pastures, which it ferociously defended against other invaders. When approached by human beings, the mares put their ears back, paw the ground with the forelegs and snap the jaws noisily. If attacked they defend themselves with teeth and hooves. This behaviour has earned Type III the reputation of bad temper and aggressiveness, although they have proved to be extremely friendly and loving creatures when tamed.

Modern descendants

Type III has numerous domestic descendants, purebred or crossed with the other types and sub-types. They come in two forms: the heavy northern horses like the Kladruber, Holsteiner, Flemish, Percheron, Hanoverian warm-bloods, and secondly the more refined southern European and Asian types, like the Sorraia, the Lusitano, the Spanish, the Barb and, in Asia, the Turkoman or Turanian and the Akhal-Teke. Many modern breeds like the Thoroughbred and all the European and American saddle horses have some contribution from Type III, explained by the morphological structure that makes it the ideal riding horse.

2.7 Theories of possible types of ancestral horse: Ebhardt's Type IV.

TYPE IV

Type IV originated as a subtropical type in high rainfall areas and is poorly known as a fossil. Sometimes called the Caspian pony, it is a medium-to-small horse, about 12.3 hands (130 cm). It includes Ewart's *celticus* pony, considered by some authors to be Type I. It lived as far north as the Pontic steppes. In historical times it was found in Mesopotamia, Iraq and as far south as North Africa (Fig. 2.7).

Characteristics

It is difficult to say what the predominant colour of Type IV was in the wild, as greys, duns and sorrel are all common coat colours. It had a small head, medium-to-broad forehead, short broad nose, dished face, round eyes, small ears, small muzzle, straight jaw, and low crowned teeth. The short back sometimes had only five lumbar vertebrae instead of the normal six, with withers higher than the croup and a short horizontal rump with the tail set high, a long, slender neck and long shoulders. The fine legs, with long round cannon bones, ended in small oval hooves with no feathering; it may have lacked chestnuts on the hind legs.

Social behaviour

The descendants of Type IV horses live in permanent family herds like Type I. The group normally moves forward grazing together. When the grass is cropped, the herd moves to another nearby spot, leaving behind a pattern of chequered grassland, and starts grazing again. Like Type I, their reaction to man is one of flight, with the whole group galloping against the wind and the stallion pressing the reluctant mares with his teeth if necessary. The behaviour patterns of Types IV and I are so similar that it is probable that they are somehow related, although showing many different characteristics.

Modern descendants

The most important is the Arabian horse. Type IV may also have contributed to the foundation of some horses of antiquity, such as the Bactrian and the Ferghana horses, and certainly to many different modern strains, like the Thoroughbred and others.

General comments

A few remarks are expedient at this point, to leave this subject as complete as possible before going on to discuss the next phase of the evolution of the horse.

All four types probably had some contact and some overlapping habitats for several millennia. It is thus obvious that crosses between two or more types have occurred, a fact that is proven by many of their modern descendants; for instance, the Arabian, the Iberian, the Barb and the Turanian horses, not to mention the wild Tarpan. It is also certain that these breeds were the result of man-made crosses occurring after domestication.

Type I and III horses were genetically bigger than the other two types and, with domestication, have produced even larger horses, a fact that enables many scientists to affirm that, without the genes of these two types, it is impossible to breed larger horses. Colin Groves observed with great clarity that:

> If there were several species during the Ice Age, capable of living in the same environment without competing for resources and without interbreeding (this we infer from the lack of intermediate specimens), then we can at once see where the heterogeneity of our domestic breeds could have come from. If people domesticated their local varieties of horses and traded them around ... some horses were found to be better for draft, others for riding, and so on ... So the breeds, starting from different initial potentialities, would diverge more and more. Different types would be interbred, as well as pure-bred; the hybrids were evidently fertile, for cross-breds survive today, and this simply indicates that the species of horse have diverged less than the species of zebra or ass. Again, animals in captivity, forced by man into an unnatural association, will interact in a way they never would in the wild, where they would not even intermingle – and will interbreed.[5]

2.8 Sculpture carved in mammoth ivory from the Volgelherd Cave, Baden-Würtemberg, south Germany, c.32,000–28,000 BC. Prehistoric 'quality' horse from northern Europe.

One important phenomenon verified many times over (with the Mustang and the Sorraia, for example) is that the original 'types' tend to come back when domestic horses escape from man's control and revert to feral status, or even sometimes when selection is abandoned. When this occurs with horses that have a high content of one of the ancestral types, the characteristics resulting from cross-breeding will be eliminated and the animals will revert to the original wild form and from then on will not change again, no matter the number of generations. By the same token, artificial man-made breeds (of all domestic animals) have been observed to fall apart if subjected to the same experience. These facts solidify and validate the four-type classification as the most exact and practical one, as reversion to the ancestral type is always observed in such cases.

Another point to observe is the recurrence of the division into two forms: a heavy and a refined horse. In Ebhardt's and in other classifications it is possible to distinguish these two basic morphological forms, i.e. Types I and II are definitely heavy horses, while Types III and IV are lighter more refined ones.

WILD HORSES

We now enter the even more confusing world of 'wild' horses. Scientific convention establishes that once a certain species has been named by its discoverer, that particular name will continue to be used to designate the species; all subsequent subspecies will be designated by that generic name plus a second specific word that will identify it as a latterly discovered subspecies. This rule can be better explained by a practical example: the first wild horse to be identified was called *Equus przewalskii,* a denomination that became the general name for all wild horses, no matter the origin. The Tarpan (South Russia's wild horse) was identified later; it was then called *Equus przewalskii gmelinii.*

The original Mongolian wild horse which first received the Przewalski name is often referred to as *Equus przewalskii przewalskii* to avoid confusion with other wild *Equus przewalskii.* Also confusing is the number of chromosomes. *Equus przewalskii* has 66 chromosomes, while the domestic horse has 64, onagers have 54 or 56, asses 62 and zebras 46 (Grévy's) and 44 (Burchell's). Although crosses between all these different species are infertile hybrids, Tarpans and Przewalski horses have produced fertile offspring with domestic horses and in crosses with each other. Dr Sándor Bökönyi wrote that according to the Soviet zoologist V. G. Heptner:

> the distribution area of Asian wild horses was fantastically vast even in histori-
> cal eras. Northwards it stretched to the 55th degree of latitude, and eastwards to
> the 85th degree of longitude. Southwards the Caucasus and the Caspian Sea
> were its boundaries, which run from the latter's north-eastern shores through
> Lake Aral and Lake Balkhash to the northern foot-hills of the Altai. It seems to
> be probable too that westwards Przevalsky [sic] horses were distributed as far as
> the Ural, and made contact with the South Russian tarpans in the regions be-
> tween the Ural and the Volga.[6]

These wild horses survived in great numbers in Northern Europe, Russia and the Ukraine, but are missing or scarce in the archaeological evidence of the Holocene (7000 to 3000 BC) in many other regions of Eurasia, spe-cially the Carpathians, the Balkans and in the Iberian Peninsula.

The Przewalski horse

In 1878 Colonel N.M. Przewalski presented the Russian Academy of Sci-ences with the remains (skull and skin) of a wild horse he had obtained in Central Asia during his explorations of that area. Colonel Przewalski's find was considered to be of the last species of wild horse still alive, and the an-imal was called *Equus przewalskii* in his honour (Figs. 2.9 and 2.10).

Describing Przewalski horses in the Prague Zoo, Colin Groves writes:

The stallion has a height of 138–46 cm, the mare 134–40 cm and the usual weight is 250–300 kg. The build is low and robust with a very strong, relatively short neck; the withers are not prominent; and the legs are relatively short and slender. The head is conical; the forehead only slightly vaulted; and the upper and lower profile lines are straight, with an angle between them of only 16–20° (in domestic horses, the two profile lines converge more strongly, the head being less oblong and more triangular, and the angle between the profile lines is 25–32°). The snout region is thus much thicker than a domestic horse, the lower jaw is not concave; and the head is relatively large.

There are two colour-types, both of which can be safely characterised as pure-bred: one is a light, livid grey-yellow, the other darker – a lively yellowish, red-brown. The foreparts, especially the neck, are clearly darker than the rest of the body. The muzzle is light coloured, even white, and there is also a light narrow ring round the eyes. The lips, the area between the nostrils and the borders of

the nostrils themselves, are very often black, and contrast strongly with the muzzle. The undersides are somewhat lighter than the general body colour, but the lower segments of the limbs – the shanks – are very dark, often black, grading at or above the knees and hocks into the overall body colour. There is a dark to black dorsal stripe, which begins at the back of the mane and runs down the middle of the back and on to the tail; in foals, it may be indistinct especially in winter. The legs show indistinct traverse stripes, which are most clearly expressed on the back of the knees of the forelegs. There is a very indistinct stripe across the shoulders, usually only a little darker than the rest of the body.

In winter, the coat grows quite long, even shaggy; the hairs can reach a length of 5–8 cm on the throat, and on the cheeks and underside of the jaw there is a distinct beard in winter. The mane, which is dark brown to black, is 16–20 cm high. It begins between the ears and reaches the withers, and is more or less upright except when slightly tilted to one side in stallions. On either side of the mane, in winter coat, there is a seam of lighter hairs which reach up to about two-thirds of its height. There is no forelock unlike domestic horses.

Most of the basal half of the tail is covered with short hairs and the normal body colour and dorsal stripe are continued on to them. The sides of most of this basal part, and the entire half of the tail have much longer, stiffer hairs; towards the base these are light-coloured and only on the latter half of the tail are they black. The tail hairs reach to the fetlocks.[7]

The Przewalski horse is preserved today in many zoos around the world and some horses are to be let free in Mongolia to repopulate that region with its indigenous wild horse.

The Tarpan

The Tarpan – the Ukrainian wild horse – whose name comes from the Turkomanian, was first described by the German Gmelin in 1769 and received the scientific name of *Equus ferus gmelinii* (Fig. 2.11). It is the horse described by Herodotus as the Scythian horse: 'The river, the Hypanis, rises in Scythia. The source of this river is a large lake on the margins of which live wild white horses.'[8]

Bökönyi paraphrases Gmelin's description of the Tarpan:

Its head is massive, the ears being pointed and sometimes rather long. The eyes are fiery, the mane is short and erect. Its tail is more or less (?) covered with hair and is shorter than that of domestic horses. The tarpan's colour is mouse-grey

2.9 (*facing above*) Przewalski stallion bred in captivity, with typical conformation.

2.10 (*facing below*) Herd of zoo-kept Przewalski horses.

(though mention is made of white and ash-grey individuals seen elsewhere), its belly is ash-grey, the legs are black downwards from their middle. The hair is very long and thick, so much so that one would rather think of a fur than of a horse's fell.

The tarpans live in small groups, each under the leadership of one stallion. The stallions often abduct domestic mares and Gmelin himself saw such a mare in the group he was chasing. The stallions are unbelievably strong; they seek fights with domestic stallions and vanquish them....

According to the Russian zoologist Heptner the last tarpan – which however lived in captivity and not in free nature – perished only in 1918–19. It was a stallion of 140–145 cm [13.3–14.1 hands] withers height, with a big head, a broad forehead and a straight profile. His ears were small and pointed, his neck was short and so was the straight back, while the rump was sway-backed. He was mouse-grey with a dorsal stripe about two cm wide running along the middle of the back and with a blurred stripe across the shoulders. His mane was very short, strikingly thick and erect.[9]

2.11 The Tarpan, the wild horse from the Ukraine, became extinct in the nineteenth century, but the Polish Konik pony is thought to be its closest descendant.

Wild horses in Eurasia lived in permanent contact with each other, a fact that led many writers to consider them a single species, with many sub-species. This has given rise to many heated discussions. There is an

enormous confusion between the Przewalski and the Tarpan, the two names being ambiguously taken to designate the same horse when they are two different animals. To make things even worse, some authors, like Heptner, for example, considered all wild horses as one single species – the Tarpan – and called it *Equus przewalskii*. He then recognized three sub-species: the steppe Tarpan, the wild horse from Russia (*Equus przewalskii gmelinii*); the forest Tarpan, from Europe (*Equus przewalskii sylvaticus*), and the Asian Tarpan, the Mongolian wild horse (*Equus przewalskii przewalskii*). According to Miklos Jankovich:

> A Hungarian expedition found horses living wild in the Mongolian mountains north of Tienshan. These were obviously the last surviving band of Przewalski's Horse. The place from which they were observed at long range is called Takhin Shar Nuru – i.e., 'Yellow Horse Mountain'. It is altogether possible that this place-name is a memorial of the golden-coated 'wild blood-horses'. The word *shar* means either 'yellow' or 'golden', and to this day the Turks call golden chestnut horses *sharylar*... It cannot be a coincidence that this locality should also be the last refuge of the true wild (as opposed to feral) horses of our time, the brown-dun or sandy-bay Takis – a hilly, waterless wilderness, remote from all human settlement.[10]

What really matters is that today these wild equines, the Tarpan, the Mongolian Przewalski and the Sorraia (now domesticated) are considered as different types, with many distinctive characteristics that place each one of them in an individual category, clearly differentiated from the others.

It is quite possible that many other wild horse types existed in Eurasia in prehistoric times, but we have no real evidence about them, except for a few vague remarks from Classical writers who may have seen the last representatives of some of these species. Herodotus, for instance, as we have seen, described a white horse he saw in today's Russia, probably a Tarpan, whose coat changed to white in winter, an occurrence that was later confirmed by modern writers who saw these horses before they became extinct. Pliny mentions wild horses in Poland and Varro describes what certainly was a Sorraia which he saw in Spain. Regarding Western Europe, Dr Bökönyi points out:

> Nor did wild horses survive for very long in the western part of Europe. The area was soon populated, the extent of cultivated land grew by leaps and bounds; livestock-keeping and animal domestication at the end of the Neolithic and the

beginning of the Bronze Age soon reduced the number of wild horses. To escape man they withdrew to forests and mountains, but they were not left in peace there either, for man hunted them. It seems likely that these wild horses did not survive even into the Middle Ages, and that those sometimes mentioned in Mediaeval sources were only feral domestic ones.[11]

The Sorraia

Dr Ruy d'Andrade, the famous Portuguese hippologist, rediscovered the Sorraia (or Merismeño) horse of Portugal and Spain. In his *Reconstrucción del Caballo Ibérico*[12] he gives much important and interesting information, indispensable to the study of the Iberian wild horses of the past (Fig. 2.12).

According to Dr d'Andrade, the first horse to be domesticated in the Iberian Peninsula was the Type I pony, the horse most frequently depicted in the Palaeolithic art of the Franco-Cantabrian caves (see Chapter 3). He points out that this heavy small horse, the *jaca* which still lives wild and almost unchanged in the cold and humid Iberian mountains, is not the

2.12 Horse from La Pileta, Spain. Possibly a 'quality' pregnant mare.

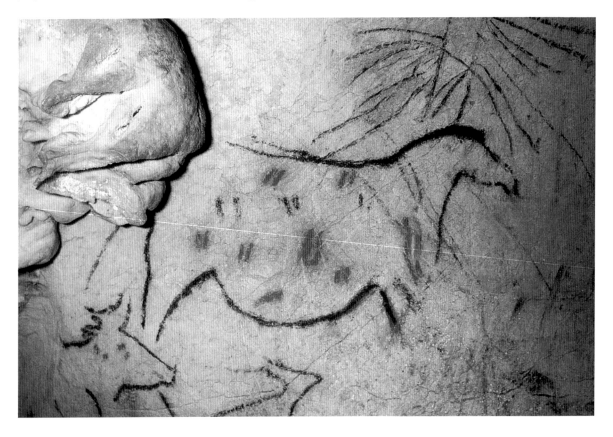

same as the bigger animal from the south of the Peninsula that became known as the 'Iberian horse'.[13]

This more refined horse, says d'Andrade, is represented in the La Pileta caves, dating back to the end of the Palaeolithic (Figs. 2.12 and 2.15), and also appears in the art of the Spanish Levant from the Mesolithic. It took its modern form (with regard to its morphology) as early as the Neolithic and subsequent periods – another very important piece of evidence that horses did not disappear from Iberia during the Mesolithic. Describing this horse, d'Andrade writes:

> This horse was some ten centimetres taller than the *jaca* and had different characteristics which became evident in the historical period. Probably, during his development, he was influenced by contacts with other horses from northern Spain with ancient Celtic and African (Capsian) inputs; so that when the present Iberian model appeared he already had the form that would for ever distinguish him. According to Strabo (C. IV, 15) and later Isidoro de Sevilla (*Etimologias* XII, 1–54), the Iberian horse had a wild ancestor.[14]

Strabo wrote the following: 'Iberia produces many deer and wild horses. ... The Celtiberian horses are like those of Parthia, he [Poseidonius] says, for not only are they faster but they are also smoother runners than the other horses.'[15]

Dr d'Andrade also tells how he discovered the Sorraia at the beginning of the 1900s:

> In 1920, I was hunting in the Coruche area, in the low Sorraia, on a property called 'Sesmaria', when I came upon a group of about 30 horses, more than half of them light dun, some of a mouse colour, many striped and with an absolutely wild and primitive look, as if they were a zebra or *hemione* [wild ass] species.
>
> Later on, concentrating my attention on these characteristics ... I observed, in all the Tagus valley region, in the Alto Alentejo and in the Guadalquivir valley, animals with that particular colour, of which I counted more than three hundred.[16]

He continues:

> They had a colour between grey and dun, with zebra stripes on the head, legs, neck, flank and back; black 'donkey dorsal stripe'... around 1.46 m [14.1 hands] in height ... and still show these primitive characteristics in some individuals in

the wild. It was easy to reproduce these characteristics when I wanted to obtain them [in horses Dr d'Andrade bred in captivity].

... I called them Sorraia, the name of the river where in ancient times they lived ... This group is similar to the old group from the low Guadalquivir, from the rivers Huelva, Algarve and Sado, but it is the group that has been preserved as the most primitive and typical among all these groups.[17]

D'Andrade then narrated his experiences in re-establishing the Sorraia:

As these animals had dispersed, it was not possible as I had hoped, to buy this group ... but I tried to obtain, in the same area, some mares with the same characteristics as I had seen before, and ended up by buying seven from various breeders from the Coruche area, and so formed one group. These mares, crossed with horses of the same origin and having the same colour characteristics, reproduced themselves and today, almost ten years later, with almost all of the original group already gone as they were old mares, their offspring is very homogeneous ...[18]

He also noted:

And as in the Andalusian herds, ... foals are frequently born dun in colour with stripes on the legs, so it was natural to conclude that this was the ancestral (ontogenetic) colour of the ancestral horses from which modern Iberian horses came ...[19]

He continues further on in the same work:

With the knowledge we have today ... we cannot have any doubt that, since the Palaeolithic, there have been *jaca* (*garrano*) type horses in the Peninsula. Also, since the Mesolithic, there have been domesticated *Merismeño* type horses, which have been ridden since the Neolithic and used for war combat. From the metal ages they began to be crossed, as can be deduced from the name Podargos (piebald) given to the mother of Achilles' horses. Primitive pure horses do not have white parts.

With regard to the origins – African or Iberian – of the horse in the Peninsula (see Chapter 4), d'Andrade is strongly in favour of an indigenous Iberian horse:

A question remains of whether the southern horse group was autochthonous from Iberia or from an African origin. Because the Spanish Levant civilization is the result of a Capsian or Saharan invasion, it is possible to ask whether the

2.13 (*above*) A group of Sorraia horses bred by the Alter Real Stud, Portugal.

2.14 A typical Sorraia horse at the Alter Real Stud, Portugal.

southern horses are originally from Iberia or from Africa. But, in La Pileta, Parpalló and other representations of the southern Spanish Palaeolithic, horses are drawn with a sub-convex profile; they must therefore be considered to be autocthonous, as these drawings date back to a much earlier era than the Capsian influence.

Dr d'Andrade gives the following description of the Sorraia:

Males measure approximately 1.46 m high at the withers and females 1.43 m. The body is solid and strong with the general aspect of a mule ... The rib-cage, high and flat, is very long in the rear, and because the kidneys are short, it reaches very close to the crupper. The chest, except in very fat males, is not very wide. The neck is short and low, inverted, of the shape known as 'ewe neck'. One of the reasons for this shape is the form of the withers, high and extending almost until the middle of the back; this explains the great weight load that these animals can support. At the top of the short neck is the large, narrow head, with relatively small, oblique and deep eyes, placed at the top of a wide face. The forehead is convex, narrow, with a not very high maxillary, and a wide muzzle, not only because the nose is long and high but also due to the large lips, sometimes exhibiting a beard ... The legs are strong, with high joints, narrow hooves, long but not very sloping shoulders. The small croup angle makes elastic movement easier. The forehand is higher than the back, specially in

2.15 Black horse from La Pileta, Spain. A refined 'quality horse' from prehistoric times.

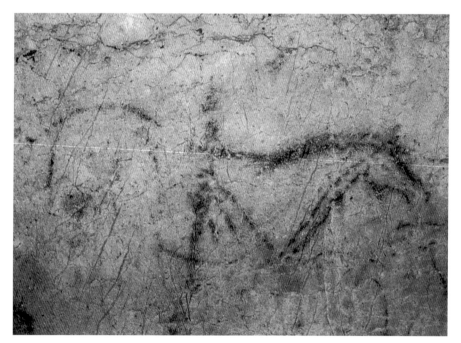

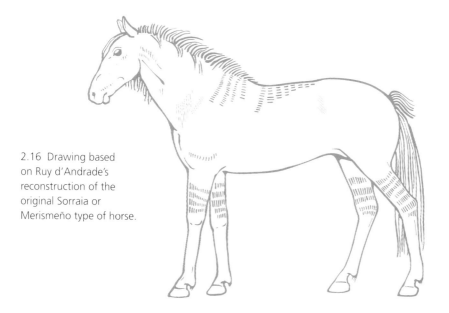

2.16 Drawing based on Ruy d'Andrade's reconstruction of the original Sorraia or Merismeño type of horse.

females. The belly is voluminous, as happens with horses that live all their lives in the field eating only very harsh, hard, heavy and low-nutrient pasture, especially in the winter. The winter coat is very long to protect them from the cold. In short, poor animals, that can be considered heavy and ugly if compared with fine and elegant Arabians. But after the winter hardships, the months from April to June are easily enough to make them fat and, once the long winter coat has changed, they develop a fine, silky coat. With bones once more covered by flesh they change completely in appearance, especially the stallions, which in full flesh show a curved neck and, so much changed, they look close-coupled and full of life, moving with a lot of elegance and gracefulness, and become beautiful Andalusian horses that can rival Arabians, as they become fine and swift, full of movement and fire. At such moments they reveal the Iberian form of the highest class of animal, on a smaller scale. The natural coat colour is grey or dun, which may possibly represent distinct primitive varieties, because the grey normally comes with few stripes, while on the other hand the dun shows abundant stripes, especially on the legs …

The mane and forelock are very full as is the tail: the colour is light grey for the outer hairs and darker underneath; the tail is full at the point of setting on. …

They are animals of exceptional vitality, resistant to all bad treatment: hunger, poor feeding and excessive work. After all, they are a natural and primitive breed.

Dr d'Andrade leaves no doubt about his conviction that the Sorraia was the wild horse of Iberia, from which all the other Iberian strains descend:

> Without any doubt this [the Sorraia] is the foundation of all Iberian horses; it was from them that, with domestication, some cross-breeding and selection, our very renowned horses were developed in Spain.

Arsênio Raposo Cordeiro explains that, during the Middle Ages, the Sorraia was known as the 'Zebro' (Zebra) and relates that a document from Lisbon, dated 1179, mentions the prices of 'skins from oxen, Zebro, and deer, each one half a maravedi'.[20] The same author also explains that during the thirteenth, fourteenth and fifteenth centuries, similar references to the Zebro are found, depicting it as a distinct horse species. It is interesting to reproduce some of Arsênio Raposo Cordeiro's observations:

> Curiously, many places called 'Zebro Valley' still exist today in Portugal, between the rivers Tagus and Guadiana, always corresponding to wild and sparsely populated areas. In this same region, places known as 'the Valley of the Mares' or 'the Valley of the Horses' are also found, clearly establishing the difference between the wild horse, the Zebro, and the already domesticated Lusitano horse, which descended from him.[21]

DOMESTICATED HORSES OF ANTIQUITY

The first domesticated horses retained many of the characteristics of their wild ancestors, especially behaviour patterns, for example reactions to men and to dangerous or unfamiliar environments and situations. This was, in no small measure, the consequence of the handling of these animals by the ancient nomadic tribes and former civilizations. It is convenient to dedicate a few lines to this important chapter of primeval horse breeding, as it may explain many present and past behaviour patterns as well as the morphology of ancient and modern breeds.

The first point to bear in mind is the alert and aggressive posture of the leading stallion in wild groups, reproduced *in toto* in fully or semi-domesticated herds. In both cases, leadership was always established by fighting, and the victory of the fittest has always been the most important factor in the survival of the species. Of no less importance is the herd instinct, the force that kept the wild horse communities close together.

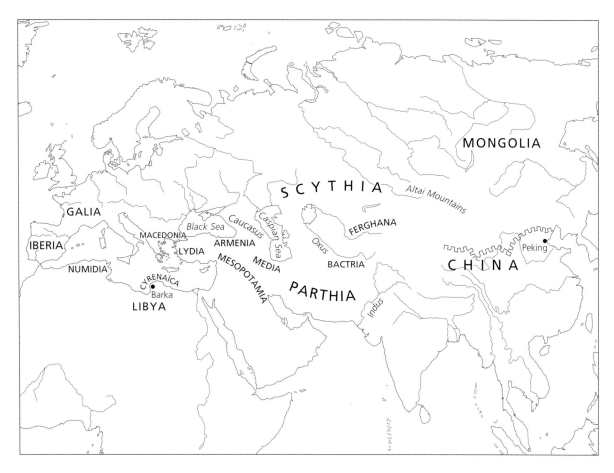

2.17 The major horse-breeding areas of ancient times, from Iberia to Mongolia.

Nomadic horse-breeding began on the Central Asian steppe, a region that stretches from Mongolia to China and westward to the Black Sea and Iran, and from where emerged, for millennia, repeated waves of raids and invasions by mounted warriors.

For centuries, the nomadic peoples of the steppe had the habit of leaving their domesticated mares free, so that they would be attracted and covered or abducted by a wild stallion, in the latter case returning to their owners before the foals were born. Primitive populations strongly believed that by acting in this way it would be possible to retain in the domesticated herd the admired qualities of the true wild stallion. Some mares would never return, which explains why observers quite frequently saw domestic mares living amongst wild herds. Runaway domestic stallions, however, did not stand a chance against the wild ones, who were much stronger and better adapted to lead the wild herd; they would simply be torn to pieces by the leader or even by younger wild horses.

2.18 Rock drawings from the Altai mountains, central Asia, showing prehistoric 'quality' horses.

Miklos Jankovich relates that these practices were confirmed by folklore traditions in Bactria and Turania:

> The Turkomans used to say that their forefathers came by the finest foals by turning out 'horsing' mares at night in the mountains, so that they would be covered by wild stallions full of quality that came out of the mountains.[22]

Some famous horse breeds of antiquity are of great interest to this work, not only for the role they played in ancient warfare, in the development of chariotry and cavalry, but also for the influence of these strains on other Eurasian breeds of ancient and Classical times. These horses may have crossed with other indigenous populations in Europe and Asia and were probably significantly infused with blood from these other strains. The most important horse breeds by far historically are the Bactrian and the Nisaean, and we will discuss them and their descendants: the Turanian (also called Turkoman or the horse from Ferghana); the Cyrenaican, and the Chinese. In addition to these oriental horses, we will also examine the influence of these ancient strains on the Arabian and the Berber (Libyan or Barb), and the eventual contacts the latter had with the Iberian and other western European breeds.

Was there more than one 'quality' horse type or breed in Asia, or do all these different names correspond to exactly the same horse? This is one of the issues that will be discussed in the rest of this chapter, the conclusion being that there were originally at least two, and more probably three, strains: the Bactrian, the Nisaean and a cross involving these two that produced the Pazyryk type and much later the Arabian horse.

Probably two kinds of 'quality' horses – one predominantly Type III and another typically Type IV – lived in Central Asia since the most remote times, and this causes some confusion, as they are very often considered as one single animal. The picture becomes even more complicated when other breeds descended from them are added to the list of Central Asian basic strains. A third level of confusion comes when some authors use the term 'Oriental horse', without a precise definition of what they mean, to designate either the Turkoman or the Arabian horse, or worse, to designate both, as if they were the same type. More of that when we discuss these and other well-known domesticated strains below.

Good land, good horses

This is an old axiom of horse breeding. It is also the sole explanation for why 'quality horses' from antiquity were only bred in fertile lands with plenty of good pastures. The Classical literature so often cited in this book is full of references to this fact: for example, descriptions in the Classical texts of Bactrian or Ferghana horses are always accompanied by extensive allusions to the excellent pastures they existed on.

The Turkish and Mongolian peoples that formed the invading hordes of later periods rode small and ugly ponies. They were Type I, Przewalski horses that lived on the Central Asian steppes and in the Mongolian mountains. One of the main characteristics of these animals was their incredible resistance to cold weather, poor nourishment and other adverse environmental conditions rendering their habitats inhospitable or

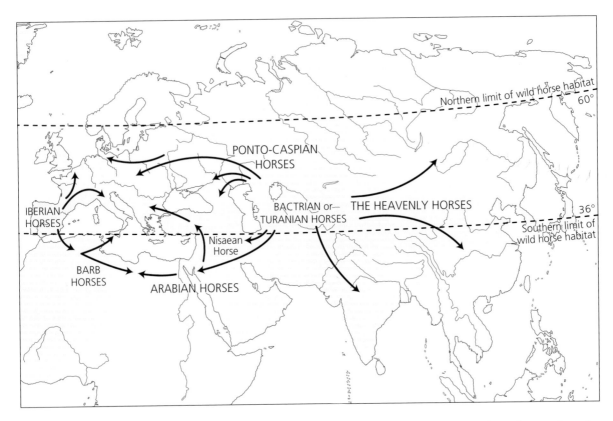

2.19 Distribution of Eurasian domesticated ancestral horses. Note that the habitat of wild horses is conventionally contained between the latitudes 60° north and 36° south.

even unviable for any other type of horse. The barbarians knew that the fine quality horses from the lands they had conquered in Asia and Eastern Europe were no match for their mounts in the severe and unfriendly conditions of eastern Asia, and so rarely remounted their cavalry with these better saddle horses, because they knew that if forced to retreat suddenly to their homelands these 'horses of quality' would not survive.

The Bactrian horse

The existence of a 'quality wild horse' in Central Asia is confirmed by various sources. The land of these fabulous horses was the Bactrian kingdom, a satrapy of the Persian Empire, located in the Afghan mountains. One special region of Bactria on the upper Syr-Darya river was known as Ferghana (or Taiyuan in Chinese). Good testimony of the existence of quality horses here are the rock-drawings from Ferghana (Aravan), dating back to the first millennium BC and depicting herds of horses, all fine animals with long, elegant, curved necks, and delicate heads with straight profiles (Fig. 2.20). The Bactrian horse has probably existed since the beginning of domestication, and Bactria was surely one of the most important sources for the supply of good horses to Near Eastern civilizations.

The first literary reference to Bactrian horses is from the fifth century BC, when the kingdom was part of the Persian Empire under the Achaemenids, and Bactrian cavalry served in the Persian Army: 'The Bactrians and Sacae both had the same kind of equipment as their infantry equivalents' (Herodotus VII, 86). Chinese documents of 126 BC mention mystical wild horses living in the mountains of Taiyuan; they were the famous 'heavenly' horses that are described below.

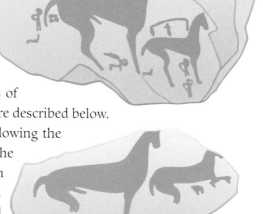

Very little is known about Bactria in the period following the reign of Yuë-chi (see p. 54). It is certain, however, that the Chinese were not the only people to obtain horses from Ferghana. The Huns too were the beneficiaries of this dispersion; it is reported that their king, Tuman, had one of these 'heavenly' horses around 200 BC.

In the eighth century AD, Bactria was conquered by the Muslims. Arab sources speak very admiringly of the Bactrian or Turanian horse, which at that time was very much appreciated in Asia and Europe. Marco Polo, writing about his travels through these countries in AD 1271, observes about the province of Balashan (in Northern Afghanistan):

2.20 The horse from Ferghana , the most famous 'quality' horse from the Ponto-Caspian, depicted in rock art of Aravan, late first century BC.

> The horses bred here are of a superior quality, and have great speed. Their hoofs are so hard that they do not require shoeing. The natives are in the practice of galloping them on declivities where other cattle could not or would not venture to run. They asserted that not long since there were still found in this province horses of the breed of Alexander's celebrated Buchephalus, which are all foaled with a particular mark in the forehead [a star and a crescent moon].

Marco Polo then describes the extinction of these particular horses:

> The whole of the breed was in the possession of one of the king's uncles, who, upon his refusal to yield them to his nephew, was put to death; whereupon his widow, exasperated at the murder, caused them all to be destroyed; and thus the race was lost to the world.[23]

With the conquest of Asia Minor by the Seljuk Turks, Turanian horse-breeding practically disappeared, as the best stock was transported to Mongolia by the conquerors. Milos Jankovich reports that Tamerlane (1336–1405) 'attempted to revive Turanian breeding by distributing five thousand brood mares among the Turkoman tribes'.[24] During the Ottoman domination, some Turkoman horses reached western Europe, including those that formed the foundation of the modern Trakehner breed.

All this information proves that Bactria, Turania and Turkestan were, for thousands of years, the original home of horses of excellent quality. Brigadier John Clabby writes that the Bactrian horse was 'from all accounts ... the same type of light fast animals as those taken by the Aryans [Indo-Europeans] to the Middle East nearly two thousand years before'.[25] This proposition is in line with the most accepted theory that the bigger, more refined riding horse came from the Kurgan area of southern Russia to Central Asia, where at the time the indigenous population was all Type I Przewalski Mongolian ponies.

More recently, in the nineteenth century, horses from the old Bactrian region became collectively known as 'Turkoman' horses, a denomination that comprised many different but blood-related breeds, such as the Akhal-Teke, the Jomali and the Jomud horses.

Chinese horses

China possessed its own indigenous herds of Przewalski-type wild horses which, from 1500 BC, were domesticated and bred, initially for chariotry. Horses had always held an important position in Chinese civilization, as demonstrated by the chariots and horses buried with the emperors (Fig. 2.21).

The Chinese, in order to improve the quality of the animals of the Imperial Studs, were always looking for good horses in the neighbouring barbarian countries. Horse-breeding was already well established in China in the late second millennium, when the Chou replaced the Shang/Yin dynasty around 1050 BC:

> Situated outside the Shang domain, this city [Chou], which was in permanent contact with the barbarian peoples of these western regions, seems to have been able to take advantage of geographical conditions favourable to horse breeding: in subsequent periods the upper valley of the Ching and the north-east of Kansu were regions given over to stud-farms. The Chou, doubtless more

warlike than the Shang, seem to have made wider use of the chariot and to have invented a new kind of harness with four horses abreast.[26]

In the first century AD, imperial envoys reported that marvellous 'blood-sweating, heavenly' horses, sired by dragons, were bred in Taiyuan (Ferghana), 3500 km to the west along the Silk Route, in the Bactrian kingdom. The legend was that in this world, they could cover three hundred miles a day at a gallop, and in the next, they would carry a human soul to the Holy Mountain and to the Land of Perpetual Peace, being destined to take the Emperor to the land of the Immortals. Initially, these horses were not used for cavalry, but for traction. Piggott reports that 'From Ferghana too were brought back seeds of lucern (*Medicago sativa*), a leguminous fodder plant appropriate to the better stock, which was then extensively grown in China'.[27]

The enormous influence of the Bactrian horse in Chinese breeding

2.21 Pair of Chinese horses from the Tang dynasty (AD 618–907), male and female.

53

and the way in which these horses were obtained by Imperial China would make a delicious historical novel. In the reign of King Yuë-chi of Bactria these horses were the object of diplomatic negotiations and military campaigns by the Emperor Wu (115 BC). First, he sent repeated embassies to Yuë-chi, trying to buy horses, with no success. Next, he tried to seduce the Bactrian king with royal gifts, sending him a thousand gold pieces and a horse of solid gold, again without any success. Indeed, Yuë-chi arrested the Chinese diplomats and had them executed when they attempted to escape. Finally the issue was decided by force, with the invasion of Bactria. According to Chinese sources, the war spoils included 30 blood-sweating horses, and 3000 half-bred mares and stallions.

Stuart Piggott gives the translation of a triumphal hymn, perhaps written by the emperor himself to commemorate the arrival of the mythical horses in China:

> The Heavenly Horses are coming
> Coming from the Far West
> They crossed the Flowing Sands
> For the barbarians are conquered,
> The Heavenly Horses are coming ...[28]

With these animals, according to Sven Hedin,[29] the Chinese emperor set up the Imperial stud-farms that were the very foundation of the fine Chinese horse-breeding of future periods. Chinese horses are abundantly represented in Han (206 BC–220 AD) and Tang (618–907 AD) art, especially in sculpture, which gives the best possible idea of the original models and leaves no doubt as to the type of horse used by the Chinese after the input of the 'heavenly' horses' blood. They are big, strong horses, with a convex head profile, strong medium to long backs, sloping rumps, good legs and strong well-angled hocks, looking very closely related to the Iberian and Barb strains. No Type IV infusion seems to be there, a fact that either proves wrong the assertion by some authors that Bactrian horses may have been 'dished faced' or, what is more probable, indicates that the newcomers were crossed with the indigenous Type I Chinese horses. On the other hand, here again we have a strong indication of at least two 'quality' horses in Central Asia in the past.

The Nisaean (Nesaean) horse

The Medes inhabited the mountainous country in the northern part of what is now Iran, south of the Caspian. The fame of the Nisaean or Nesaean horses bears witness to the high level of their horse-breeding (Fig. 2.22). The nineteenth-century historian George Rawlinson gives an excellent introduction to this region and its famous horses:

> Another [region] is Nisaea, a name which the Medes seem to have carried with them from their early eastern abodes, and to have applied to some high upland plains west of the main chain of Zagros, which were peculiarly favourable to the breeding of horses. As Alexander visited these pastures on his way from Susa to Ecbatana, they must necessarily have lain to the south of the latter city. Most probably they are to be identified with the modern plains of Khawah and Alishtar, between Behistun and Khorramabad, which are even now considered to afford the best summer pasturage in Persia.
>
> (*Note:* The proper Nisaea is the district of Nishapur in Khorasan …, whence it is probable that the famous breed of horses was originally brought. The Turcoman horses of the *Atak* are still famous throughout Persia.) [30]

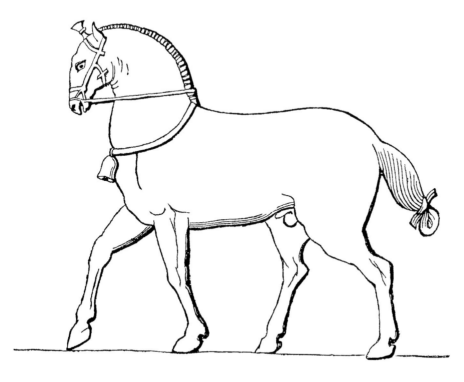

2.22 Reconstruction of the famous 'quality' horse from Nisaea, based on Assyrian wall sculptures, in *The Five Great Monarchies* by nineteenth-century writer George Rawlinson.

Miklos Jankovich translates Oppian's description of the breed as follows:

> The horses of Nisaea are the handsomest, fit only for mighty rulers. They are splendid, running swiftly under the rider, obeying the bridle willingly, with *ram-nosed heads* [my emphasis] carried high, and streaming golden manes.[31]

These horses doubtless derived from Types III and IV in Ebhardt's classification, probably with some Type I influence.

Herodotus also praises the Nisaean horse and gives more information about its presence in the Persian army:

> India, for example, … contains … living creatures, both animals and birds, which are far larger than those to be found in other countries (the only exception being that their horses are inferior to the breed in Media known as Nesaean horses) …[32]

Herodotus then tells how Xerxes' army left Sardis on the journey to cross the Hellespont and invade Greece:

> Next, magnificently caparisoned, came the ten sacred 'Nesaean' horses, named after the huge Nesaean Plain in Media which produces these tall horses. The place behind the ten horses was taken by the sacred chariot of Zeus, which was drawn by eight white horses. Following them on foot (because no human being is allowed to mount the seat of this chariot) came the charioteer, with the reins in his hands. Behind him came Xerxes himself, seated on a chariot drawn by Nesaean horses.[33]

The quality of these horses is again described by Herodotus:

> While he was in Thessaly, Xerxes had set up a horse-race, pitting his own horses against the local Thessalian stock, because he had heard that Thessalian horses were the best in Greece. As a matter of fact, though, the Greek horses were easily beaten.[34]

Obviously, to pull the emperor's heavy chariot they could not have been small horses, but must have been big, powerful animals, confirming the predominance of Type III blood, and consequently, convex or straight head profiles. They could not possibly have been the small Type IV horses, although theoretically some infusion of blood from that strain could have occurred, but in smaller percentage than the dominant Type III.

Alexander the Great remounted his famous cavalry in Nisaea, as can be inferred from Classical texts, for example:

It was on this journey that Alexander is said to have also seen the plain in which the royal mares were pastured; the plain itself was called the Nesaean and the horses Nesaean, as Herodotus tells us; and there were originally about a hundred and fifty thousand mares, but at that time Alexander found no more than fifty thousand, as most of them had been driven off by robbers.[35]

These numbers match the figures given by Diodorus Siculus, although we do not know how much Classical authors copied from each other:

Next he [Alexander] came to a land [Nisaea] which could support enormous herds of horses, where of old they say that there were one hundred and sixty thousand horses grazing, but at the time of Alexander's visit there were counted only sixty thousand.[36]

Strabo in his *Geography* mentions the favourable conditions of Media and Armenia for horse-breeding:

Now most of the country is high and cold … This, as well as Armenia, is an exceptionally good 'horse-pasturing' country; and a certain meadow there is called 'Horse-pasturing', and those who travel from Persis and Babylon to Caspian Gates pass through it; and in the time of the Persians it is said that fifty thousand mares were pastured in it and that these herds belonged to the kings. As for Nesaean horses, which the kings used because they were the best and the largest, some writers say that the breed came from here, while others say from Armenia. They are characteristically different in form, as are also the Parthian horses, as they are now called, as compared with the Helladic and other horses in our country. Further we call the grass that makes the best food for horses by the special name 'Medic', from the fact that it abounds there.[37]

Writing about Armenia, he adds:

The country is so very good for 'horse-pasturing', not even inferior to Media, that the Nesaean horses, which were used by the Persian kings, are also bred here. The satrap of Armenia used to send to the Persian king twenty thousand foals every year at the time of the Mithracina. Artavasdes, at the time when he invaded Media with Antony, showed him, apart from the rest of the cavalry, six thousand horses drawn up in battle array in full armour. Not only the Medes and the Armenians pride themselves upon this kind of cavalry, but also the Albanians, for they too use horses in full armour.[38]

The Pazyryk burial

The Pazyryk burial, a Scythian kurgan (barrow grave) in the Altai, is an extraordinary find, with some 60 horse remains of the fifth century BC. Buried deep in the frozen ground, the dead animals were very well preserved; some had the stomach contents not yet digested, making it possible to identify their diet and consequently the kind of work they were performing while still alive (Fig. 2.23).

The bodies were measured and classified by size, varying, for the adults, from 13 to 15 hands (132–152 cm). There was a clear difference of breeding, some being fine saddle horses measuring from 14 to 15 hands (142–152 cm), and others typically draught horses 13 hands high (132 cm). The more refined, clearly Type III or Type IV horses, had a dished face, short back, and well-formed limbs. They were mostly golden-dun

2.23 Drawings of the 'quality' horses found at the fifth-century BC Pazyryk tombs, buried together with 'heavy' horses and carts.

with dark manes and tail and were buried with saddles and bridles, leaving no doubt as to their use as riding horses.

The coarser ones, unmistakably Type I Przewalski individuals, were short, with long backs, short legs and sub-convex profiles, and were buried with their harness, obviously being employed to draw the four-wheel carriages buried with them. Some were geldings and the examination of the stomach contents revealed that they were fed with grain, an indication that they were kept in stables.

There was no grey or piebald, and no white stars or stockings. According to Dr Bökönyi, 'These horses had originated, in all probability, in Central Asia, though it cannot be ascertained from which territory. In [V.O.] Vitt's view they could by no means have been of Mongolian origin.'[39]

The Altai region, the country of the Mongolian Type II horse, is far north of Media and Persia. The refined 'dished-faced' horse from Pazyryk has nothing to do with the Przewalski indigenous type, and they must have been a product of genetic improvement made with the input of Nisaean or Bactrian strains, most probably the latter, as these were the horses used by the neighbouring Chinese to refine their own heavy Przewalski, Type II animals. The concave face of the Pazyryk fine horses, on the other hand, indicates that some contribution from Type IV was present, and that this input could only have come from an as yet unknown strain, other than the Nisaean or the Bactrian. It is intriguing, however, that no piebald or white marks existed in these crosses.

The horse from Cyrenaica

There were two invasions involving horses in Cyrenaica, today's Libya. The first was in 1200 BC, by the 'Sea People' from Crete, who tried to conquer Egypt only to be defeated by Ramses III (see Chapter 6). The contribution of these peoples in increasing the horse population of Africa is of minor importance and will be discussed further in Chapter 9.

Herodotus wrote the first historical report about the settlement of the Greeks from Thera in Cyrene, North Africa, in 630 BC:

> Later, things started to go badly for him [Battus] personally and for Thera in general. The Therans were unaware of the reasons for this, so they sent emissaries to Delphi to ask about the problems that were afflicting them. The Pythia replied that things would improve for them if they helped Battus found Cyrene in Libya. They subsequently fitted Battus with two penteconters and sent him

off. The explorers ... founded a settlement on an island off Libya; the name of the island ... was Platea.

Battus, the founder of the colony, ruled for forty years, and his son Arcesilaus for sixteen years. In their lifetimes the Cyrenean population remained at pretty much the level it had been when they first set out to colonize Libya. During the reign of their third king ... the Cyreneans invited settlers to come ... Soon a considerable mass of people gathered in Cyrene and took over plots of the surrounding land.[40]

Cyrenaica became a great cultural and commercial centre in ancient Africa and horse breeding was one of the main activities of this African colony. According to Herodotus, the Libyans learned from the Cyrenaican Greeks the many arts of equitation, including the use of the quadriga, a chariot with four horses abreast: 'The next tribe to the west after the Giligamae are the Asbystae ... No Libyan tribe relies on four-horse chariots more than them. By and large, they try to imitate the Cyreneans.'[41]

Miklos Jankovich makes some important remarks about the Cyrenaican horses:

In the veins of the Cyrenaican horses coursed the blood of the Bactrian Horse, already naturalized in the Near East, as is abundantly shown by North African and Greek equestrian art, as well as by documentary evidence. ...

So the Cyrenian colony played the same part in Greek history as had Bactria in the Persian. Its influence in horse-breeding in the Greek homeland persisted for centuries. Cyrenaica and Bactria had been connected, by way of the Silk Road, for centuries, so that it will have been possible at any time to reinforce the breeding-stock by a refreshing draught from the original source.[42]

It is important to recognize that, if these dates are correct, equitation was new in North Africa at that time (630 BC), coming *after* the introduction there of the war chariot. In the north-western part of the African continent, in the Maghrib, horses continued to be used and the Barb or Berber was probably established as a local breed around that date.

In his *History of Greece,* George Grote writes about the wonderful Cyrenaican horses:

Their breed of horses was excellent, and their chariots or waggons with four horses could perform feats admired even by Greeks. It was to these horses that the princes and magnates of Kyrênê [Cyrene] and Barka owed the frequent successes of their chariots in the games of Greece.[43]

Sophocles, in the *Electra* (lines 695–750), and Pindar in the *Pythian Odes* both mention these African horses.

Some authors consider the quadriga depicted in the equestrian statues of San Marco in Venice to be a copy of an ancient Greek sculpture (Fig. 2.24), the latter being a reproduction of Cyrenaican horses, particularly because the quadriga (four horses abreast) was the usual driving team used in Cyrene and Barka.

Just before the foundation of Cyrene, the famous Colaeus (Kolaios) expedition to Tartessus left from the Island of Platea near Libya to establish the first recorded commercial contacts between the Greek and Iberian populations.[44] A more detailed account of this circumnavigation is given in the section dealing with Tartessus (Chapter 8). However, this chapter cannot conclude without mentioning Bökönyi's study of the Bronze and Iron Age horses in Europe.

BÖKÖNYI'S THEORY

Dr Sándor Bökönyi, a highly respected authority on eastern European horses, is the author of a controversial theory about the evolution of European and central Asian horses of the Bronze and Iron Ages. His prolific work was undertaken in the 1960s when less information was available about Iberian and other South European horses. These are completely ignored in his writings which, like most existing archaeological literature, is almost entirely concentrated in Eastern, Central and Western Europe, north of the Pyrenees. Although his interesting conclusions do not hold up when applied to Iberia, it is valuable to be aware of his ideas.

According to Dr Bökönyi, Bronze Age horses in Europe were one single homogeneous group, and no local subgroups could be discerned among them. From the west to the east of the continent these horses were of the same type and body size. As time went by, the soil and climatic conditions in Western Europe, poorer than in the east, made the occidental horses smaller and smaller until the difference between them and their eastern counterparts reached a climax in the Iron Age. Then, Bökönyi says, two different groups of horses could definitely be recognized, as he explains:

> We have tried to set up the two groups on a geographical basis separating the finds of the territories eastwards and westwards respectively from the approximate line of Vienna–Venice. The word 'groups' we have used intentionally

2.24 The 'quadriga' from San Marco, Venice, dating from about AD 150–250. The depictions are probably of Nisaean horses.

instead of the denominations 'type' or 'breed', since the former would refer to genetical differences and the latter to the assumption of planned stock-breeding, whereas neither appears to be proved. This division on a geographical basis has been proved on grounds of the measurement data and, to a certain extent, craniologically too. The members of the eastern group are the Iron Age horses of the eastern part of Central Europe, of Eastern and Southeastern Europe, while those of the western group are horses of the Iron Age originating from the western part of Central Europe.[45]

It is obvious that this discussion is centred on northern, central and eastern Europe and does not consider the situation in southwestern Europe, especially in the Iberian Peninsula, where during the European Iron Age an indigenous breed was already known and described in Classical literature.

Dr Bökönyi considers that the foundations of the eastern group were the Scythian horses from north Iran and southern Russia, obtained by the nomadic Scythians when they invaded Europe, and that these horses expanded from Central Europe to the Altai mountains, always keeping a fairly homogeneous type. These bigger eastern horses were highly appreciated by the western inhabitants and sought after for improving their own breeds.

This opinion clearly diverges from that of Strabo, who wrote that Scythian horses were small, bad tempered and castrated – all indications of inferior animals – completely different from this image of 'horses of quality' given by Dr Bökönyi. We could of course assume that the Scythians from the time of Strabo improved their horses after they moved away from their homeland[46] and had access to finer strains in the Pontic-Caspian steppes and Persia, so that later on, in the Iron Age, they were different, better animals.

This problem and the obvious influence of the horses from Ferghana, Bactria and so on in the refinement of Iron Age eastern horses is recognized by Bökönyi:

> Anyhow, it seems that, side by side with the undoubtedly excellent Scythian horses, there existed in Central Asia smaller local groups of horses. The members of these groups were larger of body and perhaps also possessed other eminent qualities lacking in the former. They must have been valued highly by the Scythians themselves, and so it was only the leaders who came by them – and even they could only acquire few of them – since only one was found in each kurgan. Chinese sources, too, made mention of these horses. The horses in question were chiefly Ferghana horses, whose fame was well known in China too … In the excellent horses of the kurgans of Pazyryk, Vitt seems to have found this group, and demonstrated this fact on an osteological basis too. Evidently these horses had played a part in developing Persian horses, which, according to several sources were so very excellent …[47]

In his final conclusions, Dr Bökönyi sums up all his previous considerations as follows:

> The Iron Age horses of Central and Eastern Europe can be divided into two groups, which can be separated also according to the areas where they lived. One, the eastern group, can be traced back to the Scythian horses, and as such followed up in Asia as far as the Altai Mountains; in Eastern Europe and the eastern part of Central Europe up to the line of Vienna–Venice it was the only prevalent group. The other, the western group, on the other hand, belongs to

the Iron Age in the western part of Central Europe and occurred in its most characteristic form as the horse of the Celts. Out of the two groups the eastern horses were bigger of body and better from a breeder's point of view. It was for this very characteristic that they found their way from the Scythians to other people too … It seems to be highly probable that the differences between the two groups were due to the differences in climatic and soil conditions and perhaps to the different ways in which they were kept; the horses of the Bronze Age all over Europe, the ancestors of the Iron Age horses of the western part of the continent, show on grounds of the material available up to now a homogeneous picture, and this seems to contradict the idea that they may have come originally from the steppes of Eastern Europe or Asia. As for the Iron Age horses of Eastern Europe, they came at a later time from northwestern Asia.[48]

All these thoughts are more or less in agreement with the facts presented in the previous section (see pp. 46-61), including the existence of more than one 'horse of quality', a concept implied but not explicit in Bökönyi's texts. It is also clear that the influence of the famous horses of the Pontic-Caspian and Persia in the foundations of Iron Age horses was enormous, and this was recognized by the great Hungarian hippologist. How did these horses come into contact – if ever – with the Iberian horses? If we accept Bökönyi's theory, any contact – if it ever existed – was not the work of the Celts. In fact his opinion of Celtic horses is not very flattering:

First of all we must destroy the romantic hypothesis, which originated at the end of the last century … that the Celts were the best horse-breeders of the Iron Age and their horses the best individuals of the period. This assumption … was already refuted by Boessneck (1958) when he demonstrated that the Celtic horses were to be considered as the lowest link in a process of diminishing body-size; the smallest-bodied horses at the end of the chain. Now it has turned out that parallel with the Celtic horses there lived a group of horses in the eastern part of Central Europe, in Southeast and Eastern Europe whose members were larger of body than the Celtic horses … The Celts did not practice breeding selection, so they could not be expected to breed some race better than those surrounding them …[49]

The Iron Age Celtic culture belongs in the second volume of this work, which covers the historic period beginning with the Roman Empire. Chapter 8 of this volume shows that Celtic cultural values were absorbed by Iberian populations in a cultural diffusion process, without invasions or conquests. In this case it cannot be assumed that migrations of horses took place or that foreign strains were introduced. That leaves only the Indo-European migrations of pre-Celtic times, such as the 'Bell Beakers' (Chapter 6), as the sole possible agent of communication with eastern horses coming from the north, via the Atlantic or crossing the Pyrenees in prehistoric times, and reinforces the opposing hypotheses of a Mediterranean origin for this contact, which assumes Greek peoples as the agents of the introduction of agriculture and equitation on the Iberian Peninsula, as proposed by Stuart Piggott.[50] These prehistoric movements and developments on the Iberian Peninsula will now be considered in detail in the following chapters.

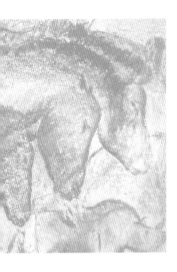

Chapter Three

THE PALAEOLITHIC

(2.4 Million to 13,000/10,000 BC)

THE DEVELOPMENT OF SOCIETY

Horses have roamed the Iberian Peninsula since the very beginning of *Equus'* existence. The first hard evidence of the presence of the horse is from the Palaeolithic archaeological sites scattered all over Iberia and the south of France. Archaeological evidence in the Iberian Peninsula goes back to the Middle Pleistocene (500,000 BC). At that time, a rather limited fauna, mostly composed of rhinoceros, deer, elephant and equines, lived in the open areas that dominated the local landscape. The climate was temperate and humid and, due to the southern location and the proximity of the ocean, the temperature differences between the glaciations and interglaciations were less intense than elsewhere in Europe.

European archaeological sites from the Pleistocene indicate the existence of human groups as long ago as 120,000 BC. In Portugal, these sites are located near the ocean, in a zone limited by the rivers Tagus and Mondego. Deserving special mention are the sites of Vilas Ruivas and Tomar. Less ancient are Figueira Brava and Montemor o Novo (Escoural Cave), the latter inhabited since 40,000 BC.

The period from 40,000 to 35,000 BC is marked by great changes, such as the extinction of the Neanderthal, eventually replaced by *Homo sapiens sapiens,* and the large increase in the number and sophistication of lithic instruments and tools.

During the last glaciation (50,000 to 13,000 BC) the Cantabrian range

3.1 Panel in the caves at Lascaux, France, c. 15,000 BC, showing a 'quality' horse, red deer and wild cattle.

was covered with permanent ice caps, the temperatures were very low and it rained copiously. At the glacial climax (18,000 BC), however, the Portuguese Atlantic coast continued to enjoy mild weather conditions, notwithstanding the influx of arctic waters. The favourable environment of grassland and steppe made the horse one of the most common animals among the local fauna. On the northern shores of the Peninsula, the freezing sea currents combined with gelid air circulation may have caused a greater temperature gradient from summer to winter, but the local climate was always friendlier to the biota than in northern Europe (Fig. 3.2).

The heavy snowfalls typical of the long glacial winters not only represented an obstacle for human and animal locomotion but also formed large glaciers which, descending from the top of the mountains, covered large areas as far as the southern Alps with ice, denuding Europe – except for the southern part of the continent – of its trees. The deforested land became steppe and tundra that offered ideal conditions for the survival of herbivores like reindeer, bison and wild horses, large herds of which followed a regular annual migration, moving from summer to winter

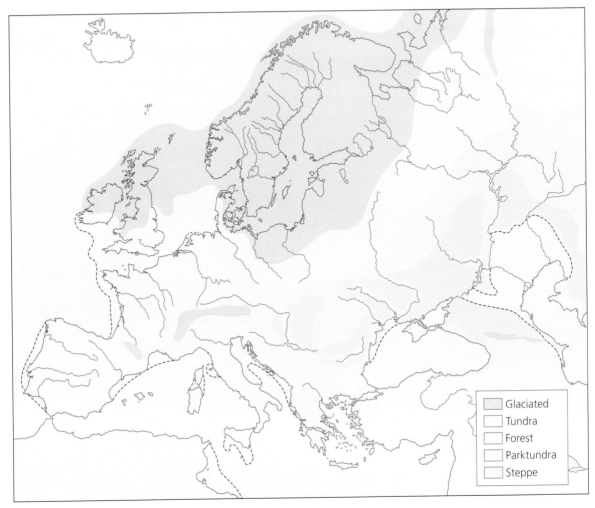

3.2 Europe at the maximum of the last glaciation (c.18,000 BC), showing major vegetation zones, the position of the ice sheets and lower sea level; note that water is even so flowing through the Strait of Gibralter.

Legend:
- Glaciated
- Tundra
- Forest
- Parktundra
- Steppe

pastures. Upper Palaeolithic men, hunter-gatherers who knew these migration routes, settled along them the better to intercept and kill the migrating animals. As a consequence, larger, more populous communities mushroomed in these ecologically favourable regions.

An alternative scenario put forward by some authors is that prehistoric man was necrophagous and searched for the carcasses of dead animals killed by the severe weather or by predators and left behind, buried and preserved in the ice. These carcasses were said to be transported to the interior of caves, defrosted by fire – already tamed by primitive man – and eaten. This would explain the bones of large animals, which could not be killed with the rudimentary weapons of prehistoric man's arsenal, found in many caves.

There are many explanations for the spread of the Upper Palaeolithic culture throughout Europe. The first question posed by archaeologist Paul Mellars is what is the origin of this cultural change. Should the transition be envisaged:

> as occurring, essentially, within the context of purely local, gradually developing populations, or does the transition reflect a much more dramatic process of population replacement, brought about by human groups who originated outside Europe, and effectively colonized the European continent over a relatively short span of time?[1]

The most recent findings tend to support his second version, of a dramatic colonization. In particular, the discovery in Palestine of 'modern human' skeletons dating from 100,000 BC, i.e. some 50,000 years before they appeared in Europe, and recent studies of the DNA of the present-day human population prove that we descended from a single common ancestor within the span of the last 200,000 years. As Mellars concludes:

> If the conclusions of the latter research are taken at face value, they would imply that the earlier 'archaic' populations of Europe (as represented by both the *Homo erectus* and later Neanderthal populations) made little if any genetic contribution to the Upper Palaeolithic and later populations of Europe.[2]

This fact would also explain the end of the Middle Palaeolithic (200,000 to 40,000 BC) and the rapid cultural transition to the Upper Palaeolithic (40,000 to 10,000 BC), as well as the amazing uniformity of the latter culture in all the territories stretching across the vast distance from Israel to the Iberian Peninsula. This transition, however, was not instantaneous; an intermediate period obviously existed with the two populations (Neanderthal and *Homo sapiens*) living together for a long time.

If the movements of humans and humanoids took place without apparent difficulty, there are much stronger reasons to assume that movements of animals, especially horses, must have been very intense. Again according to Mellars, the Upper Palaeolithic lithic technology was already firmly established in East Asia and Africa around 50,000 BC, that is at least five or ten thousand years before making its appearance in Europe. It is also probable that the invention of language accelerated the whole process of cultural uniformity. As human societies were still entirely made up of hunter-gatherers it is also certain that they moved out of Asia Minor into Europe searching for food and pursuing game, an indication that both

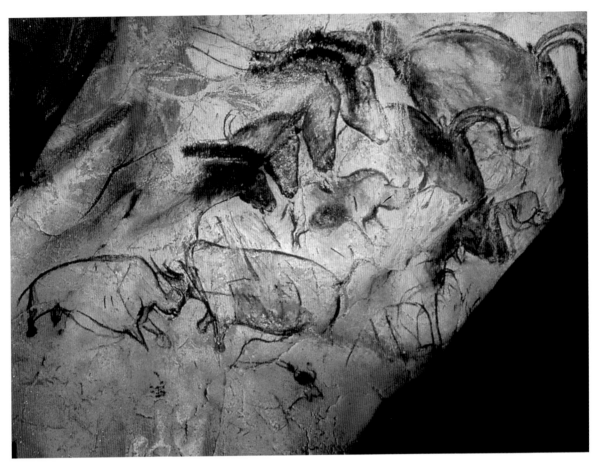

3.3 'Panel of the Horses', Chauvet Cave, France, c. 32,000 BC. Heads of four 'Przewalski' type horses, aurochs and two rhinoceros facing each other.

were abundant in the new frontier, and more strong evidence of the existence of preferred prey, including the horse, in these newly invaded parts of Europe.

The period from 20,000 to 16,000 BC of Solutrean culture is very rich in technological innovation. The specialized hunter is one of the characteristics of the Upper Palaeolithic. In different regions of Europe communities had a certain preferred type of hunting and, as said before, had the capacity to anticipate the migratory habits of the animals, locating themselves along their routes. In the tundra zone of Central-Western Europe, reindeer and wild horses were the chosen prey; further east, the choice was of typical steppe animals, such as the bison, the wild ass and even the mammoth. In the still forested areas of the Mediterranean, red deer and ibex were hunted. In the French Périgord, reindeer remains make up over 90% of the bones found in archaeological sites.

One typical illustration of the hunting culture of the time is the eponymous Solutré Rock, in France (Fig. 3.4), a place that was used to round up and kill reindeer and wild horses. Here the remains of some two thousand or more horses, which were apparently hunted intensively by man, were found. The skeletons, dated to around 12,000 BC, are from two different species – one coarse and one refined – a recurring phenomenon that has already been addressed in the previous chapter and which will be met again. Solutré is a cone-shaped mountain cut in its middle section, from top to bottom, on an angle of approximately 30 degrees. The platform created by this cross section takes the form of a horseshoe, rising from the ground to the opposite and uppermost face of the rock, which is more than 100 meters high. It is covered by grass, interrupted by hundreds of small ponds carved into the rocky soil, where snow or water accumulates, according to the season. It is the ideal environment for brood mares, bringing to mind Homer's literary image of the 'mares impregnated by the Zephir'. The local folklore is rich with stories about horses jumping to their death from the top of the rock, killing themselves to escape from predators, an image immortalized in a novel of Andrien Arcelin (*Chasseurs de Rennes à Solutré*). No animal commits suicide, nor is it credible that they

3.4 The Solutré rock, Burgundy, France. A large quantity of bones found here have given the name Solutré to the horse of this region, from Palaeolithic times.

would fall from the top of the mountain having been stampeded by local prehistoric hunters. Most probably, the horses were killed by indigenous people and then the carcasses thrown down from the rock to be dismembered at the base of the mountain and transported to the interior of the caves, where the meat was eaten. This theory is supported by the fact that large deposits of horse bones were found not at the base of the Solutré rock but several miles away.

The legends surrounding Solutré make other similar cases, where large deposits of horse bones were found and taken as a sure indication of domestication, look suspicious. According to these theories, many large Palaeolithic accumulations of horse remains, unearthed all over Eurasia, came from communities that kept herds of domesticated animals bred for food supply. Much more acceptable is the theory that the horse remains indicate interception points along the migration routes followed by wild horses. As many horses as possible had to be killed on the one occasion each year that they passed these known hunting points if they were to provide enough meat for the hunters.

CAVE ART

The cave art and rock engravings found all over Iberia and southern France are the best proof of the existence of the horse, its importance and its cultural/religious role in Palaeolithic communities.

Two controversial hypotheses surround the complex and mysterious art of the Palaeolithic: the first maintains that the art represents a close resemblance to the actual physical appearance of the animal subjects; the second postulates that any resemblance is purely accidental. The second hypothesis is vehemently refuted by some of the greatest specialists in this subject, such as Marija Gimbutas and André Leroi-Gourhan; both consider these images from Palaeolithic art as messages from their authors, who were trying to communicate with contemporaneous and future generations.

Archaeological investigations revealed that the caves were used as sacred places or as refuges for any emergencies, never as permanent dwellings. Fire was used for illumination, there being no indication that it was used for cooking.

The whole of Palaeolithic art is intimately associated with hunting, which contrary to popular belief is in fact the most ancient of all human professions. The place of meat in the diet of prehistoric man is, however, often exaggerated. According to Richard Rudgley:

A great deal of emphasis has been placed on the role of hunting in the Old Stone Age, and the gathering of plant foods has far less attention than it deserves. The detailed study of modern hunter-gatherers by anthropologists has shown that gathered foods ... often make up 80 per cent of a community's diet, with meat derived from hunting making up the rest. Hunting has been given an inordinate status both by archaeologists and by hunting peoples themselves. In the latter case this is largely due to the fact that it is the men who do most of the hunting and they therefore pride themselves on their own achievements in providing meat and tend to play down the considerable contribution of women. Prehistorians are presented with an archaeological record that contains far more information on hunting than on gathering activities. Animal bones are often found in abundance at Stone Age sites, whereas plant remains and other evidence of the gathering aspect of the economy are sparse, owing to the poor survival of botanical specimens. This has understandably led to a concentration on the available data, which can give the false impression that hunting was the most important means of getting food in the Palaeolithic period.[3]

Nonetheless, animals were widely and indiscriminately hunted and horses were one of the most important prey species for Palaeolithic man.

This long introduction is necessary to lead us to the heart of the subject, the biggest and longest lasting manifestation of the genius of our ancestors, who have left us a treasury of sophisticated forms of representation that make Palaeolithic art both a mystery and a source of admiration and perplexity for all succeeding generations; true jewels of human creativity, surely proclaiming the divine origin of humankind.

Notwithstanding the major disagreements that still exist concerning dating, artefacts and styles, Palaeolithic remains offer in broad outline a coherent inventory which allows the postulation of a relatively uncontroversial case about the lengthy period from 400,000 to 8,000 BC, a timespan much longer than the recorded existence of our species.

Our main actor, the horse, had an impressive role in the prehistory of mankind, present at all places and on all occasions, being in several instances the main theme of the artistic manifestations of our ancestors before the end of the Ice Age. There is no other way to tell the history of these remote ages than through the interpretation of these magnificent works of art, the only testimony of the evolution of *Homo sapiens sapiens* on the face of the planet.

Although it arrived in Europe from America and Asia, one of the first and oldest proofs of the existence of the genus *Equus* in prehistoric times comes from Torralba and Ambrona, near Madrid, both from the Acheulian cultural period, dating from 400,000 to 200,000 BC, when *Homo erectus,* the precursor of *Homo sapiens sapiens* who did not appear until 100,000 BC, still lived. The site at Terra Amata on the French Mediterranean coast dates from this period. Elephant and wild horse bones from animals hunted by local tribes were found at these sites. Also from Iberia but much later (30,000 to 18,000 BC) comes one of the first products of the human intellect: the rock art created at Foz Côa, Portugal (Fig. 3.12), which together with that at the Chauvet Cave (32,000 BC) in France (Figs. 3.3, 3.5, 3.11) are among the most ancient works of art known today. In both cases, the horse is a dominant theme. Next in chronological order comes a long

3.5 'Panel of the Horses', Chauvet Cave, France, c. 32,000 BC. Detail of the horses' heads from Fig. 3.3.

series of caves, the majority of which are located in one or other of these two main southern European regions.

Leroi-Gourhan's classification of styles

One of the most respected studies of cave art was carried out by Prof. André Leroi-Gourhan,[4] who personally visited hundreds of caves, trying to establish a systematic classification of prehistoric art more acceptable than the one made by the Abbé Breuil at the beginning of the twentieth century. Leroi-Gourhan proposes a methodology based on four 'Styles', according to the characteristics of different periods, adding a fifth Style or class for the art of the Mediterranean Palaeolithic, as outlined below.

Style I: Aurignacian (30,000 to 27,000 BC)

The themes in this style are predominantly of a sexual nature and are very realistic. Animals are depicted in a rudimentary and primitive way. Most of the sites included in this category are located in the French Dordogne. Foz Côa (see Fig. 3.12), from the same period, was discovered after the publication of Leroi-Gourhan's book.

Style II: Upper Périgordian and Early Solutrean (25,000 to 18,000 BC)

This style is found in practically the whole of Europe, from Iberia to Russia, and is very impressive in the uniformity of the animal representations, with great emphasis on horses, which are depicted in silhouette, showing only the dorsal outline and usually without legs. Less frequently represented are bison and aurochs. Some of the most important sites are located in the Iberian Peninsula, for instance La Peña de los Hornos and Micolon (Santander), Venta de la Perra (Vizcaya) and La Llueva (Oviedo). In France, the caves of Laussel (Dordogne), Pair-non-Pair (Gironde), Roucadour (Lot), Gargas (Pyrenees), and the female statuettes found at Laussel are equally relevant.

Style III: Upper and Middle Solutrean (18,000 to 12,000 BC)

Here the cave paintings have evolved from Style II, so that rather than the simple contours, horses are now depicted with heads and necks,

3.6 Construction of figures in Style II, according to Leroi-Gourhan. The upper line remains the same, while details are added to characterize the animals. Bison, ox, ibex and horse.

3.7 Style II figures, according to Leroi-Gourhan. Horses from Pair-non-Pair (*top*), La Croze and Labatut.

sometimes long and curved. Some art from this group could be classified as Style IV, the separation between these two styles being a little blurred. Some of the best known caves belong to this group, for example Lascaux (Dordogne; Figs. 3.1 and 3.16), Pech-Merle (Lot; see Fig. 3.19), Isturitz (Pyrenees), Altamira, El Castillo and La Passiega (all Santander).

3.8 (*left*) Principal features of Style III, according to Leroi-Gourhan. Figures from (*top to bottom*) the Périgord, the Lot, Spain and the Pyrenees. Despite geographical variations, proportions and perspectives are the same.

3.9 (*right*) Horses in Style III, according to Leroi-Gourhan. *Top row* from Lascaux, *second row* from Le Gabillou, *third row* from Pech-Merle, *bottom row* from El Castillo (Spain).

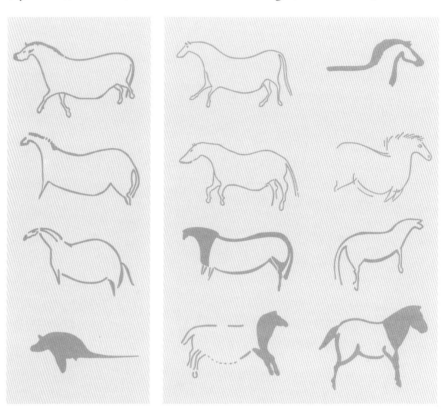

Style IV: From the Magdalenian (12,000 to 8,000 BC)

According to Leroi-Gourhan, in this style 'the animals have a form closer to photographic reality', being both an evolution and a continuation of Style III. In several instances horses are depicted with shoulder stripes and large curved bellies. Some very famous caves are included in this group, for example Les Combarelles and Font-de-Gaume (Dordogne), Grotte de Maesoulas (Haute Garonne), Le Portel (Fig. 3.14) and Niaux (Ariège; Fig. 3.17); and in Iberia, La Cullavera and Las Monedas (Santander); Pindal (Oviedo) and Ekain (Guipuzcoa), the latter being famous for the quality of the horse paintings on its walls.

Mediterranean art

In this additional group Leroi-Gourhan distinguishes a special class for Mediterranean Palaeolithic art, which covers the whole time span described above but with its own typology which does do not fit into any of the previous styles. Included in this group are the Chauvet Cave (Ardèche), dating back to 32,000 BC, and La Pileta (Malaga; see Fig. 2.12), as well as many rock shelters in Andalusia. Horses have great prominence in this group, especially in the Chauvet Cave (Figs. 3.3, 3.5, 3.11).

Portugal

In Foz Côa, horses are the main theme represented in various forms, mostly engraved by means of small perforations on rocks standing in the open (Figs. 3.12, 3.13). The prominent type is most likely the Przewalski horse (Ebhardt's Type I), and it is interesting to note that one particular carving shows a stallion mounting a mare, a rare subject in Palaeolithic art. Some of the horses are engraved over earlier engravings of aurochs, others are pecked out in a silhouette outline. Foz Côa is not the only important Portuguese site of Palaeolithic art. There are many other outstanding testimonies to the period, like the Escoural Cave (Monte Mor), which was inhabited 40,000 years ago. Manuel Farinha dos Santos, following Leroi-Gourhan's criteria, has:

> classified the Escoural paintings into two different phases: the first one is known as 'Style II of Leroi-Gourhan', that is between 25,000 and 18,000 BC, and … the second one is Style III, between 15,000 [sic] and 12,000 BC …
>
> At least eight animal pictures … as well as many symbols and signs situated in the most accessible and visible parts of the cave belong to the first group. On the other hand, the horses and other quadrupeds must be attributed to the second phase …[5]

Also very important is the Mazouco (Trás-os-Montes) archaeological station, with perforated rock engravings belonging to Styles III and IV. All the horses at Mazouco and Foz Côa are of the Przewalski type. Of the Escoural horses, the male is depicted as a more refined type and one mare, of heavier constitution, is shown pregnant.

Very interesting for showing the spread of the horse are the statistics compiled by Leroi-Gourhan, based on the 'themes' (i.e. the number of

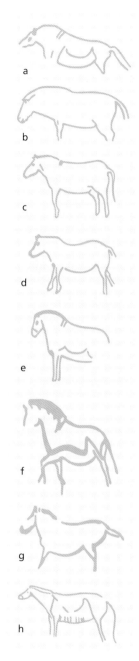

3.10 Principal features of Style IV, according to Leroi-Gourhan. a. from northern france, b–d. from Poitou-Périgord region, e–f. from the Pyrenees, g–h. from Spain.

3.11 'Panel of the Horses', Chauvet Cave, France, c. 32,000 BC. A Przewalski-type horse, the upright mane characteristic of this type being clearly visible.

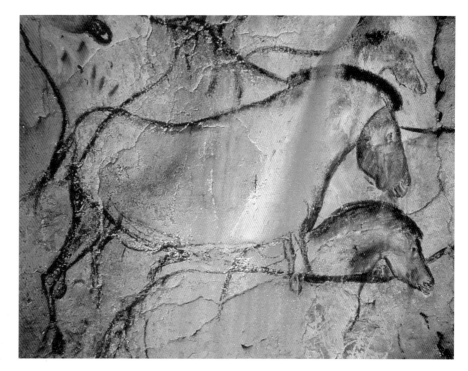

3.12 (*below*) Côa Valley, Portugal, Panel 1 of the Ribeira de Piscos. Two horses with heads intertwined, a pose typical of the courtship phase.

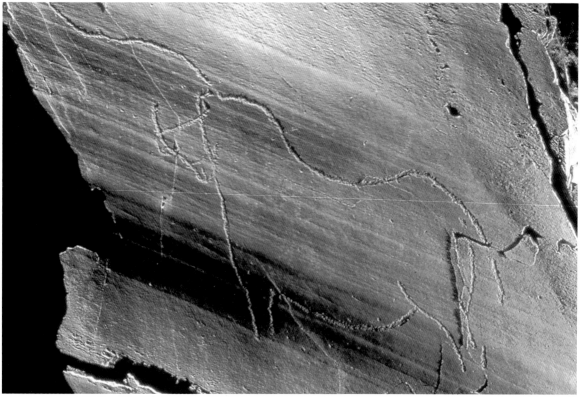

locations where an animal, for instance the horse, appears); the 'object' of the composition (i.e. the number of compositions where the motif, for instance the horse, is depicted) and, the 'number of individuals' (i.e. the number of times in which the individual motif, for instance the horse, appears at each location). This data reveals that the horse is by far the most frequently represented of all animals, as shown in the table.[6]

3.13 Côa Valley, Portugal, Panel 14 of the Canada do Inferno. 'Puncture' or pecked drawing of a heavy horse.

Presence of the horse and bison in Palaeolithic art

	Horse	Bison
Theme	60	45
Object of composition	313	209
Number of individuals	610	510

Leroi-Gourhan goes further and selects eight different important regions: the North, Périgord, Quercy, Pyrenees, Cantabria, Spain (centre and south), Rhône and Italy. The horse is again the animal most frequently represented in six of them, and takes second place in the other two: the Pyrenees (where the bison leads) and Italy (aurochs/bovine).

Leroi-Gourhan analyses the main physical characteristics of the animals represented in Style IV, considering just four distinct areas:[7]

A North (Arcy sur Cure)
B Poitou-Périgord
C Pyrenees
D Iberia

The horses from regions A and B are of the heavy type, with short legs like the little *garrano* from northern Portugal. In area C we have two types: in Marsoulas (Haute Garonne), Niaux (Ariège; Fig. 3.17) and Labastide (Pyrenees) there is one that looks like the Przewalski, and in Les Trois-Frères (Ariège; Fig. 1.4), La Baume Latrone (Gard) and Le Portel (Ariège; Fig. 3.14) there is a more refined one, with a longer, slender curved neck and longer legs. In area D the two types both occur in the northernmost areas, such as Altamira; the refined one is seen at La Peña de los Hornos (Santander). Further south in Las Chimeneas, El Pidal (Oviedo) and Los Casares (Guadalajara), the refined horse is dominant. Both types appear at Ekain (Guipuzcoa).

3.14 Horse from Le Portel, Ariège, France. A more delicate, 'quality' horse's head than the one represented at Trois Frères in the same area (Fig. 3.18).

Further study of morphological types was undertaken by one of the most renowned authorities on Palaeolithic art, Peter J. Ucko. In the book written with A. Rosenfeld,[8] he distinguishes different types of horse in the parietal (wall) paintings of Palaeolithic caves, an exercise that makes the idea of a single 'pure race', proposed by some horse specialists, difficult to support. In this book, the authors observe:

Horses are among the most commonly represented animals in Palaeolithic parietal art. The European wild horse of the late Pleistocene is *Equus caballus,* from which all modern horses derive ... It is difficult, on palaeontological evidence, to distinguish this wild horse from the Przewalski horse which still survives in Mongolia, and therefore to determine to which [form] the Pleistocene wild horses of Europe belonged. The identification of several subspecies of horse in Palaeolithic paintings has been claimed from time to time, including the Przewalski horse, the recently extinct tarpan and various hypothetical forms from which some of the modern breeds are believed to be derived. ...

Zeuner [*A History of Domesticated Animals* (London, 1963)] has suggested that some, at least, of the horses represented in Palaeolithic art are more like the tarpan than the Przewalski horse. He refers particularly to the frieze of small bichrome horses of Lascaux [Figs. 3.1 and 3.16] ... Bourdelle [in *Mammalia,* 2 (1938)] found that he could recognise three horse subtypes in Palaeolithic art; one of which corresponds quite closely to the Przewalski; one of which resembles the present-day 'nordic' horses which are larger and, especially, longer in the back than the Przewalski horse, and a third type which he compared with the present-day 'celtic' horse. However, as Windels [*The Lascaux Cave Paintings* (London, 1949)] has shown, for the Lascaux horses the characteristics of the different forms isolated by Bourdelle and others are by no means exclusive, for features such as the position of the head, the position of the mane and the position of the tail overlap considerably. Windels suggests that this overlapping of characteristics could be explained if different subspecies of horses had been in the process of differentiation and had not yet become fully characterised. Alternatively, the so-called horse types might be the result of artistic license and artistic conventions. One has only to look at the different stylistic conventions employed in different caves for showing the horse's head to see the weight of this argument. Thus, in Pech-Merle [Fig. 3.19] the head is shown as a small narrow almost shapeless projection on the neck, the 'duck-bill' head of Laming [*Lascaux* (London, 1959)]; at Lascaux the horses' heads are generally disproportionately small and narrow, but with the nostrils, and sometimes the eye shown;

3.15 Horses' heads by Palaeolithic artists from different areas, indicating the range of styles.
Row 1 Santander, Spain; 2 Lascaux; 3 Le Gabillou; 4 Pyrenees; 5 Ariège; 6 and 7 Dordogne and surrounding regions.

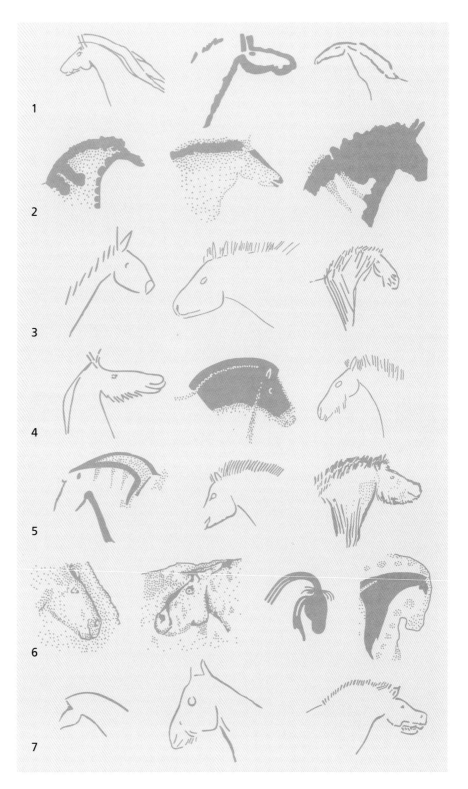

[Fig. 3.16] in contrast the horse's head from Niaux [Fig. 3.15], for example, is carefully outlined and shaded, with detail of the nostril, mouth, eye and chin hairs shown with little or no distortion. [9]

Another interesting opinion about the same issue is voiced by Colin P. Groves who, after considering cave art in general as disappointing evidence of the true appearance of a species, points out:

There are of course exceptions: there is the marvellous and exact horse from Niaux [Fig. 3.15], with its shaggy coat, thick head, bearded chops and upright mane, with nostrils, lips, eyes, all picked out with care and artistry. In such a case, there is little doubt that the artist was depicting the local tundra horse, *Equus ferus solutreensis,* and in any case only the northern pony is known with any certainty as a fossil from the Franco-Cantabrian area where this form of cave art flourished. This has not prevented several authors from finding a whole

3.16 A quality horse from Lascaux, France, c.15,000 BC, represented with short legs and upright mane.

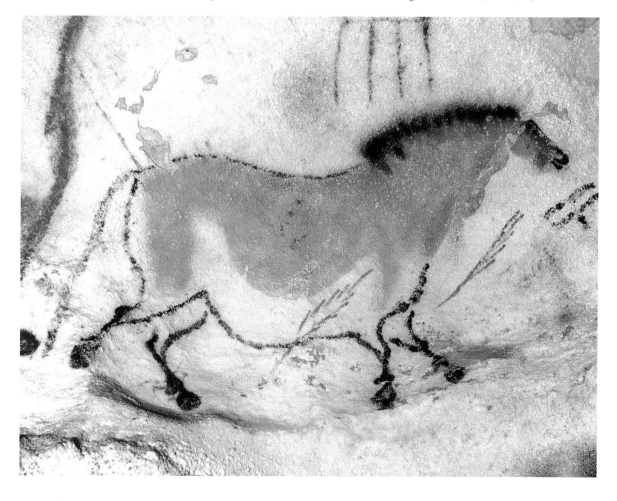

3.17 Quality horse from Niaux, France, with eyes, mane and nostrils clearly represented.

galaxy of horse species and subspecies represented on cave walls, defined by colour, head shape, body form, limb length and so on – all surely subject to the greatest artistic license.

None the less, there are one or two interesting conclusions which can, I think, validly be derived from these sources. One concerns the mane. If one has seen only Przewalski horses with upright manes, then surely one does not imagine a hanging or flowing mane out of the top of one's head? Yet a falling mane, such as characterises most domestic horses, can be found, though rarely, in Franco-Cantabrian art, such as the horse at Le Portel [Fig. 3.14], remarkable for its rhythm and movement in its execution. I would conclude from this that there must have been a type of horse with a flowing mane, living in that region at that time: probably, to judge from the ratio of erect to falling manes (about 10:1) a rather scarce species. *Equus mosbachensis,* perhaps?

Then there are the much discussed horses of Pech-Merle [Fig. 3.19]; two little fellows standing back-to-back, their rumps overlapping, with ridiculous short legs but graceful, sweeping necks and heads and, again, falling mane and forelock depicted in a darker colour.[10]

The meaning of these representations of horses and other animals – often depicted hurt or apparently dead – in the mythology of Palaeolithic peoples is also a very controversial subject, some authors postulating that animals were the object of magical or religious cults.

3.18 Przewalski-type horse from Trois Frères, Ariège, France.

3.19 (*below*) Two 'quality' horses from Pech-Merle, France. Standing back to back, with rumps over-lapping, graceful necks and heads.

The role of the hunter and his importance and association with male values are perpetual themes in the literature of all periods, from the Greek philosophers such as Plato and Aristotle to Ortega y Gasset in modern times. One of the oldest pages in literature, the Epic of Gilgamesh (2000 BC), chants about the virility of the hunter: 'I killed the bear and the hyena, the lion and the panther, the stag and the ibex, all the varieties of wild game and small creatures.' Leroi-Gourhan explains this expression of virility and masculinity and its influence on the symbolism of the horse in Palaeolithic art:

> Without overly forcing the evidence, we can view the whole of Palaeolithic figurative art as the expression of ideas concerning the natural and the super-natural organization of the living world (the two might have been one in Palae-olithic thought). Can we go further? It is possible that the truth corresponds to this frame of reference, which is still much too broad. To gain a dynamic understanding of cave art, one would still have to integrate into this framework the symbolism of the spear and the wound. Taken as symbols of sexual union and death, the spear and the wound would then be integrated in a cycle of life's renewal, the actors in which would form two parallel and complementary series: man/horse/spear, and woman/bison/wound.[11]

Following this same line of reasoning it is interesting to note that horse bones constituted a small minority (less than 15%, according to Nancy Sandars)[12] of the deposits found at Palaeolithic sites, which in a way supports Leroi-Gourhan's assumption of the magical or supernatural role of the horse in the mythology of ancient man, rather than as just a supplier of food.

CONCLUSION

The first important conclusion for the development of the theme of this book is the clear indication, from all sources, of the existence of at least two different types of horse in Western Europe since the Palaeolithic. These two types of wild horse are abundantly represented in Palaeolithic art. One type looks like the heavier Przewalski wild horse and was the most commonly represented. The other, a more refined one, is seen mostly on the Iberian side of the Pyrenees and in the southern part of the Peninsula. Both have convex head profiles and, sometimes, stripes on the shoulders and legs.

The opinion of Miklos Jankovich is interesting:

The existence of such a 'wild blood-horse' is conceivable in the light of pictures occurring in Palaeolithic cave art. In Europe these pictures present among a variety of equine types, including recognizable Northern Pony and Tarpan types, not only some markedly 'cold-blooded' specimens such as this ram-headed 'earth-horse' from Combarelles but also a stamp of horse full of quality, 'hot-blooded' in modern European parlance. Such are seen among others on the walls of caves at Altamira and Lascaux [Figs. 3.1, 3.16], and must imply that in the Cantabrian region long before domestication there was a stamp of wild horse that has vanished. One such variety, apparently about the size of Grévy's zebra among modern equines, and perhaps striped (since some European pony breeds show vestigial stripes on the legs and blurred marks on the shoulder, in combination with an eel-stripe), represents the unknown factor in the ancestry of our domestic horses.[13]

Very interesting is the description above of 'vestigial stripes on the legs and blurred marks on the shoulder', typical of the Sorraia of Portugal. It is also important to repeat that during the Palaeolithic, such a rich and varied collection of art and such strong proof of the presence of indigenous wild horses existed nowhere else other than Iberia and Southern France.

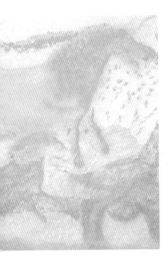

Chapter Four

THE MESOLITHIC

(13,000 to 8,000 BC)

GENERAL VIEW

The years 13,000–8,000 BC are generally accepted by convention as the beginning of the Mesolithic, an intermediary period between the end of the Ice Age and the birth of agriculture, the innovation that initiated the Neolithic (see Fig. 1.3). During the Ice Ages, the Iberian Peninsula was a true refuge for animals, men and plants, expelled by the hard weather prevailing in the north of Europe.

The end of the Palaeolithic, around 13,000 BC, came abruptly, accelerated by the temperature increase and the resulting changes in the environment. Favourable weather conditions brought with them post-glacial forests; the ice retreated and its melting down caused the sea level to rise around most of the continent.

The mild weather and greater availability of food encouraged the organization of small, mobile, self-sufficient human communities with little or no hostility between neighbours. Many groups discovering new lands with abundant food supplies ended up by putting down roots, especially near the seashore, where they developed fishing activities and larger communities which required better social relations both among their own members and with other similar groups.

Alterations in human behaviour resulting from such changes were drastic, forcing radical adaptations not only to forest hunting, very different from that conducted in the open, but also to the changes in both the quantity and type of fauna and the new physical environment. According to Paul Mellars:

> From studies of animal populations in modern environments it is clear that forested habitats can support only around 20–30 per cent of the total biomass of animal populations which can be maintained in open environments. Similarly, it is clear that the kinds of animals encountered in forested environments tend to be much less migratory in their seasonal habits, and to be distributed in smaller, more widely dispersed groups. In other words, the human groups would have needed to accommodate their behaviour not only to a sharply *reduced* overall food supply, but also to the pursuit of animals whose behaviour was very different from that of the earlier glacial species.[1]

Last but not least, ungulates such as equines and the reindeer family are open-space creatures that do not adapt well to forested environments lacking good pasturelands.

The human response to these alterations was twofold: some groups migrated northwards, following the retreat of the steppe and the animals that went in that direction; others adapted to the new environment, remaining in the same area that they had always lived in.

The dislocation of the biota following the retreat of the ice was obviously not an instantaneous phenomenon, but on the contrary a long millennial process. What happened was not a 'migration', but a very slow, secular advance, in the human case each group moving almost imperceptibly over many generations. The consequences of the changes in weather conditions were more deeply felt in northern Europe. In the south of the continent the changes were much less dramatic, with dry weather rather than low temperatures being the limiting factor of plant growth. During the first phase of the post-glacial, pine trees occupied the higher grounds while oak trees grew in the lowlands. However, in areas of low rainfall, like the south of Portugal and Greece, deciduous forests continued to prevail, now side-by-side with fields of low arboreal vegetation.

The post-glacial fauna, like the flora, also differed considerably from that of previous ages, due not only to continuous weather changes but also to intensified human activity. Many species of larger mammals like the mammoth and the rhinoceros became extinct, while reindeer followed the retreating ice northwards.

The forests that covered northern Europe by the end of the Ice Age did not constitute ideal habitat for equines and other herbivores, which were thus forced to move out to other steppe and grassland areas. Surely many migrated to the East European and Asian steppes, while others might have travelled to the Iberian Peninsula, joining the existing local populations; the inverse flow, however – a migration out of the Peninsula – is not very credible and there is not a single piece of evidence to show that it occurred.

In Iberia, hunting continued to offer the human population a good supply of meat and protein, and new methods, developed from the use of new weapons and requiring the participation of many individuals, were employed, as attested by the paintings in the Cueva de los Caballos showing a band of hunters pursuing a herd of female deer and their offspring, heading them in the direction of four companions armed with bows and arrows (Fig. 4.1). Animal traps for small animals like rabbits and hare were also developed.

The lower mobility of the animals hunted the most in the Iberian Peninsula also explains the increase in settled communities, more numerous and populous than those on the other side of the Pyrenees. Even considering the location of these settlements near the coast, where the mild climate favoured an abundant supply of seafood and thus diminished the dependence on hunting, this activity never ceased, being always responsible for an important component of the diet of these prehistoric Iberian tribes. The so-called 'concheiros' or shell middens are very typical of Mesolithic Portugal, as described below:

> The development of the type of hunter-gathering economy adopted by the post-glacial human communities from the coast and fluvial estuary areas, in the Portuguese case leads from the middle of the 6th millennium BC to the surge of shell middens, which sometimes formed compact volumes of several thousand cubic meters, mainly at the estuaries of the rivers Sado and Tagus, specially in Muge, over a vast time span that corresponds to the High Mesolithic, which extends until the 3rd millennium BC – when these shell midden communities had already settled at those regions – these shell middens being very rich and diverse archaeological sites. There the remains of consumed fauna are identified, as well as stone and horn utensils – of which the geometric microliths attract special attention – different decorative objects, house structures and the graves of adults and children. The consumed fauna, although in quantitative terms dominated by shellfish, is qualitatively varied with the mammals (boar, deer, *horse* [my emphasis], aurochs), fish and birds contributing approximately half the caloric value of the diet.[2]

4.1 Rock art from the Spanish Levant, the Cueva de los Caballos. Red deer are driven towards a hunting party.

Steven J. Mithen has interesting comments on this subject:

Large terrestrial mammals have, for many years, been assumed to be the essence of Mesolithic economies. Their pre-eminence is gradually being eroded, however, as the productivity of the marine and freshwater environments are appreciated and as studies of human bone provide direct evidence for a significant amount of aquatic foods in the diet. Nevertheless, the hunting of large terrestrial mammals remains central to the Mesolithic, for, even if they were not the staple food supply in all areas, they may have required the greatest time to exploit, and they had considerable social significance.[3]

In Iberia, there were never the mass killings of horses which elsewhere indicated the urgent need to intercept and hunt them on the one annual occasion when they passed strategic points along their seasonal migratory routes. In comparison with other sites in northern Europe, where archaeological objects are rare and scattered over large areas, in the Iberian Peninsula both the most primitive cave settlements and those in the open occur in great density, indicating that through all the cycles of the Pleistocene, the regions of southern Europe and the Mediterranean were occupied continuously on a uniform basis, making it clear that food, including meat, was always available. Ceramics, considered a technology of the Neolithic, already existed in a rudimentary form in some regions of Mesolithic Europe, a sign of sedentary or semi-sedentary communities.

It was also during the Mesolithic that the first ocean-going fishing boats made their debut, and human settlements were established on many islands, indicating that these boats were large enough to navigate the high seas. Again, according to Steven Mithen:

> Efficient water transport would have been essential for the Mesolithic communities of Europe for various subsistence activities, to move between different habitats, and for communication between groups. During the Mesolithic, many offshore islands were colonized, such as the Hebrides and those of the Mediterranean, and substantial boats would have been necessary for the sea crossings.[4]

It is not impossible that the first overseas transportation of horses from the Iberian Peninsula to North Africa, aboard these primitive boats, took place during the Mesolithic. If true, this implies that horses were already domesticated.

As in previous periods, during the Mesolithic stone tools were preponderant, but were now associated with microliths, minor stone objects used mainly for arrow heads and other hunting weapons. The microlith, the most typical and important artefact of the period, comes in a variety of forms, but it is the arrow head, in its various formats, that really indicates the changes in hunting style and way of life. As Prof. Leroi-Gourhan writes: 'This arsenal of miniscule arrow points and little blades evokes bow hunting, fishing, the harvest of wild graminae with the aid of small flint scythes.'[5]

4.2 Paintings at Alpera, Albacete, Spain, depicting archers hunting ibex and domesticated cattle.

Microlith parts have been found with many human and animal bones encrusted on to them, denoting that they were used to kill enemies and for hunting. Wood, horns and bones were also extensively used. In addition, more sophisticated houses were built during the Mesolithic, notably at Moita do Sebastião on the Muge valley in Portugal, dating back to 5000 BC.

Mesolithic societies had a basic organization and good knowledge about the environment, the habits of their prey and seasonal changes. Consequently different types of settlements were built, from transitory camps for short stays to permanent villages occupied by a large number of residents. Temporary camps predominated in the north of Europe while in Iberia more permanent settlements were found, as for instance those of the Asturian culture of the north coast of Spain (7500–6500 BC).

Also dating from the Mesolithic are the first cemeteries, which took the place of the individual tombs until then dominant. The cemetery indicates larger populations and occurs more frequently near the coast or on river and lakeshores, more prosperous regions with better food supplies which made them the home of the first large communities. Many skeletons from the Mesolithic show injuries caused by the impact of projectiles, possibly the result of hunting accidents or fights among rival groups. Some tombs had objects buried with the deceased, indicating some sort of funereal rites, and this differentiation among the dead marks the birth of the early hierarchical societies in Europe. The western European and Iberian tombs, unlike the Pontic-Caspian ones, never had horses buried with their masters, a fact that may indicate that the horse was already domesticated in the west before any Indo-European invasion and importation of customs occurred. We thus lack this important testimony so plentiful in the steppes, as will be discussed later.

While Palaeolithic men are known as 'great hunters', their Mesolithic heirs are considered as 'small hunters' who consumed meat from small animals and molluscs. Gabriel Camps describes this traditional (yet false) conception of Mesolithic peoples:

> These [Mesolithic] men are often depicted as miserable beachcombers, wandering in search of shellfish and other gifts of nature swept in by the tides. The next stage in this gloomy vision is to imagine these emaciated peoples trapped between a hostile forest and a still inaccessible ocean, living in a chronic state of anxiety about the future, all their energies being devoted to day-to-day survival.[6]

MESOLITHIC ART

Mesolithic art is not monumental, mysterious or even to any extent religious, unlike Palaeolithic art; it is mostly schematic, geometric and, except for that of the Spanish Levant, no longer figurative as in the Palaeolithic. It now contains small human figures, totally absent before (Fig. 4.3). The Iberian Peninsula still deserves special attention. The predominant subjects are related to hunting and gathering, and constitute some of the little information we have about daily life in prehistoric Europe. Some of the art shows horses being led by men, which puts them culturally in the Neolithic, when horses have been proven to have been domesticated.

At the important sites, as for example the already mentioned Cueva de los Caballos, the men are armed with bows, arrows and lances and are

4.3 Mesolithic engravings from the Iberian Levant, c. 5000 BC, showing domesticated horses led by hand. This proves that horses were present in Iberia during the Mesolithic period.

shown killing boar and red deer. This leads us to the next prehistoric puzzle: why did the whole magnificent complex of Palaeolithic art, comparable to the highest human creative work of all time, disappear so suddenly at the end of the Ice Age?

The two main centres of Mesolithic art were, without any doubt, the Spanish Levant and North Africa. The North African artistic environment began with the Iberomaurusian complex around 14,000 BC. Over a vast region of the African continent, a very powerful and dynamic culture known as the Capsian evolved (see Chapter 9). The art is generally monochromatic and depicts scenes from daily life, clearly denoting African influences. According to Nancy Sandars: 'The real continuation of Palaeolithic art is not in the Pyrenees nor round the Baltic and the Arctic Ocean, but in that Mediterranean landscape where descendants of Palaeolithic hunters lived on, in Calabria, in Sicily, and above all in Spain.'[7] She continues:

> The archaeology of the Iberian peninsula south of Cantabria and Asturias was distinctive even during the Paleolithic, having many links with North Africa and beginning at some still unfixed time. Around 9000 B.C. new composite tools that required tiny flint blades (microliths) had come into use in North Africa. This technique … crossed the Straits of Gibraltar and entered Spain, where it survived for many centuries. The later population of Iberia was made up partly of descendants of Upper Paleolithic hunters and partly of people from Africa. Only the extreme north was unaffected by the change. The Azilian Mesolithic was entrenched on both sides of the Pyrenees, while the 'Levantine' paintings are clustered south-east of a diagonal running from Lérida to Cádiz.[8]

As Camps points out:

> The sudden disappearance of the great tradition of Magdalenian art would be the consequence of these new living conditions. According to the traditional conception of prehistoric art as motivated by a preoccupation with magic, this people of whelk-eaters and rabbit hunters had no reason to continue to depict large animals, some of which had by then died out in any case. Since collecting shellfish presented no dangers comparable to those of the hunt for aurochs or bison, the magical effect of imagery was no longer needed.[9]

Today this image has been somewhat refined, with the Mesolithic groups being considered as dynamic, creative peoples responsible for the transition from hunter-gatherer groups to productive Neolithic agricultural societies. As Nancy Sandars observes:

> Great as were the changes in climate and environment, they do not alone explain the disappearance of Paleolithic art. On the part played by isolation and lost mobility when forest, dense and deciduous, spread over parkland and steppe, I have already said something… [the population] must have experienced

a concrete rupture with the past, a shock to the elusive influence of place on art. The old sanctuaries could not attract and dominate as they once did, except, and to a much lesser extent, round the Mediterranean in southern Spain, Italy and Sicily. Even more disconcerting than the cessation of large-scale art is the disappearance, about the same time, of small-scale artist's and craftsman's work. Compared with the delicate engraved and carved Magdalenian spear-throwers and 'bâtons', the Mesolithic fish-spears, leister prongs, and so on, are almost without exception monotonous utilitarian objects.[10]

Coming back to our main theme, it is intriguing to note that in the new Mesolithic artistic style, represented in Iberia at a large number of important sites, the horse is no longer depicted as the central subject or even as a secondary figure, being now substituted by hunting themes where goats, deer and other smaller animals are the prey.

This fact has led some authors to jump to the conclusion that horses had become extinct in the Iberian Peninsula during the Mesolithic, as happened in northern Europe, only returning with the Indo-European invaders in the third millennium BC, as a domesticated animal (Fig. 4.4). In other words, these authors believe that during a time span of 5000 years, horses had mysteriously disappeared from Iberia, where favourable conditions for herbivores continued to exist, as proved by the many other mammals such as deer, bovines, ovines and caprines that continued to prosper there. For example, when trying to prove that rock engravings with horses as the central subject at Foz Côa are more than 10,000 years old (they are actually more than 30,000 years old), Chris Scarre writes:

> The position regarding the extinction of the horse is a little less sure. Some archaeologists believe it survived in limited numbers after the Ice Age, but overall it is much more likely that, like the ibex, it disappeared from the region around 10,000 years ago and was absent for the next 5,000 years. Horses were reintroduced to Spain and Portugal as a domestic animal by humans during the third millennium BC.[11]

With all due respect, this is a hasty conclusion, as the author himself recognizes at the beginning of the quoted paragraph. The absence of the horse in Iberian Mesolithic art is certainly puzzling inasmuch as it happened so soon after being the most important subject of Palaeolithic art, as demonstrated above. This fact alone, however, does not justify the conclusion that it became extinct in the area. Many other factors have to

4.4 Cantabrian Palaeolithic art: 1. Palaeolithic horse; 2. Palaeolithic horse's head with halter; 3 & 4. Palaeolithic horses from La Pileta; 5 & 6. Mesolithic horses from the Iberian Levant.

be considered. As we have seen, the Iberian Peninsula never suffered the dramatic shifts in weather conditions imposed by glaciations and inter-glaciations. The local environment was always friendly and favourable to all herbivores, except those biologically adapted to the cold weather, like reindeer and mammoth, which without a doubt moved out following the retreat of the ice. During the climax of the weather disturbances referred to above and when the Ice Age ended it is much more probable that horses leaving the south of France may have entered the Iberian Peninsula look-ing for pastures that had always been there, rather than the inverse move-ment of equines leaving Iberia and going to inhospitable environments north of the Pyrenees. Some Mesolithic species may have disappeared as a consequence of excess hunting, but as Steven J. Mithen writes:

> It is very difficult, however, to make detailed reconstructions of past environ-ments as the majority of animal and plant remains are recovered from archaeo-logical sites and hence pass through a 'cultural filter'. If a particular species is absent, it is often unclear as to whether it was not present in the early post-gla-cial environment or simply not exploited by the Mesolithic hunter-gatherers.[12]

The bow, so often represented in the art of the Spanish Levant, although a Mesolithic invention, was widely used and perfected during the Neolithic. It probably did not exist in the Palaeolithic. Another hypothesis attributes the absence of the horse in the art of the period to the invention and spread of the use of both bow and arrow, as the main hunting and fighting weapon of the age (Fig. 4.5). This technological innovation made small animal hunting a more interesting proposition. These swift little creatures must have been very difficult to catch – probably mostly with primitive traps – before bows and arrows were available. On the other hand, bigger quadrupeds like horses are not so easy to kill with the primitive microlith pointed arrows used by Mesolithic hunters and, what is more, the horse may by then already have been domesticated for utilitarian purposes. The combination of these two new developments, domestication and the archer, may be the reason behind the end of the hunting of horses in Mesolithic Iberia.

A study made by Jean-Georges Rozoy has shown that pointed projectiles thrown by hand or from specialized instruments must have a certain weight to be efficient, with mass compensating for the low speed of the projectile.[13] Bows give a much greater speed to the projectile (30 metres per second), thus compensating for the low weight of the arrows. The part played by this new weapon in the Mesolithic scenario is not well accepted, however, by Gabriel Camps:

> Nobody will accept that hunting stags instead of reindeer would have had so profound an effect on forms of artistic expression. Neither do I accept J. Rozoy's suggestion that the invention of the bow was the cause of this change: that since hunting became easier thanks to this new weapon, recourse to magic would no longer be necessary to ensure success. If this explanation is to be believed, it must be accepted that Palaeolithic art was a means of invoking magical forces. It must furthermore be noted that the fine wall paintings of the Spanish Levant are the work of deer hunters armed with bows.[14]

But he admits to Mesolithic man's preference for hunting small animals, as confirmed by the art of the period: 'The animals portrayed in Levantine art represent four main species: all are sought-after game animals, first deer, then the ibex, the aurochs and the wild boar. *Horses* [my emphasis] were also hunted but rarely depicted.'[15]

Some authors suggest that the survival and continuous transmission to future generations of the mystical respect the Palaeolithic peoples had for

4.5 Mesolithic art from Les Dogues, Ares del Maestre, Castellón, Spain. Combat between two bands of archers.

the horse preserved it during the Mesolithic, when hunters much preferred to kill smaller animals, abundant and much easier to hunt with arrows, than the horse, an animal they still revered, respected and feared. Besides, the majority if not all of Mesolithic art in Spain is contemporaneous with the first Neolithic farmers, already established in neighbouring areas and thus undoubtedly part of the new era of the recently domesticated horse. The horse's conspicuous absence from art may thus indicate the beginnings of domestication, i.e. a phase during which horses were neither hunted nor yet used for any type of work.

Another more logical explanation suggests that the displacement of peoples is linked to the above-mentioned movement of Mesolithic communities to the seashores, now rich with fish and shellfish as a result of the warming of the oceans. As we have seen, shell middens are an eloquent testimony of this change in the lives of the Iberian populations at that time. Fishing not only fixed the tribes near the ocean but also reduced their dependence on hunting, which became more difficult as the animals generally lived deeper in the hinterland. Seafood and small animals and birds living near the coast could satisfactorily provide the protein requirements of these communities.

It can also be stated that during this intermediate period, pre-dating the emergence of agriculture and domestication – the two essential characteristics of the Neolithic – horses were still wild and not part of the domestic lives of local communities, the subject often represented in Mesolithic art. Therefore they are absent from the art, but this absence alone is not sufficient to conclude that they were extinct.[16]

By the end of the Pleistocene mankind was still living in the same way as during the previous 30,000 years, that is, in mobile egalitarian societies. During the next 5000 years three factors completely altered this situation: social differences arose, agriculture developed and man increased his interference with nature and the environment. The various populations that spread all over Europe kept in common elements of the hunter-gatherer lifestyle, still predominant, but developed throughout the period social and economic inequalities arising from different cultural traditions and environments. The social and economic phenomena of the Neolithic are analysed in Chapter 5. Before we enter this new period, however, it is important to emphasize that Mesolithic Iberia presented an unusual situation with regard to its population, a fact that may have had led to major consequences in the future, as will be discussed below. According to Colin Renfrew:

> In cases where the mesolithic population was much denser – perhaps in Brittany or on the shores of Portugal, where the shell middens suggest a fairly flourishing mesolithic community – their contribution might have been larger, and where the local mesolithic population actually took up farming itself, it too would undergo much the same increase in population density. In such a case its language would have a greater probability of surviving. On this model, that could be the explanation for the occasional pockets of non-Indo-European languages which survived into historic times, such as Etruscan or Basque, and no doubt many others which survived for a while but are now extinct.[16]

The contacts between man and horse in Iberia, however, have been very intense since the Mesolithic. This is certified by the authority Dr Ruy d'Andrade, who wrote:

> The contact between men and horses in the Iberian Peninsula is very ancient. Horses being led date back to the Mesolithic in the Spanish Levant, some 6,000 years BC. The Neolithic halberd [Fig. 4.6] indicates that at that time (around 5,000 BC) this weapon, suitable for unseating a horseman, was already in use in the Peninsula.[17]

Dr d'Andrade also writes that the first horse to be domesticated in the Iberian Peninsula was the Type I pony from the northern mountains of Portugal, the *garrano* or *jaca* (its Portuguese and Spanish names

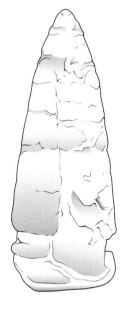

4.6 Halberd from Mesolithic or Neolithic times, used to unseat horsemen.

respectively). It is, as we have seen, the type most often depicted in the Franco-Cantabrian caves. D'Andrade points out that this heavy small horse, that still exists today almost unchanged in the cold and humid Iberian mountains, is not the same as the bigger animal from the south of the Peninsula that became known as the 'Iberian horse'. This more refined horse, says d'Andrade, is represented in the cave at La Pileta (see Fig. 2.12), and dates back to the end of the Palaeolithic. It also appears in Spanish Levantine art from the Mesolithic and had taken its current form by the Neolithic – more important evidence that horses did not, after all, disappear from Iberia during the Mesolithic. However, in Parpalló, La Pileta and other southern Spanish Mesolithic sites, horses are depicted with subconvex heads, which makes the Iberian origin of these horses certain, as the drawings date from a much earlier period than the Capsian influence.[18]

It is therefore certain that horses never left the Peninsula. In spite of being endangered by the indiscriminate hunting of indigenous peoples, there is no evidence that they ever became extinct; quite the contrary, they were no doubt able to find a favourable environment in the friendly interior of the Iberian world where they could continue to live in large herds.

CONCLUSION

Mesolithic art had its apogee in the Spanish Levant; it no longer has the horse as its main theme, a fact that may indicate the beginning of domestication and the consequent cessation of the hunting of the horse in that area. The bow and arrow, introduced during this period, may have been a principal cause behind the changes in hunting habits and the reduced presence of horses in Mesolithic art.

The early stage of domestication, combined with all the facts mentioned above, is probably the major cause of the disappearance of the horse from the artistic works and testimonies about the animals hunted by Mesolithic man. This has contributed to the acceptance of the erroneous idea that the horse became extinct in Iberia during that period. In all likelihood horses never left the Peninsula, in spite of having been previously exposed to indiscriminate hunting.

All these are still moot points, however, and we are far from reaching any consensus over these controversial themes.

Chapter Five

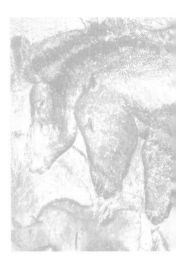

THE NEOLITHIC

(8000 to 4000 BC)

GENERAL VIEW

The Neolithic is characterized by the advent of full-blown agriculture, born from the primitive horticulture practised until then; by the technical evolution of ceramics and textiles; and by the development of animal breeding and domestication, especially of the horse. The almost simultaneous occurrence of these developments in societies as far apart as Asia Minor, the Far East and America, with different regional variants, is an intriguing phenomenon which has yet to be satisfactorily explained. The first European arable communities were established around 7000 BC in a vast area stretching from the Black Sea to the north of France, including the Mediterranean and the Danube valley. This technological revolution was initiated with cereals imported from Asia. According to many historians the revolution was brought about by foreign invasions; according to others it happened with the progressive absorption of new techniques by local populations.

In the Iberian Peninsula, the climate was more humid and warmer than in previous geological periods; deciduous forests developed and the first signs of food-producing activities came with deforestation to clear land for agriculture. Grain production and animal breeding, probably starting with the domestication of ovi-caprines (sheep and goats), were the main economic activities. Cardial ceramics made their first appearance and land occupation increased. Hunting continued to be a very important source of food, with deer, aurochs, boar and hare being the animals most commonly

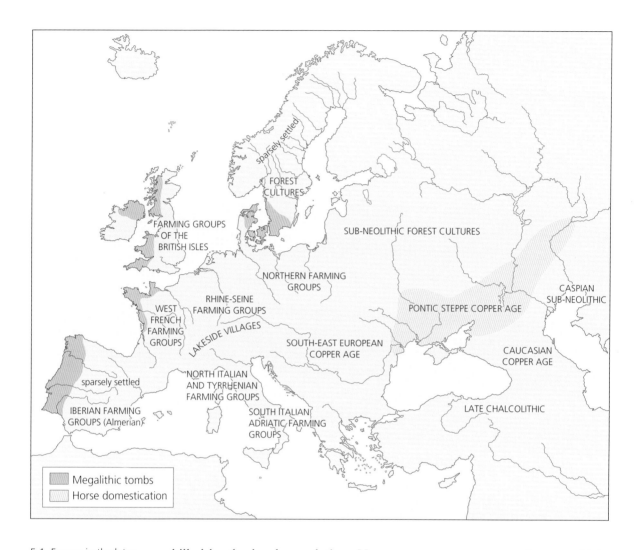

5.1 Europe in the later Neolithic and earlier Copper Age (4500–3500 BC), showing different farming groups. Megalithic building began on the Atlantic Coast, while copper working was developing in south-east Europe. Horse domestication was beginning in the Pontic steppes.

killed by the local population. Horses, as we saw, were no longer widely hunted in the Mesolithic, possibly because of domestication.

Fishing communities can be identified from around 6000 BC in Italy, France, Corsica and the Balearic Islands, indicating that navigation was already known in the Mediterranean. In Portugal, 'shell middens' continued to exist on the estuaries of the Tagus and Sado rivers.

Not much can be said about the expansion of agriculture, because of the very limited knowledge we have of this period in the Iberian Peninsula. The little we know about the commercial and cultural relations at that time does not enable us to answer one very pertinent question: was the introduction of Neolithic agriculture made by way of the Mediterranean coast, independently and not contemporaneously with the continental

European process, or did it come much later, by way of the Atlantic coast or from southern France through the Pyrenees, with the Indo-European or other invaders? This question will be addressed in the next section, but here we can anticipate opinions such as that of Prof. Renfrew:

> The farming economy of western Greece reached Italy by sea, and soon Sardinia and Corsica, southern France and the Mediterranean coasts of Iberia. In each of these areas there is pottery decorated with impressions which has given its name to the Impressed Ware cultures. Farming was soon practised throughout much of Iberia, and in central and northern France.[1]

During the Middle Neolithic (6500 to 5000 BC) caves were abandoned, progressively replaced by open-air settlements. The expansion of commercial exchanges involving raw materials and products can be detected, and the first megalithic monuments date from this period, the Portuguese coast being one of the most ancient and important centres of this European cultural phenomenon (Fig. 5.2). According to Andrew Sherratt, the

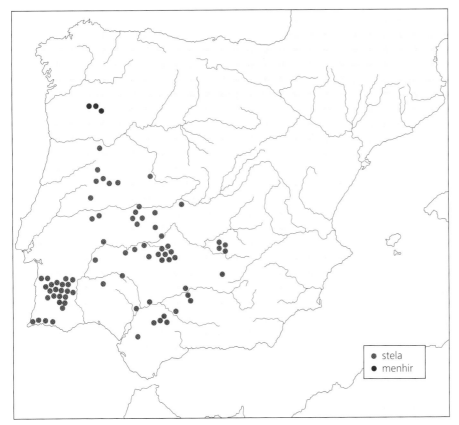

5.2 Distribution of megalithic monuments in the form of stelae and menhirs – standing stones – in Iberia.

megalith in Neolithic Europe is typical of zones where large communities did not exist, the two things (megaliths and villages) being mutually exclusive, i.e. where one existed the other did not occur. Sherrat believes that the megaliths exerted the same role as the large Neolithic settlements of Central Europe, being a focal point of reunion for people living scattered around them, and consequently acting as a meeting point for the organization of agricultural activities.[2]

Megaliths also indicate that extensive and active communication networks existed along the Atlantic coast, connecting peoples from Scotland, England, France and Iberia already familiar with the land and ocean routes of western Europe.

The agricultural revolution occurred much later than it did in the Orient – where settled agriculture really started during the prehistoric period – and continued to develop autonomously, not affected by the technological improvements achieved in Asia Minor, like irrigation and the plough, which provided the basic conditions necessary for the establishment of the first urban communities in the east. European agricultural history varies

5.3 Megalithic group of standing stones, France.

from place to place, but always stems from the introduction of non-native food staples, like grains, and working animals, some locally domesticated. To make all this possible, it was imperative that cultural exchanges take place, and the big question is to discover who was responsible for these movements: Europeans going to Asia, learning and returning, or a true colonization from the East? Both movements may have taken place, but colonization from Asia was certainly greater than migration into that continent. In southeast Europe, around 5000 BC, colonization as well as local development are evident; in the central and western Mediterranean the picture may indicate a slower local evolution. In central and eastern Europe colonization was clearly dominant.

In other words, the agro-techno complex known as the 'Asia Minor (traction, agriculture or Neolithic) package' introduced in Europe around 4000–3500 BC included cereals, horticulture, animal breeding and domestication, ceramics and villages with timber houses (Fig. 5.4). It was not, however, a continuous homogeneous process for the whole continent. In Central Europe, as mentioned above, the acceptance of this package was integral to and always associated with the rise of large villages of timber houses. On the Atlantic coast and the Mediterranean, on the other hand, only selective items of the package were absorbed; the association there was with megaliths, and the population did not undergo any radical transformation. This is confirmed by Cavalli-Sforza, who postulates the 'demic (demotic) hypothesis', which holds that agriculture expanded out of Asia Minor as a result of the immigration of farming peoples, rather than from the cultural diffusion of the new technique. Ethnographic studies reveal that the chronological rate of expansion of European farmers is compatible with the rates of mobility and fertility of these same primitive populations, thereby giving support to the theory that it was the farmers that invaded new areas and not agriculture that expanded, to be absorbed by pre-existing indigenous populations.

After 3500 BC, the influence exerted by the great civilizations of Asia Minor was intense and responsible for the birth of the palatial cities of Minos and Mycene in Greece. Navigation developed quickly, mainly in the Aegean. Animal traction on the one hand expanded the cultivated areas and productivity in agriculture, while on the other hand its impact on inland transportation made possible contacts with neighbouring communities including those of the steppe, accelerating cultural changes. The so-called 'Kurgan Culture' developed at that time, the name deriving from the

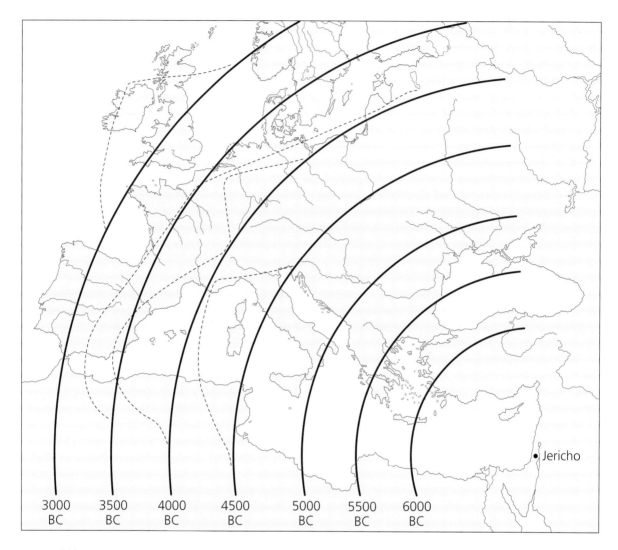

3000 BC   3500 BC   4000 BC   4500 BC   5000 BC   5500 BC   6000 BC

• Jericho

5.4 Neolithic expansion from the east. From its beginnings in the east, Neolithic culture expanded westwards over several millennia.

underground tumuli covered by wooden beams and circular mounds, or *kurgans* in Russian. These graves, some containing just solid wooden wheels and others complete chariots, reached from the Danube to the Urals and the Caspian. Later on, following the course of the Hungarian valleys, they entered western Europe, introducing to this new frontier not only funereal rites but also metallurgy, wool sheep and the double mould for better finishing of smelted objects.

These influences and innovations caused many radical transformations in Western Europe. Corded Ware ceramics – born in the steppes and later introduced into Europe – date back to this period, the name coming from the decorative rope motifs engraved on the ceramic articles produced by this culture. Following the advance of the Corded Ware culture, also from the steppes, came the pastoral way of life, with more mobile herders taking the place of the former settled agriculturalists, and the advent of the 'Bell Beaker' culture, intimately associated with its predecessor the 'Corded Ware' (Fig. 5.5). All of this is explained more fully in Chapter 6.

The most important phenomenon of the Neolithic, intimately connected with the spread of the domesticated horse, was the Indo-European expansion, which we turn to now.

THE INDO-EUROPEANS

The emphasis now changes from archaeology to etymology and linguistics. Although the Neolithic sites produced copious material for archaeological studies, it was the languages spoken by the Indo-Europeans that give us the best clues to the history of this period, especially the expansion of agriculture and the domestication of the horse.

The origin and expansion of the Indo-Europeans are very complex and controversial themes, with as many hypotheses as there are idioms and tribes belonging to this large linguistic family. Although none of the various hypotheses can so far be proved beyond doubt, the majority tend to accept the 'Pontic-Caspian' origin of the Indo-Europeans as the most plausible. The real issue is that we face a mystery, not yet deciphered, of a linguistic family born in the region of the Black and Caspian Seas, which between 4500 and 2500 BC spread over the whole of Europe, Asia Minor and India, reaching the very borders of China.

Many respected modern authorities on this subject, for example Marija Gimbutas, Colin Renfrew, Bernard Sergent and J.P. Mallory, have produced remarkable scholarly works proposing different hypotheses for this great prehistoric enigma. More recently the geneticist Prof. Luca Cavalli-Sforza has contributed a new approach to this multidisciplinary discussion.

We will briefly discuss these ideas, beginning with one of the greatest authorities on the subject, J. P. Mallory. In his famous work, *In Search of the Indo-Europeans,* he examines exhaustively the origins, expansion and legacy of the Indo-Europeans and the intimate connections that always existed between these peoples and the horse. The horse was present throughout their history and in their daily life, both in a utilitarian form as a traction or riding animal and an instrument of war, and in its role in the mystical and religious traditions of these warlike societies.

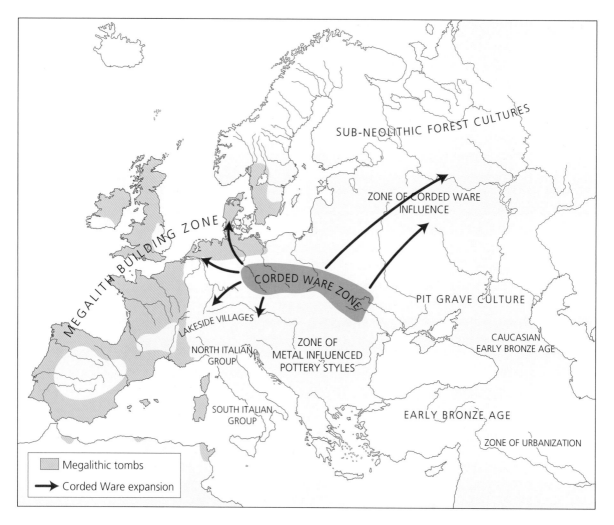

5.5 Europe in the later Neolithic (3500-2500 BC). Megalithic culture is indicated by the shaded area; the Corded Ware expansion is also shown.

The intimate association between the horse and these people is constantly present in the Indo-European lexicon, and linguistic analysis can give us the key to solving the mystery of the Indo-European's past. Investigating the evidence provided by words derived from the root *ekwos* (horse) in the many Indo-European idioms was true detective work, and enabled the renowned author Mallory to develop one of the best descriptions available about European prehistory. The study of these proto-Indo-European cultures reveals that these groups were formed mainly by pastoral warriors, agriculture being relegated to a secondary place. Mallory affirms that:

> The most significant linguistic-archaeological correlation among the domestic animals is the horse, which is known at least from the fourth millennium BC, or

earlier from the Dnieper east to the southern Urals. It is not simply present, but all the evidence indicates intense exploitation and a role in ritual. All of this helps underwrite the apparently equo-centric practices that are shared by many Indo-European peoples. Where the horse occurs either to the south or immediately west of the Pontic-Caspian, this is generally explained by contacts with the natural home of the horse. This strengthens the Pontic-Caspian's claim to homeland status [of the Indo-Europeans] though it does not entirely secure it against other areas.[3]

The perfect symbiosis between the Indo-Europeans and horses can also be demonstrated by a series of linguistic associations. Mallory gives some examples:

> Hieroglyphic Luwian *a-su-wa;* Mitanni *a-as-su-us-sa-an-ni* 'horse trainer'; Sanskrit *asva;* Avestan *aspa-;* Tocharian A *yuk;* Tocharian B *yakwe;* Mycenaean *i-qo;* Greek *hippos;* Latin *equus;* Venetic *eku-;* Old English *eoh;* Gaulish *epo-;* Old Irish *ech;* while Lithuanian retains the feminine *asva* 'mare'.[4]

As all these words were used to designate the domesticated horse, we can assume that the proto-Indo-European *ekwos* was also a domesticated equine. However, if one assumes that the word *ekwos* designates both the wild and the domestic animal, it is possible, according to Mallory, to distinguish three different areas as candidates for the Indo-European homeland. The first corresponds to most of the Near East, including Anatolia and the Balkans:

> The earliest horses in Greece do not appear prior to about 2000 BC which is consistent with a late Indo-Europeanizing of Greece … There is no evidence whatsoever for horses in the Neolithic period of the Carpathian Basin although very small numbers of horses do begin to appear, again from the east, during the fourth millennium BC. …
>
> The second category includes areas where horses appear to have survived the Late Pleistocene and continued to be exploited through the Neolithic, albeit as wild animals … It refers basically to Central and Northern European sites.
>
> The third category is the actual centre of the natural range of wild herds of horses, specifically the tarpan, and the earliest-known centre of horse domestication. The main core of this region is to be found from the Dnieper river east to the Volga, and possibly on into Asia…. During the fourth millennium BC, the domestic horse appears to have expanded westwards and accounts for the increasing percentages of horse remains in the northwest Pontic and the

earliest appearance of the horse in the Balkans and Carpathian basin. Thus, if one wishes to confine *ekwos to the domestic horse, then linguistic palaeontology suggests that the border of the homeland should not lie much further west than the Black Sea.[5]

It is obvious that Mallory was preoccupied with the limitation of the possible regions that could pretend to be the original Indo-European homeland and the very intimate association of these peoples with the domesticated horse. He was not discussing the existence or the domestication of wild horses, wherever it might have taken place. He recognizes Iberia as an equine territory, but as there is no archaeological or other evidence of the domesticated horse there at the age of the proto-Indo-Europeans, he considers the Peninsula as situated beyond the geographical contour of his anthropological/linguistic analysis, and affirms:

> The other regions excluded from the primary range of the horse lie outside of serious homeland [for the Indo-Europeans] consideration, for example, the Apennine peninsula, southern Iberia, and Ireland, *although they further emphasize the later movements of Indo-Europeans into these regions* [my emphasis]. If the horse, either wild or domestic, is employed as a major marker of the Proto-Indo-Europeans, then we would exclude most of Southeastern Europe from the homeland.[6]

Many authors think that the domestication of the horse may have taken place almost simultaneously in many different parts of Eurasia, both by endogenous initiatives and by imported technology, acquired through contacts – that existed but cannot be proved – with other cultures.

As we will see in Chapter 7, going deeper into his analysis, Mallory cites the works of other experts showing that the words for wheeled carts in Indo-European languages always contain the root *kwel,* which means rotation. Although these occurrences do not prove that Indo-Europeans invented the wheeled vehicle, it indicates that they had contacts with other peoples who were already familiar with it in the fourth millennium (see Fig. 7.7).

We must now refer to the hypothesis of Marija Gimbutas, who identifies the Kurgan culture, originally from south Ukraine and Russia, as the cradle of the Indo-Europeans. The peoples from this Indo-European culture were familiar with not only the domesticated horse, but also the wheeled vehicle, and they followed a funereal ritual, burying their dead in shallow stone or earth graves covered by short mounds called *kurgan* in Russian. This warlike people from the Volga–Ural steppe region advanced westward, invading Central and Eastern Europe; heading south they entered Mesopotamia and went as far as India. According to Gimbutas one of the most important indications of these invasions, which would have occurred in three successive waves, is the expansion of equitation from the steppes to the Danube valley, which can be proved by many wood and antler objects such as bridles, bits and batons with carved horsehead tops, all of them typical of the Kurgan culture.

That the Indo-Europeans one way or another became masters of the war chariot is undeniable. The French author Bernard Sergent writes:

> In the myths and in the history of the second and first millennia BC, the perpetrators of the most damaging raids and the most formidable conquests had a very impressive weapon but it was only usable in groups and during the day: the war chariot … The chariot followed all the Indo-Europeans, Greeks, Anatolians, Indo-Iranians, Celts and even Romans … when they emerged into history. Archaeology confirms the antiquity of the chariot. In the Kurgan culture, the war chiefs appear to have been mounted: *equitation seems to have anticipated the charioteers* [my emphasis] … and the principal strength of the Indo-European warriors may have been based on it. In any case, mounted or driven, it is patently clear that the horse was *par excellence* the means of the Indo-European successes. The developing mentality – the specialization of some men in warfare, the heroic spirit – could have been equally important, but perhaps it was the easy initial successes due to the domestication of an animal ideal for war that is at the origin of the dynamics by which men turn towards pillage and external conquests.[7]

This interpretation is supported by Edgar Polomé:

> Archaeological data were not yet clear on its formation, but there seemed to be a Mesolithic group in an originally limited area between the Don and the southern Urals. As early as the fifth millennium BC, it is supposed to have had *domesticated horses at its disposal, and in the following millennium, it is deemed to have introduced wheeled vehicles* [my emphasis] in the steppe area … With increased mobility, growing herds and population, the Kurgan warrior nobility strove for expansion, hence a series of movements took place towards the Balkan-Danubian area during the first half of the fourth millennium BC, whence they conquered northern Europe.[8]

It is important to say that Mallory's version is not the only one accepted by archaeologists. Other hypotheses have been put forward by experts (Prof. Renfrew, for instance) linking the Indo-European expansion in Europe with agriculture's Neolithic diffusion, the above-mentioned 'package' that would have been introduced with the migrations originating in Asia Minor. Over many generations, these colonizers progressively advanced into the Mediterranean and the Balkans, continued along the Danube Basin as far as the Atlantic and the Baltic, while others advancing from the Black Sea and the steppes enabled a huge exchange of experience and cultural dissemination to take place, with the absorption of different customs and lifestyles, mainly agriculture and animal husbandry. According to Renfrew:

> In surveying European prehistory I do not believe that we can see any one process, nor any series of processes at once sufficiently profound in social and demographic consequences and so wide-spread geographically as to suggest a viable background for such radical linguistic changes, until we go right back to the time of the spread of farming. Of course there remain other possibilities, even if that point is accepted. It would still be logically possible for the changes in question to have occurred *before* the spread of farming, a possibility which takes the argument back to the palaeolithic era. And of course it is possible to argue, as some have done, that an explanation in terms of the *spread* of some early Indo-European language or languages is not the right approach. Some different, in some senses more static, model could be proposed.[9]

Renfrew has enunciated the hypothesis that Neolithic farmers colonizing Europe from Anatolia spread Indo-European languages. In the same work he also asserts two different hypotheses. The first one, which he calls 'A',

> suggests that the zone of early farmers speaking Proto-Indo-European extended east to northern Iran and even to Turkmenia at the outset. The spread of Indo-European speech to the south, to the Iranian plateau and to north India and Pakistan, can then be seen as part of an analogous dispersal, related to the demographic changes associated with the adoption of farming.[10]

The second one, hypothesis 'B',

> suggests instead that the crucial development for the eastern area was the development in the Eurasian steppes of nomad pastoralism, and that this took place first at the western end of the steppes. In this way, it was argued, the

nomad pastoralists of the steppes spoke an Indo-European language at the outset. Their later dominance in Iran and in the Indus is then ascribed to their military effectiveness, based largely upon the use of the horse.

This theory of the dissemination of the horse as a by-product of Neolithic agricultural diffusion has been strongly reinforced by the work of the geneticist Cavalli-Sforza, who arrived at the same conclusions following different paths in this now multidisciplinary investigation. Using Professor L. Luca Cavalli-Sforza's own words:

In 1976, Paolo Menozzi, Alberto Piazza and I began to study the genetics of Europe by a new method that allowed us to synthesize the geographic information of many genes ... The work of synthesizing the geographic maps of Europe for 39 genes, published in 1978, showed that the most important pattern hidden behind the crowd of numbers, representing the frequencies of the different forms of 39 genes (like ABO, Rh, etc. in hundreds of European populations) was in excellent agreement with the hypothesis that farmers of the Middle East had slowly expanded to settle beyond the limits of the original area, and had spread towards the extreme borders of Europe. The map of archaeological dates, and that of the most important latent pattern of European genes (usually called in statistical terminology the first component, or first PC), were so similar that merely looking at them, one was easily convinced that that was very likely to be the same cause behind both maps – namely, an expansion of people, the Neolithic farmers, into a Europe inhabited by a sparse population of Mesolithic hunter-gatherers. The geographic map of the first principal component of European genes showed a gradient which must have been generated by the slow, progressive admixture of the slowly migrating farmers with the local foragers [Figs. 5.6 and 5.7] ...

The first principal component confirmed an expansion originating in Eastern Europe, but the maximum moved somewhat eastwards, just above the Caucasus. As is well known, there has been a great many hypotheses on the area of origin of Indo-European languages (see for instance Mallory 1989). Gimbutas (1965) was, to my knowledge, the first to hypothesize that the Kurgan pit-grave cultures, located north of the Black Sea and south of the Urals (in Kazhakstan, in the Don–Volga–Ural region) were responsible for the expansion of Indo-European speakers beginning in the Early Bronze Age and continuing throughout the later Bronze Ages.[11]

Cavalli-Sforza continues: 'What can we conclude from our observations? They support the idea that there was a major expansion of people from the

5.6 First farmers of western Europe. The probable routes followed by the expansion of farming are shown, indicating its arrival in Iberia via the Mediterranean. Farming was first established in south-east Europe about 7000 BC.

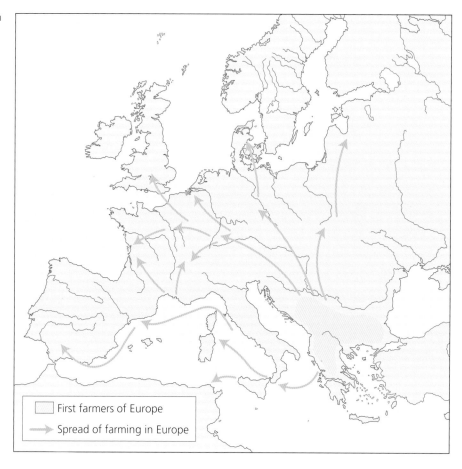

First farmers of Europe

Spread of farming in Europe

Kurgan area, that is from the steppe region north of the Black Sea, the Caucasus and the Caspian Sea.' And concludes:

> It seems to me that one cannot, at this stage, exclude that both Gimbutas' and Renfrew's hypotheses are right; i.e., that the Neolithic expansion brought a pre-Proto-Indo-European language to the Volga–Don region, from where, three or four thousand years later, Proto-Indo-European languages were spread west and southeast by the Kurgan people.

To conclude this theme, the following text was written by Edgar Polomé:

> After all the dust settled, the main tenets of Marija Gimbuta's theory remained valid:
>
> (1) the Proto-Indo-European culture, essentially patrilinear and patrilocal, spread from humble beginnings, at least four millennia BC, all over Europe, the Middle East, the South Asian subcontinent and even Chinese Turkestan in

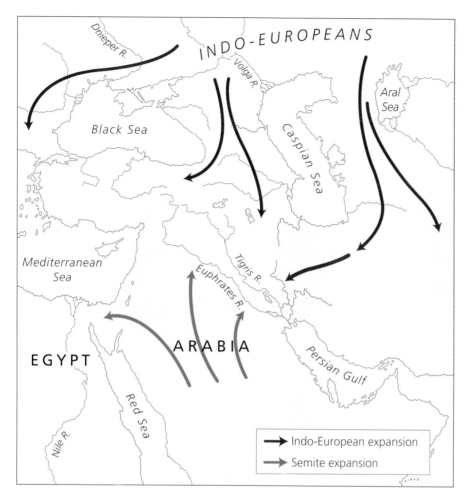

5.7 Movement of nomadic peoples to cultivatable lands. Indo-Europeans moved from the Ponto-Caspian steppe to central and western Europe, Asia Minor and Mesopotamia. Semitic peoples from the Arabian Peninsula invaded Egypt and Mesopotamia. Formerly nomads, these people settled down as agriculturalists.

steady waves of diffusion; (2) the domestication of the horse and, secondarily, the introduction of wheeled vehicles facilitated this diffusion; (3) it is possible to capture through artifacts as well as the archaic lexicon, the main tenets of PIE civilization, as Benveniste and the French school (Dumézil, Sergent, Haudry, etc.) have demonstrated; linguistic paleontology provides reliable clues on the ecology of its homeland; (4) the Pontic steppe area is a quite plausible location for the original core of the Indo-Europeans.[12]

All the above scholarly opinions overturn the until now consensual wisdom that held that horses were first domesticated for traction and only much later for equitation. This also changes the picture relative to the advent of domestication in the Iberian Peninsula as, up until this revised theory was put forward, one of the strongest arguments used to dismiss out of hand the possible existence of domesticated horses there, before the

Indo-European invasions, was the absence of wheeled vehicles and chariots, which only appeared in the first millennium BC, imported from Asia Minor, as symbols of the status and power of the local aristocrats. The admission of the inverted order of events in the domestication of horses makes the introduction of these prestige vehicles in Iberia more logical and understandable; they could only be absorbed by a society already familiar with the domestic horse, a necessary condition without which their introduction would not be possible, i.e. wagons without horses do not make any sense.

There is thus strong evidence that the horse was first domesticated for riding and only later for traction. Riding did not initially prosper because horses were too small. According to Dr Sergent:

> It is estimated that approximately thirty generations are necessary for changes due to domestication to modify the biology of a species; in fact, the S'ézz'ee cemetery of the Samara culture, which is the most ancient among the so-called Kurgan cultures, from around 5000 BP, produced horse skulls and statuettes; horses were thus domesticated for meat, and later no doubt for riding, in the steppe zones between 5000 and 5500 BP [before present] and were descendants of the tarpan ...
>
> The Kurgan horses were small (maximum 145 cm [14.1 hands] at the withers) and, aside from an initial phase in which they were ridden, it was the chariot that gave them military value.[13]

The sacrifice of horses in Indo-European communities is another confirmation of the ever prominent role played by the horse in all prehistoric and protohistoric societies. It represented his perennial value to all these peoples as a noble and valuable possession, deserving of the gods to which he was immolated or of the owner with whom he was buried to be of use in his next life. The preponderance of horses amongst sacrificial animals and his dominant position in the Indo-European lexicon, as explained above, thoroughly demonstrate his place in these peoples' culture. One of the most eloquent indications of this is the recurring presence of the mythological twins, as for example, Asvin Indo horsemen, the Greek Castor and Pollux, the legendary Anglo-Saxon Hengist and Horsa (stallion and horse) and the Irish twins born from Macha after she completed a horse race, as Mallory explains:

> The major ritual enactment of horse-centred myth is supported by evidence from ancient India and Rome and, more distantly, medieval Ireland. The Indic

ritual is the *asvamedha,* probably the most spectacular of the ancient Indic cere-
monies. It began in the spring under the direction of four priests ... A prized
stallion was selected as the victim and after rituals ... was set free to wander for
an entire year, 400 warriors trailing behind to ensure that the course of the stallion was neither interfered with nor that it had contact with mares. Ancillary rituals took place throughout the year until the horse was returned for the final
three day finale. This involved, among other things, the horse pulling the king's
chariot, a large sacrifice of a variety of animals, and the smothering of the horse,
after which the king's favourite wife 'co-habited' with the dead stallion under
covers. The horse was then dismembered into three portions, each dedicated to
deities who played out the canonical order of Dumézil's three 'functions'.[14]

The Roman October Equus was similar:

Following a horse race on the ides of October, the right-sided horse of the team
was dispatched by a spear and then dismembered, again in such a fashion as to
indicate its 'functional' division into the three estates. As with the Indic ritual,
the major recipient of the sacrifice was the warrior-god (Mars).[15]

Many Indo-European ritual traditions involved the copulation of a stallion
with a feminine personage of the highest local nobility, resulting in the
birth of twin godly horses. It is also interesting to note that in all these rituals the right-side horse was always the one sacrificed, a fact that assumes
special significance when it is known that it is always the best one in the
pair (in the Hittite civilization, a mule on the left side pulled the vehicle
under the leadership of the horse on the right).

In the treaty celebrated between Matizawa, king of Mitani, and his opponent the king of the Hittites, the former invokes the Indic divinities
Mitra, Varuna and Indra and the Natsayas. Indra is the war god *par excel-
lence,* while the Natsayas are twins intimately associated with horses.

In Iberia no civilization that practised similar rituals ever existed. What
is found at burials are chariot parts, weapons, and 'stelae' with horse and
chariot engravings, but never the remains of immolated animals. On the
one hand, this is an indication of the non-penetration of cultural values
from the steppes, as was the case with many items of the 'Neolithic package', and on the other hand it demonstrates, once more – as was the case
in the Mesolithic – deep cultural differences between the Iberians and the
pastoral nomads of the east. The remote location of Iberia and its isolation
from the rest of Eurasia once more preserved it from external influences,

giving breathing space for the appearance of well-differentiated local cultures, less influenced by outside values (Fig. 5.8).

The Indo-Europeans moved out from the Pontic-Caspian and occupied vast areas of Asia and Europe, disseminating language, religious cults, technologies and cultural values that most certainly moulded European civilization as we know it today. They were also, as already pointed out, the most important agents in the expansion of equine culture on the continent, thus being of enormous interest for our subject.

In Asia, the Indo-European expansion seems to have started around 4000 BC and continued for millennia, until it was interrupted by the opposite invasion of Turkish tribes. The first Indo-European Asiatic culture is that of Afanasievo, which spread eastwards to the Altai mountains. The Afanasievos had domesticated horses and most probably had wheeled vehicles. The Okunevo culture, derived from the Afanasievo, had horse-drawn vehicles.

Later on, in the second millennium, the Andronovo culture appears

5.8 Main Neolithic sites in Iberia. The Neolithic expansion in Iberia had its maximum development on the Atlantic and Mediterranean coasts.

5.9 Non-Indo-European languages (Tartessian, Iberian and Basque) and Indo-European Hispano-Celtic languages in the Iberian peninsula. Basque is the only surviving non-Indo-European language in Iberia.

east of the Urals; this culture used horses both for traction and riding. The archaeological sites from all these cultures are rich with objects, chariots and sacrificial horse remains, as well as ruins of ancient settlements with timber-built houses. In Anatolia the case is more complex. Although horses were not known to have lived there before the Bronze Age, horse remains, wild or domestic, were found in many tombs, probably from animals imported from southeast Europe.

Finally reference should be made to the 'Battle-Axe' peoples (Fig. 5.10). The Middle East kingdoms, none of them horse-breeding countries, had their first contact with equitation and wheeled vehicles through the 'Battle-Axe' people, in the second millennium. These Indo-Europeans who migrated from Kurgan areas in Russia were so called from their custom of burying stone battle-axes with their dead. As we shall see when discussing the chariots and horses of antiquity (Chapter 7), these peoples were, most probably, the agents for the introduction of 'quality horses' into Central Asia.

5.10 Beaker, amber beads, battle-axe, flat axe and dagger, found in Holland. The Battle-Axe and Beaker peoples are intimately associated with the spread of equitation.

CONCLUSION

The Indo-Europeans, whose most probable origin was southern Russia, spread out of their homeland to conquer and occupy vast territories all over Eurasia between 4500 and 2500 BC.

The first known Indo-European raiders were the so-called 'Battle-Axe' peoples. What most strongly characterized the Indo-Europeans was the perfect symbiosis they had with the horse, abundantly demonstrated by aseries of linguistic associations and also by their mastery of the war chariot, the vehicle which gave them the irresistible power to conquer and dominate several other peoples and civilizations.

The Indo-European invasions did not reach Iberia, where horse domestication and riding were possibly locally developed.

Chapter Six

THE BRONZE AND
IRON AGES

(4000–600 BC)

THE EMERGENCE OF THE ELITES (2500–1300 BC)

The great Aegean civilizations, like the more ancient Asian ones that pre-ceded them, did not exert a notable influence on the development of west-ern Europe, contrary to the situation one millennium later, when the Phoenicians and Greeks established strong commercial links with the less developed populations of the Mediterranean and of the Iberian Peninsula.

During this period, Indo-European peoples from the Pontic steppes ex-panded towards Asia, temporarily reversing their unrelenting advance upon eastern Europe. These peoples were the agents of major change, such as the introduction of metallurgy and the spread of riding, driving and the war chariot. As well as these improvements in land transport, new navigational techniques were rapidly developing in this period, and all these modernizing factors resulted not only in a vast increase in mobility and new territorial exploration, but also in the adoption of these techno-logical improvements as power and prestige symbols for the hereditary elites that arose all over the Eurasian and African continents.

South of the Carpathians, fortifications and large collective burial sites indicate settled societies, whose greater objectives and power base were land ownership. Northern and western Europe, on the other hand, were conspicuous for the absence of large villages and for evidence of a prepon-derance of pastoralism, in other words, of mobile groups over the fixed societies typical of large sedentary populations.

Ceramics continued to prosper in all regions of Eurasia, with local styles and various levels of sophistication. The experience of these primitive potters in the transformation of different materials by the application of heat eventually led them to dominate metallurgy, the next technical revolution of mankind.

6.1 A Bell Beaker vessel from Tarragona. The inverted bell shape gave the name to this most important culture which became established from c. 3000 BC.

During the cultural period of Corded Ware ceramics, from 3000 BC, vestiges of settlements and villages became scarcer throughout the area, while Corded Ware ceramics, with the eponymous cord motifs, and individual graves, both steppe-imported cultural elements, proliferated. On the Atlantic coast, however, greater resistance to change gave an added lifespan to the megalithic cultures, and the above-mentioned new customs only arrived around 2000 BC, with the Bell Beaker culture. It was during the Beaker period too that copper metallurgy, introduced in Europe by the Corded Ware peoples, flourished. Although gold, silver and other metals were known, bronze was the most important material of that time; from this copper and tin amalgam were made the prestigious objects and weapons which, by their abundance, justify the name Bronze Age, by which the period became known in history. Together with bronze, equitation, war chariots and the weaponry and military tactics associated with them spread over the ancient world.

The Bell Beakers

The Bell Beaker culture is of enormous interest for the core subject of this book (Fig. 6.2). Probably derived from the Corded Ware culture, of which it would have been a variant born in the Rhine delta, the Beaker peoples spread over the whole of the Atlantic coast and southwestern Europe around 3000 BC, reaching countries as far as Sicily in the Mediterranean and the Maghrib in North Africa. Besides the drinking vessels with an inverted bell format that gave the culture its name, other equally important elements such as individual graves covered by mounds, and weapons and artefacts made from stone or metal characterize the Bell Beakers. The early Bell Beaker ceramics exhibit the same corded motifs that are typical of the preceding Corded Ware period.

The importance of the Bell Beakers for our theme is that they are one of the most probable agents of the diffusion of equitation in Western Europe. This makes the discussion of their possible origins, migrations and destinations a priority. According to many respected authors, the origin of these peoples was Portugal; according to others Hungary, Yugoslavia or even Scandinavia.

Bell Beaker ceramics, together with weapons, initially made in stone and later in bronze, appear in many Iberian tombs. The type of grave, covered by a mound, and the ritual associated with the objects buried with the deceased, such as leather and later fabric capes, tied on with ornamental

6.2 Distribution of Bell Beaker objects in Europe and North Africa. The North African presence indicates cultural influences there from Iberia. Equitation may have been part of this process.

horn buckles, indicate that these were warriors' graves. This same kind of warrior is later depicted on 'menhirs', 'stelae' and other Iberian funereal monuments which also exhibit swords, lances, daggers and horse bits, demonstrating the importance of horses and warriors in the local societies. Unlike the Corded Ware peoples (the Battle-Axe peoples) who were buried with stone axes (Fig. 6.3), the Bell Beakers were normally interred with daggers and arrow heads, initially of stone and, after they learned to work with metals, in copper and finally in bronze.

The earliest indications of the Bell Beaker culture appeared in Portugal, a fact that made some authors suppose that they came via the Atlantic, spreading out very rapidly all over the Peninsula. There are also many vestiges of the Beakers in North Africa, reinforcing the opinion that these were a people with great sailing skills who adventured on risky long-range voyages. Arriving in Iberia, these intrepid newcomers met with local Chalcolithic (copper-using) cultures living in fortified settlements, but there is no indication of any violent confrontation. The indigenous populations rapidly absorbed the new symbols of prestige, including (according to some authors) equitation, which may have accompanied these Indo-European invaders, who found in Iberia rich supplies of metals and wild horses

6.3 Drinking vessels and battle-axes from Denmark (3000–2400 BC) of the Corded Ware culture, from which the Bell Beaker culture originated.

of excellent quality, as well as new ceramic motifs with geometrical patterns. Other Bell Beaker groups may have entered Iberia from France. Some authors consider that the intimate association of Bell Beaker ceramics with the ridden horse in Iberia, Italy and Majorca is so impressive that it suggests a common origin for both, possibly Anatolia. In that case, the Beakers would have come from the eastern Mediterranean, arriving first in Iberia and from there spreading to North Africa and, possibly, to the rest of Western Europe in the movements described above.

Andrew Sherratt has a different theory about the Bell Beaker phenomenon in Iberia, in contrast to those given above. According to him, the Beakers arrived in Portugal as merchantmen, via the Atlantic, all evidence indicating the interest of these groups in exploring uncharted territories. According to Sherratt:

> In Portugal and southern Spain they encountered the already complex and copper-using groups living in elaborate fortified centres, and beakers occur both in settlements such as Vila Nova de São Pedro and Los Millares … There were no revolutionary consequences to this encounter, however, but rather peaceful relations and the exchange of status symbols. Iberian populations acquired horses [or perhaps he should say 'equitation'], probably some quaint northern recipes for food and drink, and a geometric decorative repertoire that was widely adopted on local pottery shapes such as wide bowls, and spread beyond the area of immediate beaker influence. In return, beaker groups and their successors in Brittany acquired Iberian copper (sometimes specifically in the form of local arrowhead shapes), and rare objects of silver. A comparable penetration of eastern Spain took place from adjacent areas of southern France, bringing other beaker-using groups to the Mediterranean.[1]

The opposing theory, defended by equally respected scholars, is that the Bell Beakers originated in Portugal, and travelling via the Atlantic reached Brittany and the British Isles, and via the Rhine went as far as Central Europe and the Danube valley. Stuart Piggott proposes such a theory for the Bell Beaker phenomenon.[2] According to him, at the end of the third millennium Chalcolithic settlements, probably Greek colonies, came to a violent end (as attested to by the remains of Vila Nova de São Pedro in Portugal), being destroyed and replaced by local tribes possessing beaker ceramics with engraved esparto motifs, indicating that these indigenous groups already knew how to make ceramic objects before the arrival of the colonizers from the Aegean. The same local groups probably learned the primitive techniques of copper metallurgy from the Greek colonizers, which they later spread through the remaining Neolithic areas of Western Europe. By the end of the third millennium, these Bell Beakers moved north-westwards from a region close to the Tagus river estuary in Portugal, disseminating in the course of their incursions both beaker ceramics and copper metallurgy. In support of this hypothesis is the surprising homogeneity and uniformity of Beaker ceramics produced at such distant places as England and Germany, almost identical to the models produced in Iberia. This uniformity, over such a vast area, also indicates that these movements must have happened over a short time span. Following the northbound movement out of Iberia came the reverse colonization, called the 'Great Reflux', starting from the above-mentioned northern European lands and reaching still virgin regions of France, Sardinia, Sicily and North Africa, as well as Britain and Iberia itself.

In this movement back, the Beakers may have been influenced by Corded Ware culture, and brought for example Indo-European idioms into the Iberian Peninsula. These 'flux' and 'reflux' movements were responsible for the spread of equitation; in the initial phase, heading northwards, they were the agent of the dissemination of riding techniques, as suggested by Uerpmann,[3] and on the return phase brought with them improvements learned by the central European populations from the steppe peoples, with whom they had contacts in the valley of the Danube. Both movements would also have opened up and increased horse traffic from the Iberian Peninsula to north and central Europe (and from there to the steppes) and vice versa, giving rise to the second of many meetings between the horses of the east and the west (the first being caused by the Indo-European 'Battle-Axe' peoples, as already described). This explains the great similarities and almost certain blood relationship between the Iberian and the Turkoman horse (Fig. 6.4).

As Andrew Sherratt observes:

There is also a similar Bell-Beaker burial from Moravia, while the well-known Hungarian Bell-Beaker site of Csepel Haros (Bökönyi 1978) seems to have been a specialized breeding centre, potentially supplying the adjacent Bell-Beaker network with the central-European type of horses.

These occurrences suggest successive westward extensions of the domesticated horse, presumably as a riding-animal, reaching western Europe (the British Isles, France, Iberia) in the Bell-Beaker period of the latter third millennium (van

Wijngaarden-Bakker 1974, 345–7 for horses at Newgrange). Uerpmann (1990) has emphasized that Spanish populations were derived from local stock; indeed, he views the domestication process as having begun not in east Europe but in the far west of Europe in the third millennium. Underlying this are the twin ideas of direct Near Eastern influence in Spanish Chalcolithic fortified sites ('colonies')

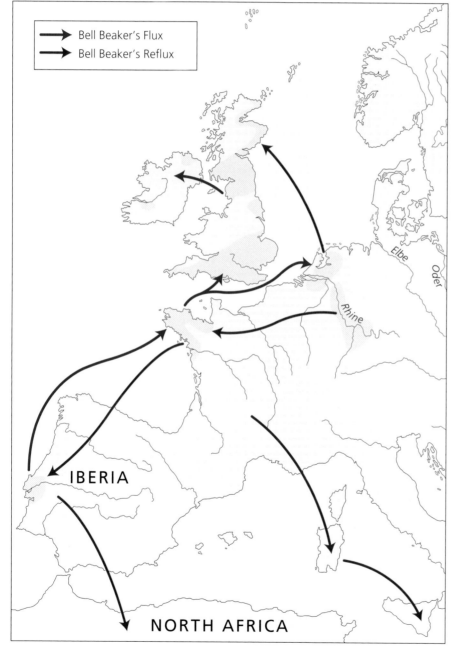

→ Bell Beaker's Flux
→ Bell Beaker's Reflux

IBERIA

NORTH AFRICA

6.4 General distribution and movements of the Bell Beaker peoples. They originated from Portugal (c. 3000 BC) and reached Brittany, the British Isles and Germany. From there they travelled up the Rhine to the Danube. In the other direction, the 'Great Reflux' of Bell Beakers returned to Iberia via France and reached as far as Sardinia and North Africa.

like Los Millares, in contact with the area where donkeys were already domesticated, and of a Bell-Beaker expansion from the Iberian peninsula.

Sherratt then concludes:

> This multi-centric model of several unrelated domestication-episodes of small relict populations seems to me implausible; the reconstruction of a single, large-scale episode of horse domestication on the Pontic steppes in the later fourth millennium, whose effects were felt in eastern and central Europe in the later fourth millennium and in western Europe in the third millennium, seems more persuasive than any postulated alternative.[4]

Stephen Shennan affirms this:

> We have, then, in the Bell Beaker phase, at the very beginning of the Bronze Age a highly significant pattern of contact linking virtually the whole of central and western Europe in what is essentially a time of innovation diffusion and adoption in various spheres ... including ritual and ideology, in a number of very different local situations.[5]

According to Renfrew:

> Instead of the old explanation in terms of migration and diffusion it is possible in many cases to recognize a process of what has been termed 'peer polity integration', where a number of local communities, none more prominent than the next, interact together. In this way a new 'nuclear area', a new 'style zone' comes about, and new things are created and diffused. This is what seems to have happened in the case of the Bell Beakers.[6]

Summing up this survey of sometimes partially conflicting opinions, it can be said that whatever the theory of each individual author, all the different texts agree on one point: that an ancient nucleus of domesticated and ridden horses existed in Iberia, either locally developed or imported from other Asian or European origins, long before many other centres of equine culture, wrongly named as the sources of these techniques, even existed.

The Bell Beaker influence was absorbed by the local Chalcolithic societies which, beginning in 2000 BC, developed a preponderance of pastoral activities and fortified settlements on hilltops, typical of the 'El Agar' culture and totally different from the previous agricultural communities. The archaeological treasure troves of the period have produced among the many bronze objects a large number of swords, daggers and halberds (see Figs. 4.6 and 8.13), the latter being, according to Dr Ruy d'Andrade, a typical weapon used against cavalrymen, its presence indicating the existence of the ridden horse (see Chapter 8).

THE PERIOD FROM 1300 TO 600 BC

Europe in the fourteenth century BC was a vast mosaic of small communities with varying degrees of development, social castes and economic hierarchies that created huge differences between their members. Subsistence was assured by agriculture and animal breeding. Beginning in 1200 BC the explosion of metallurgy occurred both quantitatively and qualitatively, and from 1000 BC onwards, bronze, until then the dominant metal, lost its importance in the face of the irresistible advance of iron. In Iberia, however, bronze continued to dominate until the eighth century BC.

The Great Catastrophe

The first large European city was born in the third millennium on the isle of Crete, an important cultural centre and the cradle of the Minoan and Mycenaean civilizations, which dominated Greece and the Asiatic margins of the Aegean in the second millennium. All these magnificent cultural complexes collapsed around 1200 BC in the disaster called the Great Catastrophe, a series of invasions by the 'Sea Peoples', nomad warriors who destroyed not only the great civilizations of Greece and Asia Minor but also the Hittite Empire, only being contained by the pharaoh Ramses III (1184–1153 BC), who defeated them in the first big naval battle in world history (Figs. 6.5 and 7.15).

The military victories achieved by the 'Sea Peoples' are attributed to the use of iron weapons and cavalry, both as yet unfamiliar to their enemies. The 'Great Catastrophe' marks the end of the age of chariotry (see Chapter 7), during which time these heavy vehicles had been the masters of the battlefield. Iron weaponry was much less expensive and more resistant than the bronze equivalent, making viable the formation of larger armed forces at a lower cost. In addition, iron weapons introduced a new style of direct soldier-to-soldier combat, until then impossible as bronze weapons lacked the resistance, impact and penetrating power of iron. Even more revolutionary in warfare strategy was the ability to assemble large cavalry corps (Fig. 6.6), as opposed to the elitist chariot formations whose forbidding costs limited use to a few rich members of the local aristocracy.

6.5 Battle of Ramses III against the 'Sea-Peoples'. The Sea-Peoples, protagonists of the 'Great Catastrophe', were finally contained by Ramses III of Egypt. Relief from Medinet Habu, Egypt.

The immediate result of the introduction of iron weapons was the incentive to take part in bellicose activities and the whetting of an appetite for conquests, bringing in a new, never-ending age of armed conflict. This increase in armed conflict was the underlying cause of new waves of migration, as defeated peoples, sometimes whole nations displaced by invading armies, wandered through most of Eurasia, creating serious disturbances with major consequences.

The Celts

While all this turmoil was taking place in the Mediterranean, around the end of the second millennium to the north on the Black Sea shores, semi-nomad horsemen from the steppes who dominated both equitation and

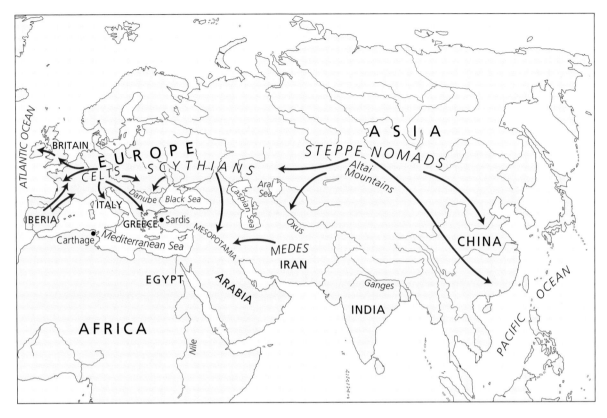

chariotry developed the 'Catacomb Culture', so called because of their custom of burying the dead in large tombs, with weapons, riding equipment such as bits and headgear, and spoked-wheel vehicles. Further east, in the Volga basin, the 'Timber Grave Culture', developed by other nomadic horsemen, expanded westwards, dominating and taking over the land of the Catacomb people. According to Herodotus, the Catacomb people were the Cimmerians and the Timber Grave people the Scythians. These movements of nomadic horsemen had a domino effect, with the displaced Cimmerians invading the Hungarian plains and the Scythians – who started all the unrest – moving forward into Asia Minor. All these invasions provoked a series of other peoples having to leave their homelands. Herodotus wrote:

> the Scythians were a nomadic tribe living in Asia, and that once, by force of arms, they were driven by the Massagetae across the River Araxes and into Cimmerian land – that is, the land currently occupied by Scythians, which is said to have belonged originally to the Cimmerians. In view of this Scythian invasion, and especially given that the invading force was so large, the Cimmerians tried to

6.6 The cavalry revolution (600–500 BC). The steppe nomads, the Scythians and the Celts, in that chronological order, were the main vectors of cavalry expansion during this period.

133

decide what to do ... Having made this decision, they formed themselves into separate groups, each containing an equal number of men, and fought one another. Then the Cimmerian people of the general populace buried them [the Royal family] by the River Tyras (where their grave can still be seen) and emigrated, so that the Scythians invaded and took possession of an empty land. ...

It seems clear that the Cimmerians fled into Asia to escape the Scythians and settled in the peninsula where the Greek town of Sinope is established nowadays. And it is also clear that it was because they took the wrong route that the Scythians entered Median territory during their pursuit of the Cimmerians. For the Cimmerians fled along the coast, whereas the pursuing Scythians kept the Caucasian mountains to their right until they entered Median territory, by turning inland.[7]

Strabo also wrote about the Scythians, the Cimmerians and the Sarmatians: 'It is a peculiarity of the whole Scythian and Sarmatian race that they castrate their horses to make them easy to manage; for although the horses are small, they are exceedingly quick and hard to manage.'[8]

From these quoted Classics, one can deduce that these nomads originally came with the coarser Mongolian ponies which Strabo tells us were small and castrated. In the Pontic-Caspian and in Iran they obtained much better mounts, which certainly replaced the ones they arrived on.

The invading steppe nomads, establishing themselves on the fringes of the European 'Urnfield Culture' homeland, met with horse-loving communities who were well capable of training, breeding and riding their horses and, therefore, the nomads found an attractive and active market in quality horses. The Scythians – who until then rode on steppe or Mongolian ponies – obtained a better strain of horse with which they went further west into Europe, disseminating these superior animals and new riding techniques. This migration might have met with the movement of the Bell Beakers from Iberia and therefore be the vector of the cultural exchanges that would have taken place.

Coming back to the Scythians and other nomadic horsemen, their invasions provoked, as mentioned before, great disturbances in eastern Europe. In the period from 750 to 600 BC Urnfield peoples of Central Europe developed what became known as the Hallstatt Culture, from which came the Celts. Barry Cunliffe observes:

Within the old Urnfield zone of western central Europe, bounded on the west by the communities of the Atlantic arc, on the east by the 'Pontic' communities of the Great Hungarian Plain, and on the south by the Alps, significant changes can be detected after the middle of the eighth century BC. This period, dating from c. 750–600 BC, is referred to as the Hallstatt C culture … It is at the aristocratic level that the culture is at its most universal, being reflected in the widespread distribution of warrior gear, in particular the Hallstatt long sword of iron or bronze … and the trappings for horses both as cavalry beasts and yoked in pairs for pulling vehicles.[9]

Also characterizing this culture are weapons, accoutrements, and four-wheeled chariots found in the tombs of noble warriors.

It is practically impossible to be precise about the mutual influence, if any, that may have existed between the Mediterranean Greeks and the southern German Hallstatt cultures. There are indications of Greek traders penetrating up the Rhône and contributing to the appetite for luxuries of the northern elites. Would the ridden horse and the chariot also have reached Germany by the same route at that same time?

If the answer is yes, who transmitted what to whom? Did the steppe riding techniques come to the western Mediterranean following these routes in the reverse direction? Or did the Asian chariots go up-river to satisfy the desire of the Hallstatt peoples for ostentatious goods? Beginning with the period known as Hallstatt 2–3 (530 BC), this culture expanded westwards, coming into the whole area delimited by the great river basins of the Danube, the Rhône, the Seine and the Rhine.

It was then that the La Tène Culture (450–370 BC), derived from the Hallstatt, made its appearance, in a climate of extreme violence and destruction (Fig. 6.7). The upcoming La Tène elites preferred burials to include the weapons of war and two-wheeled war chariots, instead of the hunting weapons and four-wheeled chariots of the Hallstatt burials. The La Tène tribes formed an alliance or confederation amongst themselves, typical of barbarians, with no unity of command, which became known as the Celts. The Celtic tribes penetrating western Europe put down roots, adopted agricultural activities and abandoned their original nomadism, which continued to be the *raison d'être* of the eastern Celts. Among the former, those who lived in Dacia (the present Romania) and in Thracia (the present Bulgaria) are the most famous. Among the latter we find the Getanes, who occupied the Pontic steppes, followed eastwards by the Roxolanes, the Iaziges, the Sarmatians and the Alans.

The raid was the characteristic war tactic of the eastern Celts, who always lived from pillage, never having permanent territorial ambitions.

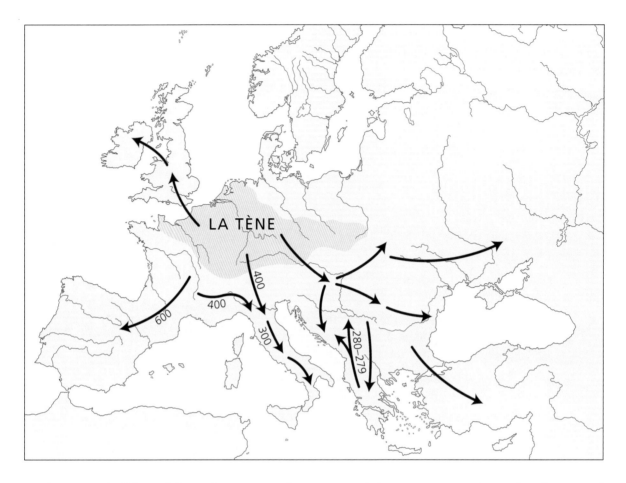

6.7 The 'La Tène' (Celtic) expansion in the first millennium BC. The influence of the La Tène culture on the Iberian substratum produced the Celtiberian culture in Iberia.

Many times over, they extracted heavy ransoms from the threatened nations, obtaining by extortion what might have been achieved by military force.

The history of the Celts and their important presence in the military events that moulded the final centuries BC will be dealt with in the second volume of this work.

CONCLUSION

It is possible to distinguish at least four different agents who could have been responsible for the introduction of equitation into Europe during the Bronze Age. Initially, we mentioned the Indo-European peoples from the Pontic-Caspian or south Russia (probably the so-called 'Battle-Axe' peoples) who, in 3000–2500 BC, expanded eastwards into Asia. In 2500 BC came the 'Bell Beaker' phenomenon in western Europe, for which we have two possible alternatives: either they started in Portugal and expanded northwards, returning later on the 'reflux', or they came from northern Europe arriving in Iberia via the Atlantic coast or across the Pyrenees. Whichever was the case, these peoples may have been the vector for the introduction of equitation into the areas which they penetrated. Around 1200 BC we have two important movements: the Urnfield tribes from 1300 BC, who planted the roots of the future Hallstatt and La Tène cultures from which the Celts were derived, and the Great Catastrophe which destroyed the civilizations of Asia Minor and Greece. These 'Sea Peoples' were the first users of cavalry as an effective war tactic at the beginning of the Iron Age. Finally, during the last millennium BC we have the rise of the Celtic peoples, and Greek and Phoenician colonization in the Mediterranean. These latter two events will be addressed more fully in the second volume.

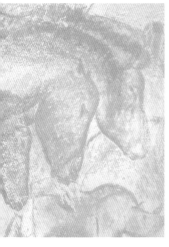

Chapter Seven

CHARIOTS, WARFARE AND DOMESTICATION

As shown in previous chapters, after the end of the Ice Ages horses survived in the steppe lands of Eurasia, in the Iberian Peninsula, and maybe in much smaller numbers in some parts of forested western and central Europe. It was suggested that many of the most respected authorities on the subject maintain that equitation anticipated traction, both techniques coming to Europe with the spread of agriculture. Animals, equids included, were first domesticated for human consumption and only later for work, beginning with bovines, followed by onagers and asses and lastly by equines, which although much easier to teach and docile of character did not then have the physical size and power necessary for traction or equitation. It was selection by primitive man, probably learned from the genetic improvement of bovines and ovi-caprines, that finally produced the 'modern' horse, fit to work.

Camelid and equid domestication began around the fifth millennium BC, almost simultaneously in Egypt and Arabia for camels, and from Russia to Turkestan for equids. Onagers were first used for traction in the Middle East, later being substituted by asses whose habitat stretched from Algeria to the Sinai. The hardiness, temperament and low subsistence needs of the ass made him a useful complement to the horse, including for the production of mules, which until the development of navigation were widely used by the caravans that traded goods between North Africa and the Middle East. With the increase of traffic on the Mediterranean, camels replaced mules on the auxiliary land routes across desert sand, unfit for equids but ideal for camels.

7.1 Cart miniatures in clay from Hungary, 10 cm high, c. 3000 BC.

Until the second millennium, equids in Mesopotamia were harnessed with a rope noseband, while in the same period on the Eurasian steppes bits were already known and equids were employed to pull light-weight vehicles, with spoked wooden wheels. The dominant opinion is that the first mouth control pieces made of antler or bone were developed for chariot driving, and later adapted for riding which also began with nose-strap control. There is also some evidence of camels pulling heavy carts in the steppes, but no evidence whatsoever of animal traction in Africa until the second millennium.

For most authors, the scenario of how and where the first domestication of equines took place was in the pastoralist communities of non-agricultural peoples of the middle Dnieper. At one of these places, Dereivka, south of Kiev, horse bones dating from 3500 years ago were found, and the problem is to determine whether they come from domesticated animals or from hunted wild horses. Dr Bernard Sergent expands the 'Kurgan' theory, as already mentioned in Chapter 5:

> The oldest skull of a horse showing the particular characteristics indicating domestication (modifications of the marks on tooth enamel) was found in Dereikva, a village of the Kurgan culture on the Dnieper. It was carbon-14 dated from 3500 BP … It is estimated that approximately thirty generations are necessary for changes due to domestication to modify the biology of a species …[1]

Another candidate for primacy in the domestication of the horse is Botai, in north Kazakhstan, where copious remains of horse bones were found, dating from the end of the fourth millennium. The most accepted theory for the origin of equitation is the one that puts it on the Pontic-Caspian steppes, spreading from there to Asia Minor and to eastern Europe by the end of the fourth millennium and to western Europe by the third millennium. According to other respected opinions, however, horse riding was a technique developed locally – independently or through external contacts and influences – in many different places at about the same time, using the indigenous horse populations.

One of these theories attributes the innovation to the Iberian Peninsula. H. P. Uerpmann affirms that the Iberian horses belong to an indigenous race and that equitation started not in central but in western Europe, probably in the Iberian Peninsula, during the third millennium.[2] This technique was brought about as a result of contacts between Bronze Age Peninsular peoples with the Middle East, where donkeys and onagers had already been domesticated. The other Iberian hypothesis attributes the spread of the ridden horse to the 'Bell Beakers', as already discussed.

It was at this time that maritime commerce connecting the Mediterranean islands started. While Asia Minor and the Aegean entered the international 'Oriental Mediterranean Bronze Phase', the western side of this land-locked sea remained in the European prehistoric stage, notwithstanding the fact that Italy, Sicily, Sardinia and North Africa were in touch, through seafaring activities, with these more advanced civilizations.

As mentioned in Chapter 5, Edgar Polomé affirms that Mesolithic groups, located between the Don and the Urals, had already domesticated the horse by the fourth millennium BC, and Marija Gimbutas' Kurgan theory suggested that domestic horses disseminated from south Russia between 4500 and 2500 BC. This opinion is supported by most writers, as for example Dr Bernard Sergent. In his opinion, it was the horse, whether driven or ridden, that was responsible for the success of the Indo-Europeans.[3]

All these academic opinions, as will be seen below, reverse the previous consensus that horses were first domesticated for traction and only much later for riding. They also modify in some way the Iberian scenario regarding horse domestication: one of the arguments sometimes used to suggest that domesticated horses did not exist in Iberia before the arrival of Indo-Europeans was exactly the absence of chariots and other wheeled vehicles, which only appeared during the first millennium BC, as discussed in Chapter 6. The admission of the reverse order in equine domestication makes the introduction of these prestige vehicles into Iberia much more logical.

The small stature of the first domesticated horses forced the rider to sit in an advanced position above the animal's front legs (Fig. 7.2), or at the back over the rump, but never in the control position in the middle of the back as is done nowadays. These primitive riding positions were used until the last millennium BC, when the first organized cavalry troops were created, employing more advanced techniques, like bits, bridles – but not yet saddles – and obviously bigger and stronger animals. All these improvements were the result of practices perfected after centuries of chariotry.

Horses had been ridden in the civilised world since the second millennium. Riding is represented in Egyptian art as early as 1350 BC and reliefs from the twelfth century show mounted soldiers … None, however, is a cavalryman. All ride bareback, without stirrups, and straddle the horse toward its rump, not a control position. That indicates, indeed, that the horses were not yet strong enough in the back to be ridden in the modern style. By the eighth century BC, however, selective breeding had produced a horse that Assyrians could ride from the forward seat, with their weight over the shoulders, and a sufficient mutuality had developed between steed and rider for the man to use a bow while in motion. Mutuality, or perhaps horsemanship, was not so far advanced, all the same, that riders were ready to release the reins: an Assyrian bas-relief shows cavalrymen working in pairs, one shooting his composite bow, the other holding the reins of both horses. This, as William McNeill [*The Rise of the West,* p. 15] observes, is really charioteering without the chariot.[4]

7.2 Cavalry soldiers of the time of Sennacherib (704-681 BC). Note the rider, protected with armour, seated in a forward position over the horse's legs. Drawings reconstructed from Assyrian art.

The horse was a luxury, valuable and expensive to maintain, reserved for the elite, except in the Asian steppe, where the absence of sea outlets and navigable rivers plus the favourable ecological conditions and the extraordinary resistance of the local pony made him the only means of transportation available. It is not by accident that the chariot was born there.

WHEELED VEHICLES AND TRACTION

Human experiments with traction started with wooden sledges, first used in Arctic Europe around 7000 BC, probably drawn by dogs. Sledges were later used on the steppes around 4000 BC, as attested from sites of the Tripolye culture in Russia.

Wheeled vehicles, an improvement over sledges, came later, in the fourth millennium, and were pulled by a pair of bovines. Heavy solid disc wheels (Fig. 7.3) were unearthed in the Pontic steppes from the tomb of a local chieftain of the third millennium. The large dimensions of these tombs gave the name 'Catacomb Grave' to this culture. Later on, onagers and mules were employed for traction in the Middle East. Mules are more suitable than horses for carrying heavy loads. Having a harder skin less liable to damage they can also better endure extreme weather conditions and lack of water.

The Sumerians in the west and the Bronze civilizations of the Indus Valley in the east definitely had ox-drawn vehicles by the third millennium. Also from Sumer comes the first evidence of the driving of equids. The tombs of the Third Dynasty Royal Cemetery at Ur contains both solid-wheeled ox-drawn vehicles and lighter vehicles pulled by a pair of donkeys. A four-wheeled vehicle pulled by four donkeys was found in a grave at Kish. Many other findings attest the transition from oxen to donkeys, onagers and finally horses.

Wagons and other vehicles were originally built to be drawn by oxen, using two animals attached by yoke and pole, a method that took advantage of the oxen's hump to keep the harness in place. This method was also tried with equines, with poor results for two reasons: first, the absence of a hump at the withers made the yoke slide back and forth and, secondly, the throat harness compressed the windpipe, suffocating the horse. This problem was later solved with the adoption of parallel lateral shafts, which replaced the yoke and pole, while the throat harness was replaced by the

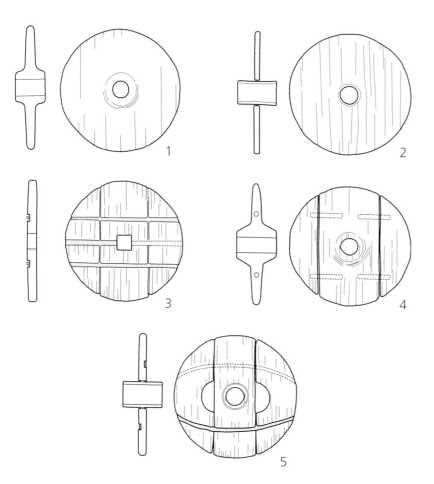

7.3 Prehistoric solid wooden wheels. (1) single piece, integral nave; (2) single piece, inserted nave; (3) tripartite disc, external battens, turning axle; (4) tripartite disc, integral nave, internal dowels; (5) tripartite disc, inserted nave, curved battens, lunate openings.

stiff collar, transferring pressure from the throat to the shoulders and chest of the animal.

The technological contribution of China in the development of driving and equitation was so important that it is imperative to recall some of its most innovative influences on these equine arts, soon adopted by all other civilizations in antiquity and the Classical world. Horse breeding, traction and equitation arrived in China sometime in the second millennium, brought in by the Mongolian invaders, who in their turn learned it from the western Asian nomads, most probably the 'Battle-Axe' Indo-European peoples. Although equine traction and equitation were imported practices, the Chinese greatly improved both arts, being the inventors or disseminators of, among other improvements, the collar harness (4th century BC) and stirrups (2nd century AD), the latter probably introduced by the Sarmatians.

According to Jacques Gernet:

The cart with a pole and two horses harnessed with a neck-yoke gave way at the time of the Warring States [fifth to third centuries BC] to the cart with two shafts. And it seems that at the same time the neck-yoke – which was to remain for a very long time the only method of harnessing known in the rest of the world – was replaced by the breast harness. This new device, and also the horse-collar, which was to appear between the fifth and ninth centuries A.D., were important pieces of progress in the field of animal traction. By freeing the horses from the pressure of the yoke, which tended to choke them, they made driving easier and rendered it possible to pull heavier loads. One single horse would suffice where formerly two or sometimes even four were required.[5]

Linguistics can also provide some interesting information on this fascinating subject, as for example, that given by Prof. Mallory and already briefly mentioned when discussing the Indo-Europeans (Chapter 5):

The earliest evidence for wheeled vehicles outside of territories either demonstrably non-Indo-European, for example, Sumer, or implausibly Proto-Indo-European – such as the Kuro-Araxes culture of south Transcaucasia where Hurro-Urartian languages appear – is to be found among a number of fourth-millennium BC cultures in Europe. These include the TRB culture of Northern Europe which reveals an acquaintance with wheeled vehicles by the mid-fourth millennium BC; the Late Copper Age Baden culture in the Carpathian Basin and other late Copper Age cultures of northern Italy which date from the latter half of the fourth millennium BC; and the Pontic-Caspian region where numerous remains of wheeled vehicles begin to emerge towards the end of the fourth millennium BC. Tomas Gamkrelidze and Vyachislav Ivanov, interestingly enough, have noted that one of our words associated with wheeled vehicles, Proto-Indo-European *kwekwlo-* bears striking similarity to the words for vehicles in Sumerian *gigir,* Semitic **galgal-,* and Kartvelian **grgar.* With the putative origin of wheeled vehicles set variously to the Pontic-Caspian, Transcaucasia or to Sumer, we may be witnessing the original word for a wheeled vehicle in four different language families. Furthermore, as the Proto-Indo-European form is built on an Indo-European verbal root **kwel-* 'to turn, to twist', it is unlikely that the Indo-European borrowed their word from one of the other languages. This need not, of course, indicate that the Indo-Europeans invented wheeled vehicles, but it might suggest that they were in some form of contact relation with these Near Eastern languages in the fourth millennium BC.[6]

Heavy carts, the wagons that antedated war chariots, came in three different wheel versions: (a) one made from criss-crossed planks, i.e. all planks vertical on one side and horizontal on the reverse side; (b) the crossbar model, where the empty space in the interior of the wheel circumference was occupied by two horizontal bars connected by a small vertical plank perforated in the middle for the passage of the axle; and (c) the spoked wheel, with several spokes going from the hub to the felloe (Fig. 7.5). As one can easily guess the first type was employed on heavy vehicles and the third type on light ones. The second type was rarely used. Vehicles could have two or four wheels. The heavy four-wheeled vehicles were pulled by oxen and had either fixed or movable axles, i.e. the front axle could rotate around the centre to facilitate turning. On smaller vehicles, the axle was fixed, and

7.4 Soldiers from Iran, on foot, on horseback and in carts. Assyrian relief from Niniveh, North Palace.

145

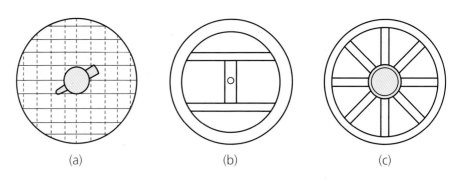

7.5 Wheel types from ancient carts. (a) criss-crossed planks, i.e. all planks vertical in one side and horizontal on the reverse side; (b) the crossbar model, where the empty space in the interior of the wheel circumference was occupied by two horizontal bars; (c) spoked wheel.

(a)   (b)   (c)

the wheels turned round on a stub to which they were attached by a lynch pin that kept them in place. On heavier vehicles, the wheels were fixed directly to the axle and both rotated together.

CHARIOTS

Wheeled transportation was quickly accepted throughout most of the Ancient World. The great advantages of the chariot over the existing heavy vehicles were the spoked wheels and the structure, both made of light hardwoods (Fig. 7.6). This made possible the use of the horse as a draught animal and all the resulting tactical advantages on the battlefield, such as speed and the platform provided by the chariot for shooting missiles. Artillery was enormously improved by another newly invented offensive weapon: the composite bow. Before its invention, archers could only hit targets situated no more than 50 meters away, and the impact was small as the arrows lacked speed. With the composite bow (see below) everything changed.

It was in the seventeenth century BC that the combination of the chariot and composite bow made its appearance as a new and formidable war machine. The chariot crew was composed of two warriors: the charioteer who drove the vehicle and the bowman who shot a barrage of arrows on to the enemy formations. Before then, chariots were used only for transporting warriors to the battlefield; once arriving at the combat zone they dismounted from the vehicles and fought on foot, as so often described by Homer in *The Iliad*.[7]

The war chariot that appeared around 2000 BC was a technological revolution in warfare. It was the first advanced, sophisticated product developed for military purposes and, as has always happened since in similar

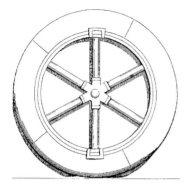  

7.6 Three Assyrian chariot-wheel models, (1) from the early empire; (2) from c. 900 BC; (3) from c. 700 BC. Drawings reconstructed from contemporary Assyrian art.

circumstances, its control gave a dominant position and supremacy to those who could build and operate it. But there is no consensus on where these vehicles came from. Evidence exists of two-wheeled vehicles in the second millennium among the Hurrites, a people originating in Armenia, who invaded Mesopotamia and are considered as the possible 'inventors' of the light, spoked-wheel vehicle drawn by one or two horses.

Some authors argue that the manufacturing process of the chariot – the invention and production of spoked wheels, the leatherwork, the carpentry and all the specialized workmanship and technology that went into these sophisticated war machines – was way beyond the skills of the barbarian horse-raiders from the steppes, a fact that puts in doubt Armenia and neighbouring Pontic areas as candidates for the cradle of the chariot. William McNeill writes:

Through the mediation of agricultural communities in their midst, these pastoralists became increasingly exposed to influences radiating from the distant Mesopotamian culture center. In this setting, not long before 1700 B.C., a critically important fusion of civilized technique with barbarian prowess seems to have occurred, for it was here, in all probability, that the light two-wheeled chariot, soon to become the supreme arbiter of the battlefield in all Eurasia, was invented, or perhaps merely perfected.[8]

The great military historian John Keegan has formulated what is certainly the best answer to this controversial question:

Whence came these charioteers? Clearly not from the still-forested lands of western Europe, even though pockets of wild horses may have survived there; its forests formed an obstacle that delayed the arrival of chariot aristocrats for at least 500 years. Nor again from the alluvial plains of the great rivers, since there the horse did not roam. The steppe – dry, treeless and offering good going in all directions – was unquestionably the main home of the wild horse but, though highly suitable for the passage of wheeled vehicles at all periods outside the spring and autumn *rasputitsa,* it is so deficient in the metals and woods necessary for chariot construction that it too may be discounted as the place of origin. By a process of elimination, therefore, the proposition that chariots and charioteers first appeared in the borderlands between the steppe and the civilised river lands seems convincing.[9]

The war chariot was thus perfected in the steppes and from there spread to the Middle East, where it became a powerful weapon and a symbol of prestige, a privilege of the highest nobility. Egypt, always trailing in technological innovations, only adopted the chariot in the sixteenth century BC after the Hyksos invasion. In the Greek world, the vehicle made its appearance in Crete and Mycenae by the end of the third millennium. As Mallory points out:

> We know that wheeled vehicles were employed in Mesopotamia by 3000 BC in early Sumer, and their presence in southern Mesopotamia has no obvious direct association with the Indo-Europeans. These vehicles were basically drawn by bovids, although there was a gradual increase in the use of equid draught in Western Asia. This, however, was primarily the onager or ass, and at no time prior to the second millennium BC can we regard Southwest Asia at practising the horse- and chariot-centred warfare that one finds among the Indo-Aryans. The earliest evidence for the horse in Western Asia is presently limited to Tal-i Iblis in south-central Iran (3500 BC) and Selenkahiyeh in Syria (2400–2000 BC), and its attestation in cuneiform texts appears to be similarly late and dates to the end of the third millennium BC. But from early in the second millennium BC we find unequivocal evidence for both the horse and the chariot, and by the seventeenth–sixteenth centuries this form of warfare is found from northern Anatolia south to Nubia, which illustrates the rapid spread of this revolutionary technology.[10]

The war chariot was already well established in China by the time of the Shang dynasty (1766–1122 BC). This fact is well described by Charles O. Hucker:

> War seems to have been the principal occupation of the chariot-riding ruling class, which regularly called out commoner draftees in groups of 1,000, 3,000, or 5,000 for expeditions against surrounding non-Chinese 'barbarians'. The

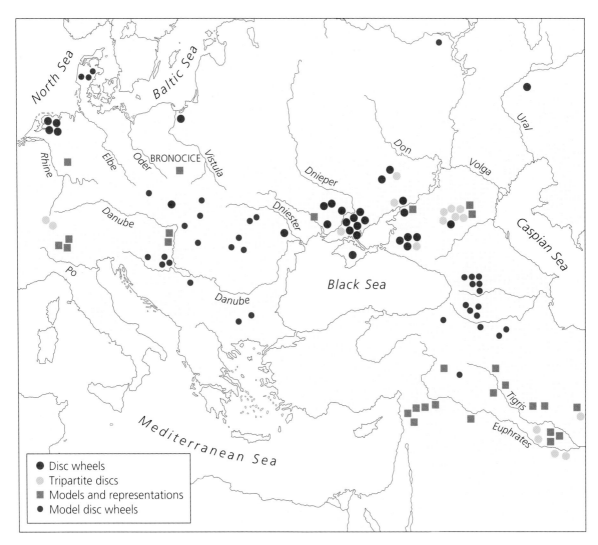

Disc wheels
Tripartite discs
Models and representations
Model disc wheels

7.7 Distribution of wheeled vehicles and models of wheeled vehicles in Eurasia before 2000 BC.

ways in which chariots were used in the fighting are not clear. Battles seem to have been man-to-man melées, joined with spear and bow and fought by aristocrats and commoners together. The Shang bow, made of wood, bone, and horn, was of the compound sort that later came to be the standard weapon of the steppe nomads and was known to Westerners as the Turkish bow.[11]

Charioteers and sometimes horses were protected with armour (Figs. 7.9 and 7.10). Archaeological sites in Crete, Mycenae and Greece have yielded many corselets and helmets, made in leather or metal. Homer describes these shining pieces of armour in *The Iliad*.[12]

Regarding the materials employed for chariot construction, the qualities required were toughness and lightness, which made the speed of

149

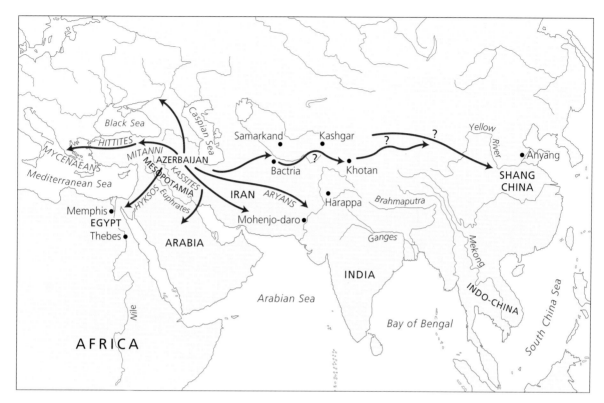

7.8 (*above*) Charioteers'
expansion (1700–1400 BC).
Chariots spread from the
Pontic-Caspian to Asia and
Europe.

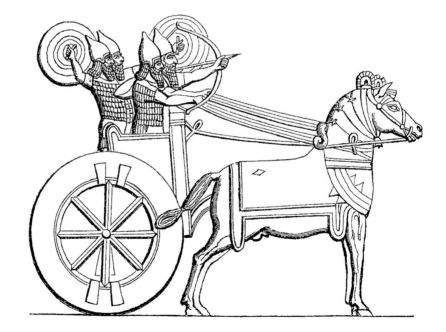

7.9 Assyrian war chariot
with four armoured
warriors (drawn according
to the sculptures at the
Koyunjik palace at Nineveh,
c. 700 BC). As well as the
driver and archer, there are
two shield-carrying soldiers
to protect the first two.

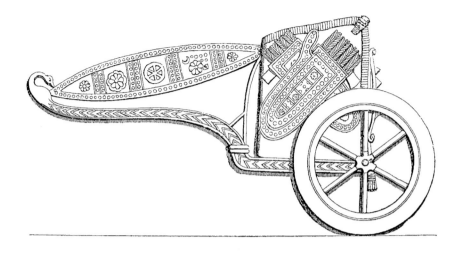

7.10 Early Assyrian war chariot (from the sculptures at Nimrud, c. 875–860 BC).

horse-drawn vehicles possible. These requirements were achieved by the use of light but strong woods, and new techniques were developed for bending the wood and joining it with glue to metals and leather, as well as the substitution of the new light spoked wheels for the old solid heavy ones. The final product, the sophisticated war machine, demanded constant skilled upkeep. Damage arising from wear and tear, accidents and combat engagements were frequent, requiring quick repair. Thorough maintenance required a group of very specialized and expensive craftsmen. Even when inactive, the chariots needed special care, such as removing the light spoked wheels to avoid them being deformed, and the placement of the remaining structure on top of a wooden support base or leaning against a wall. This practice is described by Homer in *The Iliad:*

> The Seasons loosed the purebred sleek-maned team,
> tethered them to their stalls, piled on ambrosia
> and leaned the chariot up against the polished walls
> that shimmered in the sun ...

> ... Quick at Zeus's side
> the famous lord of earthquakes freed the team,
> canted the battle-chariot firmly on its base
> and wrapped it well with a heavy canvas shroud.

and again in *The Odyssey:*

They loosed the sweating team from under the yoke,
tethered them fast by reins inside the horse-stalls,
tossing feed at their hoofs, white barley mixed with wheat,
and canted the chariot up against the polished walls,
shimmering in the sun ...[13]

The oldest treatise on driving and equitation, written by Kikulli of Mitani who was hired by the Hittites as a horse trainer in the fifteenth century BC, tells us about the difficulties to be overcome in the training, upbringing and feeding of horses for war chariots. When in use, these horses demanded not only special training but substantial nourishment, which besides green forage included hay and grains. Above all, as these horses had to be stabled and have special care, a large number of specialized workers were necessary. John Keegan speaks about a 'dearth of suitable horses' as a limiting factor in the expansion of chariot warfare:

> The chariot horse had to be a selected and highly schooled animal. The earliest known schooling of horses, apparently to dressage standard if an elaborate contemporary vocabulary of horsemastership is a reliable indication, can be dated from a group of Mesopotamian texts of the thirteenth and twelfth centuries BC; then as now, the young horse was intransigent in any language spoken to it.[14]

All these factors limited the use of chariots to monarchs and powerful chiefs who could command the wealth required for their upkeep, as explained in such a masterly fashion by Stuart Piggott and deserving of a full transcription:

> In the first place the motive power was the horse, an animal with a natural habitat in the temperate climatic zones of Eurasia, and with regional variants. An adequate supply of wild or feral horses had to be available, at hand or by import through reciprocal exchange, to be available for selection and training if not for deliberate breeding of improved stock. Training for working in matched pairs could be highly organized and elaborate ... Such highly trained animals needed adequate housing, foddering and watering by skilled stable staff. There is from the beginning the need for horse traders and trainers, grooms, stable lads and the like on the domestic or institutional pay-roll, and they appear in the palace archives of the eighteenth century BC at Chagar Bazar and Mari in Mesopotamia ...
> So too trained constructional and maintenance staff would need to be a part

of any large establishment for the building and repair of the chariots and their harness, with provision of stocks of raw materials – special seasoned woods, leather, glue and metal for structural and decorative use, paints and colourings. Here joiners and wheelwrights as well as metal-workers and artists combined their skills in creating a costly product which would need housing and storage, dismembering and re-assembling as well as emergency work after accidents …

In action, the high-performance horse needed not only special exercise and training but in addition to pasturage, hay, grain and other fodder not needed by the less demanding hay-eating ox … Such fodder requirements could draw quite heavily on cereal resources, especially in simple agriculture communities …

Finally, when these requirements of what were no more than essential back-up facilities had been provided for, the driving of the chariot with its trained and mettlesome pair of horses demanded a skilled charioteer, whether for solemn parade and festive or ritual display, or for the more risky exploits of hunting or war …

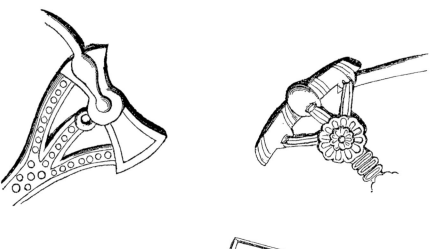

7.11 The bits of Assyrian chariot horses (from the sculptures at Nimrud, c. 875–860 BC).

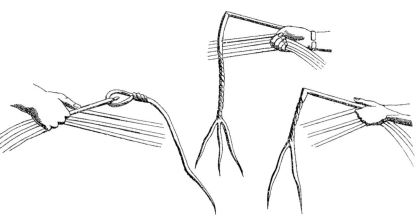

7.12 Driving-whips of Assyrian charioteers (from contemporary sculptures).

This then is what became by early second millennium BC the expensive package-deal offered to those seeking power and prestige and able to pay for it; it was a deal involving not only things but people. As Robert Drews put it recently: 'When ... an ambitious ... prince acquired chariotry for himself, he did not simply purchase vehicles. He also acquired teams of trained chariot horses; but even good horses and good chariots would by themselves have been useless. The most important ingredient would have been the men who knew how to repair the vehicles, to care for the horses, to drive them in battle, and to fight from a fast-moving chariot' (R. Drews, *The Coming of the Greeks* (Princeton, 1988), p. 176).[15]

Chariots in battle

Around 1700 BC, the chariot became the weapon of the barbarian raiders from the steppes, who initiated the age of chariot terror, with frequent and successful attacks upon civilizations located in the rich valleys of the great rivers, where the topography was ideal for the deployment of chariots and confrontation with other chariot or infantry armies from rival kingdoms. As the barbarian horsemen absorbed the new technology, they became a power to be reckoned with and few kingdoms could resist their incursions. The Hyksos in Egypt, the Mitanni in Syria and the Kassites in Mesopotamia are just a few eloquent examples of chariot-using barbarians conquering centres of civilization. According to Robert Drews:

> The earliest chariot warfare seems to have occurred in Asia Minor. Troy VI may have been established soon after 1700 B.C. by chariot warriors, and there is evidence that by ca. 1650 chariots were used by the king of Hatti, by Umman Manda at Aleppo, and by the *hyksos* who took over Egypt ... By 1600 chariot warriors were in control at Mycenae and elsewhere in Greece, and not long thereafter charioteers took over northwestern India.[16]

The history of the period between 1700 and 1200 BC was summarized by William McNeill:

> As the great wave of barbarian chariot invasions subsided about 1500 B.C., 'native reactions' against the intruders gained headway. In Egypt, the expulsion of the Hyksos by a native dynasty led to the creation of the Egyptian empire (1465-1165 B.C.) ... In the north and east, native reaction was less pronounced, for Mitannian, Kassite and Hittite rulers accepted the cultural traditions of their subjects to a large degree, in that sense ceasing to be alien. Nevertheless, native kings of Assyria who threw off the Mitannian overlordship (ca. 1380

B.C.), rapidly raised their state to the rank of a first-class power, strong enough to destroy the Mitanni empire about 1270 B.C., and to subordinate the Kassite kingdom. The Assyrians thus emerged as imperial rivals to the distant Hittites and Egyptians.[17]

Chariots went to battle in groups or squadrons, each one of them identified by a different colour of the box. There were also right-handed and left-handed chariots, probably used to attack the corresponding flank of the enemy's formation.

Most authors diverge on the subject of chariot formations and tactics in battles. Some visualize the chariots providing a protective screen for the infantry troops at the inception of the battle, and then moving sidewise whilst shooting at the enemy at right angles and thus opening the way for the incoming foot soldier's attack. After the battle ended, the chariots would return to pursue the retreating enemies. Others suggest that the chariots were kept in reserve, waiting for the battle climax, when they would move in against the enemy, helping to decide the victor. The other possible scenario would be the opposing chariot corps moving against each other, shooting arrows and trying to kill or wound the enemy's horses, immobilizing as many of the opponent's chariots as possible (Figs. 7.9, 7.13 and 7.14).

It is important to point out that infantry troops were always present and had a major role in chariot warfare. The 'runners', as the name suggests, were soldiers who ran alongside the chariots performing multiple tasks, such as killing fallen enemies or rescuing comrades. As Robert Drews observes: 'We might say that whereas in Greek and Roman times horse troops supported the infantry formation, in chariot warfare infantrymen as individuals or in small squads supported the horse troop to which they were attached.'[18]

The end of chariot warfare in the 'Catastrophe'

The Great Catastrophe marks the abrupt end of the palace-centred world represented by the civilizations of Asia Minor and Greece. Circa 1200 BC, the 'Sea Peoples', whose origins are still very debatable, invaded and destroyed all these, until then, powerful kingdoms (see Chapter 6). Only when they tried to extend their raids into the Nile, allied with the Libyans, were they driven back by Ramses III (1184–1153 BC). The Catastrophe marks the end of the Bronze Age in the eastern Mediterranean and the

7.13 (above) Royal lion hunt with chariot (Assyrian relief from Nimrud, North-West Palace, c. 875–860 BC). As in battle, the king uses the bow while the driver controls the three horses drawing the chariot.

7.14 Assyrian war chariot (from the sculptures at Koyunjik, c. 700 BC), drawn by a pair of Type III horses. Note the resemblance to the chariot above.

birth of the Iron Age. It also signals the end of chariotry as the most powerful and dominant weapon of war, replaced by infantry troops which held the leading role until cavalry rose to prominence among the barbarians much later, in the twelfth century BC. The reasons for the Sea People's triumph have been attributed both to iron weapons – which they used before they were known to other peoples – and to the tactics they adopted, deploying large infantry groups that overwhelmed the chariot formations of the more developed kingdoms.

In the decades of the Catastrophe, archaeological evidence supports the thesis that a significant change in weaponry took place, attesting to the transition from chariot to infantry warfare. According to Robert Drews, bows and lances, the weapons of the charioteers, were far more numerous before the Catastrophe than after. He points out that:

> Javelins, on the other hand, thrown on the run by skirmishers, seem to have proliferated at the end of the Bronze Age, and in the Near East remained important through the twelfth and eleventh centuries. The spear, the weapon par excellence of the close-order infantryman, is well attested for the early Iron Age. In Dark Age Greece a single spear normally accompanied a dead man to the afterlife. …
>
> On the basis of the circumstantial evidence we may therefore conclude that chariot warfare ended in the Catastrophe, the raiders and city-sackers having found a way to defeat the greatest chariot armies of the time. [19]

7.15 Ramses III in battle with the land forces of the 'Sea-Peoples'. Ramses III defeated the 'Sea-Peoples' and other raiders. Relief from north wall of the temple of Ramses III, Medinet Habu, Egypt.

In China also, this phenomenon took place at approximately the same time, as mentioned by the historian Jacques Gernet:

> From the fifth to the third centuries the development of the infantry was gradually to reduce the role of the chariots and was eventually to destroy the aristocratic mode of life bound up with the driving of teams ... As for cavalry, swifter and more mobile than chariots, it appears in the fourth century B.C. in the northern kingdoms, where it was adopted in imitation of the nomads at the same time as the dress of the horsemen of the steppes (tunic and trousers).[20]

CAVALRY

While chariotry was the essential war machine of the Late Bronze Age and infantry the dominant force on the battlefields in the Iron Age, cavalry slowly began to replace it as an offensive weapon from about 1200 BC.

It was very difficult for the rider, with neither saddle nor stirrups, to control his horse and use his bow simultaneously (Fig. 7.16). The solution was to ride in pairs, one cavalryman holding the reins of both horses, leaving the other with both hands free to shoot his bow.

7.16 Horse archer from Assyria, after 700 BC. A stirrupless rider in the forward position, using armour and a composite bow. Drawing from contemporary art.

It appears, then, that the use of cavalry began in the twelfth century, that by the tenth century some kings employed thousands of cavalrymen, and that the ninth-century Assyrian kings had at least as many horses in their cavalry as in their chariotry. The final obsolescence of chariotry came with the discovery, in the eighth century, of new techniques for reining a ridden horse. The new method, apparent in the reliefs of Tiglath-Pileser III, allowed cavalrymen to operate independently rather than in pairs, each rider now controlling his own mount. With every rider an archer, the 'fire-power' on the backs of a hundred cavalry horses was double the firepower drawn by a hundred chariot horses. Thus by ca. 750 B.C. the replacement of chariots by cavalry was more or less complete. …

From the twelfth century to the end of antiquity horse troops did not establish the battle but played a supporting role. On occasion, as at Issus or Adrianople, that supporting role might be decisive, and we even hear of armies (the Parthians at Carrhae) that consisted almost entirely of cavalry. But the normal expectation of Chaldaeans, Persians, Carthaginians, Greeks, and Romans was that a battle was in essence a clash of infantries.[21]

The ascension of cavalry as outlined above by Robert Drews is certainly the main cause behind the subversion of the established political/military order in Asia and Eastern Europe at that time. An interesting description of this critical period is given by McNeill:

As these invasions subsided soon after 1100 B.C., a second native reaction gained headway, this time centering primarily in Assyria. Through almost incessant and peculiarly bloodthirsty campaigns, the Assyrians gradually extended their power, until the empire at its height (745–612 B.C.) came close to uniting the entire civilized area of the Middle East into a single body politic … recurrent rebellion in Babylonia and endemic disorder in Egypt and Palestine presented the Assyrians with a problem they were never able to solve.

Hence the Assyrian empire rested on insecure foundations … the classic combination of barbarian assault (Medes from Iran and Scythians from the northern steppes) with domestic revolt (centering in Babylonia) brought the Assyrian power suddenly to ruin (612–606 B.C.) …

After a brief interlude, during which the Medes, the Chaldaeans, and the Egyptians divided the legacy of fallen Assyria, still another semi-barbarous conqueror upset the rather precarious balance of power among these three peoples. Cyrus the Persian emerged about 550 B.C. from the southwestern part of the Iranian plateau, and within an amazingly short period overran most of the Middle East ...

   With this achievement, the political evolution of the ancient Orient came to a logical, if not to a historical, conclusion.[22]

The turmoil, war and destruction suffered by these Asiatic civilizations and specifically the consequences of such tragedies upon Tyre resulted in drastic changes in the western Mediterranean and were responsible for the Punic presence in Iberia as discussed in Chapter 10. Stuart Piggott describes the ascension of horse power in a concise and objective manner:

cavalry was taking over from chariotry in Assyria by the ninth century BC and the king Shalmaneser III (858–824 BC) is depicted as riding on horseback. Thenceforward the monarch as a warrior on horseback became the accepted convention in the ancient Orient. By the seventh century BC momentous re-alignments of power were taking place, and new people with a tradition of mobile horsemanship from the west Asiatic steppe were establishing themselves in the ancient centres of authority; Nineveh was destroyed by the Medes in 606 BC, Babylon conquered by Cyrus, founder of the Persian Achaemenid dynasty, in 539 BC. The tribes known to the Assyrians as the Ishkuzai and Gimirrai (the Scythians and the Cimmerians) were raiding the Caucasian kingdom of Urartu from the time of Sargon II (721–705) and continued their raids of devastation into Asia Minor, the Cimmerians destroying the kingdoms of Phrygia and Lydia before their defeat by Assurbanipal (668–626). The Scythians moved eastwards, establishing themselves round Lake Urmia, where they invaded Median territory in the mid seventh century. The peoples all shared an economic and military structure based on the mastery of the ridden horse and the use of the bow, barbarian and at least partly nomadic in origin but by the time of the Achaemenids integrated into the sophisticated literate civilized culture of ancient Persia. It was this horse-riding Persia that was to confront the Greeks at the end of the fifth century BC, before being itself invaded and conquered by the forces of Alexander, who died in 323 BC. The Greek Seleucid dynasty was established by before 280 BC and maintained until it in turn was superseded by the Parthians, who remained the dominant power in Persia until the beginning of the third century AD, when Sassanian kings rose to prominence until conquered by the Arabs around AD 650.[23]

With respect to Europe, Anthony Harding confirms these facts:

Finally, we should not forget the role of the cavalry in Urnfield and early Iron Age warfare. Since the adoption of the horse to pull chariots (and later for riding) in large parts of Europe after 2000 BC, its versatility and power had been increasingly appreciated. A series of bridle fittings in bone and antler in the first half of the second millennium was increasingly supplemented by metal pieces, both the bits themselves and, much more common, the cheekpieces to which the bit and the rest of the bridle were attached. An increasing use of horses, in ceremony and perhaps also in warfare, can be seen, but the really dramatic change occurred after about 800 BC, when graves containing horse-riding equipment began to appear over a wide area of eastern and central Europe. Their interpretation as 'Thraco-Cimmerian' reflects the traditions recorded by Herodotus of a movement of peoples from the steppelands to the east, westward into Europe at a time that preceded the Scythian settlements.[24]

These historical events will be discussed in the following chapters, and as we shall see, all these new conquerors, like the Celts and other barbarians after them, were either horse-peoples or utilized mercenary cavalry as their main offensive weapon.

THE SUPPLY OF HORSES FOR WARFARE

While the literature about wagons, carts and chariots is very rich and varied, the same cannot be said about the horse, the most important element in the assemblage; the engine without which the chariot would not move. The same applies to the art of the period: while chariots and carts are well depicted, draught animals are not shown in sufficiently accurate morphological detail to permit their identification; it is difficult to discern what kind of equid is represented in Mesopotamian art of the middle third millennium BC.

As was the case with the Palaeolithic artists, we have to accept some creativity and maybe even more freedom of conception, but some common characteristics repeatedly appear in a numerous group of works scattered over the vast area from Egypt to Asia Minor. These represent a valid view of the probable morphological type of the horses of that age. The only conclusion which can be drawn after surveying the works is that these horses were mostly Type III or Type IV (see Chapter 2).

The consensus amongst scholars is that horses existed throughout the huge tract of land stretching from northern Syria, the Black Sea and Anatolia all the way to central Asia and Mongolia, and that this was

7.17 Assyrian war chariot (from the sculptures at Koyunjik), pulled by a pair of Type III horses. Two warriors, possibly archers or an archer and runner, have disembarked.

always, through intermediaries, the main source of the supply of horses to Mesopotamia. As pointed out by Brigadier John Clabby:

> the first appearance of the horse on the Middle Eastern scene was in a fairly peaceful and unspectacular role: pulling the little wagons of the gypsy-like Aryan migrants who, at the end of the third millennium BC, had trekked down from the north of the Caspian, through the mountains of the Caucasus and Armenia, to infiltrate most of the eastern Mediterranean area. These people brought with them not only the horses that became the nucleus of the breeding stock of this previously horseless region but also, most likely because they must have been expert wheelwrights, the idea for the design of the new spoke-wheeled chariot. A similar Aryan migration in about 1500 BC took the horse to India.[25]

Mallory confirms this theory:

> We have diplomatic correspondence between Egypt and Mitanni where the former requests both horses and chariots from the latter, indicating the Mitanni's reputation for horsemanship throughout the Near East. We have already seen in the linguistic evidence, such as Kikkuli's manual on horsemanship, that the terminology of chariotry included a distinctly Indo-Aryan vocabulary. Furthermore, the earliest evidence for the domestic horse is from the Pontic-Caspian region, and all present evidence suggests that it diffused

7.18 Mounted Assyrian spearman of the time of Sargon (c. 700 BC). Stirrupless, seated in the advanced position, riding what is possibly a Type IV horse.

from there through the Caucasus into Anatolia and perhaps around the eastern Caspian into northeast Iran.[26]

Homer mentions Thessaly (Perea) as the origin of the fabulous mares bred by Apollo:

> The best by far of the teams were Eumelus' mares
> and Pheres' grandson drove them – swift as birds,
> matched in age and their glossy coats and matched
> to a builder's level flat across their backs.[27]

This non-Mesopotamian, northern origin is again reported by Homer when he mentions Thrace:

> ... Zeus himself, his shining eyes turned north,
> gazed a world away to the land of Thracian horsemen,
> the Mysian fighters hand-to-hand and the lordly Hippemolgi
> who drink the milk of mares, and the Abii, most decent men alive.[28]

John Keegan places the chronology very clearly, avoiding the confusion between the chariot-drawing horse and the cavalry horse that came much later. It is instructive to reproduce some of his observations on this point:

Out on the steppe, however, man may have been riding even earlier than in the civilised lands, and it is possible that the use of the bow from horseback bled back from the Assyrians across the steppe frontier and was taken up by peoples who were better advanced in horsemanship. We know that as late as the reign of Sargon II the supply of horses still ran from the steppe, where unbroken foals were caught yearly for training and then sale, to Assyria; it is not improbable that the skills of mounted archery went in the opposite direction.[29]

This supply route is also confirmed by Amélie Kuhrt:

With the routes into the Zagros and Iran firmly in their grip, the Kassites were probably able to procure fine horses from the Iranian mountains, later so highly prized by Assyrian and Persian kings. Formal gifts from Babylonia to Egypt included teams of horses, i.e. horses trained ready for use. This impression is strengthened by the fact that they are accompanied by an equivalent number of chariots. Such a present was the ancient equivalent of being sent an equipped jet-fighter.[30]

Better-bred horses came much later with the Scythians and Cimmerians, as was discussed in Chapter 6. It is appropriate here, however, to say something about the type of horse that existed at that time. Florence Malbran-Labat examines the Assyrian and Babylonian letters from the Sargonide period (725–627 BC), written on tablets now in the British Museum, which contain a number of references about the supply of horses at the time of the kings Sargon II, Sennacherib, Asarhaddon and Assurbanipal.[31] These tablets indicate that there were at least *two types* of horse, one for traction and another for saddle, and that they came mostly from Syria and Persia. Although there is no description of the morphological types, one tablet indicates that the predominant colour was black, the grey horses being less frequent and more valuable.

According to Stuart Piggott:

The domesticated, broken-in, trained horse was in itself as much an artifact as the chariot, but the 'equid of the mountains' was, in wild or domestic form, a foreigner from its natural habitat, in the temperate climatic zone of the north and the open pasturage of steppe or semi-steppe …

It is this region then, around the Black Sea and from the areas to the south from Transcaucasia westward into Anatolia, that would provide a natural reservoir from which Mesopotamian horse supplies could ultimately be drawn through intermediaries who would have domesticated and trained chariot stock.

The appearance of the horse in ancient Mesopotamia comes at the point of time when equid burials die out, but texts increase around 2000 BC ... All early horses were within the modern pony class in withers height: Przewalsky's horse averages 135 cm (13½ hands). From the earlier seventeenth century BC we have horse burials in Egypt and Anatolia – at Buhen c. 1675 BC, at Osmanskayasi seventeenth–sixteenth century, at Thebes 1430–1400 – with heights from 140 to 150 cm; the yoke heights of surviving Egyptian chariots average 135 cm ... The bone report on the horse remains from Troy VI (c. 1800–1300 BC) described them as of 'oriental type', presumably implying the same characteristics. It looks then as if the first ancient Near Eastern chariot horses included or perhaps were predominantly of Bökönyi's Eastern group.[32]

There is a lot of confusion here, as well as in other scholarly texts, mostly as a result of the comparative lack of interest that historians have in hippology, their main concern being quite rightly historical facts rather than zoology. Historical texts confound the 'Oriental' and the 'Arab' horse – which are two different animals – frequently assuming them to be the same horse. The 'Oriental' is the Pontic-Caspian, Turkmenian or Turanian horse, i.e. Type III, a blood-strain present in the Turk and the Iberian horses. The 'Arab' is a much more recent development and comes from Type IV, as discussed in Chapter 2. Caution must be taken when reading these texts to identify what type of horse the authors really mean to designate in the various references and descriptions.

However, horses 'still ran from the steppe' which had been the main if not the only source of supply for the Middle East kingdoms and Egypt since the Bronze Age. It is obvious that these horses, coming from the Pontic steppe, were of the predominant type available there, which means the Type III, Turkmenian horse. Coming from the east these were often referred to as 'oriental' by Greek and Roman authors. Arab horses did not exist then.

In Europe, at that time, wild horses existed in larger or smaller herds, as pointed out by Anthony Harding:

Horses were also present, of course, though never as a main food source; their usefulness as draught animals and for riding, appreciated since before 2000 BC, took on a new aspect during the early centuries of the first millennium as items of horse harness in bronze and iron begin to appear in graves over a wide tract of eastern Europe. Much has been written about the significance of these finds in ethnic terms; the widespread presence of horses that is attested perhaps indicates the start of the appreciation of the horse as a noble animal fit to accompany the warrior into battle.[33]

The French historian, Dr Sergent, gives more information about the Kurgans and their horses:

Putting it in a different way, archaeology identifies the events that correspond exactly to the processes of Indo-Europeanization that history advances as a necessary hypothesis.

There is no equivalent to these events in Oriental Europe. The Kurgan peoples conquered the whole of Europe and thus were able to impose their languages; never the contrary.

This point is entirely validated by the history of the domesticated horse. The majority of the Quaternarian horse species disappeared at the end of the Wurm glaciations (soon after 10,000 BP). In the Neolithic, two Euro-Asiatic breeds survived, the tarpan in the west (Ukraine, South Russia), the taki or Przewalski horse in the east.[34]

7.19 Chariot horse protected by clothing (from the sculptures at Koyunjik, c. 700 BC). A Type III horse with breast harness.

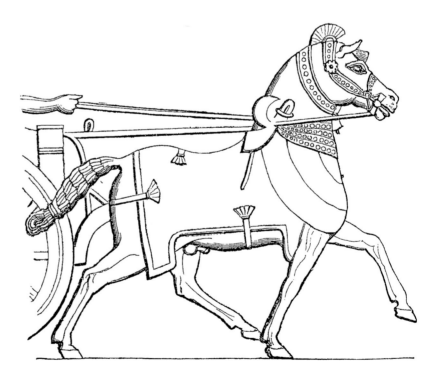

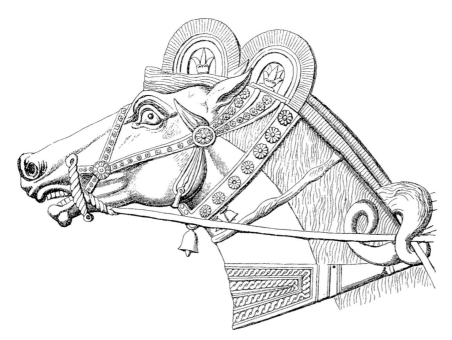

7.20 Head of a chariot horse showing a rich, sophisticated harness with bells attached to the collar (from the sculptures at Koyunjik, c. 700 BC).

7.21 (*below*) The king in procession (Assyrian reliefs from Nimrud, South-West Palace, c. 730 BC). Ceremonial chariot pulled by a pair of richly harnessed Type III horses.

7.22 Assyrian war chariot (from the sculptures at Koyunjik, c. 700 BC). Probably built with two shafts for a single horse.

TECHNICAL INNOVATIONS AFFECTING WARFARE

The composite bow

The origin of the composite bow, which was known to have its first use in the third millennium BC amongst the Sumerians, is still a mystery. Certainly, as with the war chariot, it must have gone through many changes and improvements before the definitive model was produced, which then did not alter much. John Keegan gives an excellent description of its manufacture:

> The composite bow began as five pieces of plain or laminated wood – a central grip, two arms and two tips. Once glued together, this timber 'skeleton' was then steamed into a curve, opposite to that it would assume when strung, and steamed strips of horn were glued to the 'belly'. It was then bent into a complete circle, again against its strung shape, and tendons were glued to its 'back' [Fig. 7.23a]. It was then left to 'cure' and only when all its elements had indissolubly married was it untied and strung for the first time [Fig. 7.23b]. Stringing a composite bow, against its natural relaxed shape, required both great strength and dexterity; its 'weight', conventionally measured in 'pounds', might amount to 150, against only a few for a simple or 'self' bow made from a length of sapling.

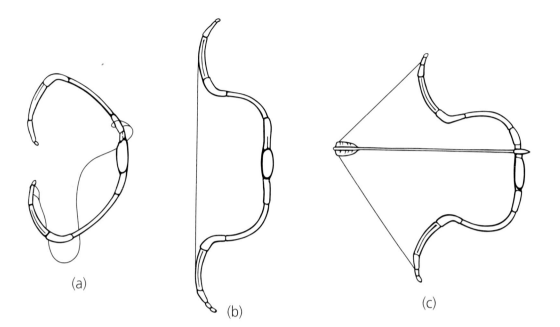

(a)

(b)

(c)

He continues:

> The composite bow was short, reaching only from the top of a man's head to
> his waist when strung, and therefore suiting itself perfectly to use from a char-
> iot or horse. It shot a lighter arrow – the best weight was about an ounce – than
> the long bow would [Fig. 7.23c], but could still carry to 300 yards with great ac-
> curacy … and penetrate armour at a hundred yards. The lightness of the arrow
> was actually an advantage, since it allowed the pastoral warrior to carry a large
> number – up to fifty in his quiver – into battle, which he counted on winning by
> subjecting the enemy to a disabling hail of missiles.[35]

The versatility and ease of operation made the composite bow an ideal
weapon for both charioteer and cavalryman, and its range and effectiveness against flesh and armour, combined with the operational possibilities
of the horse and chariot, made the bow plus horse or chariot a formidable
deadly weapon.

7.23 The composite bow:
(a) bent in a complete circle
against the strung shape;
(b) strung; (c) drawn and
ready to shoot.

Boats

The seaborne transportation of horses is fundamental to all the information and conclusions presented here. It is of paramount importance to
investigate and understand how, in prehistoric times, equines could be

169

transported over large distances aboard primitive boats guided by unso-phisticated navigational systems. It is a story worth telling.

The first real boats, that is, floating equipment made of wood, were probably developed by the Egyptians in the fourth millennium BC. Men learned how to use paddles and navigate over short distances in open seas, and at the end of that millennium sails were invented and the force of the wind partially replaced human power as the main propulsion. All these developments happened, not surprisingly, in the Mediterranean, where more advanced civilizations flourished and environmental conditions were favourable. In the 'internal sea', distances between islands and continents were shorter and waters normally calmer than in the Atlantic, but most importantly, winds had a reliable, predictable pattern which made naviga-tion less risky. These conditions are very clearly explained by Lionel Casson:

> the prevailing winds in the eastern Mediterranean and Black Sea ... during the ancient mariner's sailing season are from the north; in the Aegean, for example, summer northerlies were so constant that the Greeks called them the Etesian, 'annual', winds ... A skipper leaving Athens on the Black Sea run had to fight his way out there but could boom home with a following breeze. For those who handled Egyptian grain, the reverse was true: they sailed downhill before northerlies from Athens to Rhodes and before northwesterlies from there to Egypt but had to work against them all the way back, and the best course they could lay was a roundabout one by way of Cyprus; it helped somewhat that be-tween Egypt and Rhodes they were willing to sail all year round. A skipper headed for Sicily had the wind behind him only as far as the southern tip of Greece, and from that point on he had to work against it; conditions were, of course, just the reverse on the homeward leg. An ancient freighter could make between four and six knots with the wind, only two or a bit more against it. This meant that the round trip to Egypt or the Crimea involved three weeks at sea, to Sicily about two.[36]

Another breakthrough was the improvement in sailing that resulted from the discovery of bitumen caulking. As Fernand Braudel wrote, the 'pitch miracle' was the discovery that made long sea voyages possible:

> The miracle of the Phoenician voyages, the first systematic use of the sea, was at first sight due to human skill and courage. But perhaps there was something else. The Phoenicians possessed abundant supplies of bitumen, if only that of

the nearby Dead Sea, which had been in use from time immemorial. Pierre Cintas writes: 'I am inclined to believe that their success at sea was largely due to the use of bitumen for caulking their vessels.' Leaks and inadequate water-tightness were indeed the enemies of early navigation. In those far-off days, ships were invariably pulled up out of the water, either on to the sand for the night, or in port, where the hull could be exposed to the air for checking and careening. Bitumen, a kind of natural tar, was certainly used for this purpose by the Phoenician sailors.[37]

Transportation of horses across the Mediterranean waters was practised since the earliest times. Homer mentions several instances when this occurred, as for example:

So tribe on tribe, pouring out of the ships and shelters,
marched across the Scamander plain and the earth shook,
tremendous thunder from under trampling men and horses
drawing into position down the Scamander meadow flats …[38]

In Classical times, the Greeks destined the least seaworthy of their boats to that task, as explained by Lionel Casson:

a more discriminating system of four categories was introduced [in the Athenian navy]: 'selects', 'first-class', 'second-class', and 'third-class'. Ships that failed to measure up to even the last category could get a stay of execution by being converted into transports to ferry the cavalry's horses;… An unusual item that formed part of the regular gear was a set of 'undergirdles'; each ship normally carried at least two, often a few more as spares, and, when converted to transport horses with all their extra weight, four.…

The penteconter was a thing of the past, completely replaced by the trireme. The latter was far from being only a ship of the line, designed solely for use against enemy units. It was a general workhorse and carried out a multitude of tasks. Stripped of many of its rowers it transported troops; with the oarsmen reduced to sixty it carried horses, thirty to a ship.[39]

As reiterated several times in the course of the present book, horses obviously had to be domesticated in order to be transportable aboard these ancient ships. The first references to these voyages coincide with the period

7.24 Trireme, full size replica *Olympia* at sea.

of the war chariot, making it most likely that the horses were draught animals. The voyages were certainly short-distance affairs, as indicated by the size of the boats and the number of animals per ship, which would create a logistical problem of feeding and watering. In fact, things did not change much between ancient times and the days of Columbus, except for the larger tonnage and distances travelled of the sailboats.

Chapter Eight

THE IBERIAN PENINSULA

GENERAL VIEW

Geographically speaking, the Iberian Peninsula is an appendage of Europe, connected but at the same time separated from the continent by the Cantabrian and the Pyrenean mountain ranges. These barriers constitute a true wall that reduces Iberia to an enclosed territory, making incoming and outgoing travel difficult for both people and animals. It is also isolated from the environmental conditions prevailing on the rest of the continent, possessing quite a different ecology and a climate which has always been more favourable to the survival of the fauna and flora. For these and other reasons, the behaviour of the biota there was always different from the rest of Europe. North of the Pyrenees, the thermal variations are more extreme and the temperature gradients steeper, not only in the annual cycle between summer and winter, but also in the long term, between the maxima and minima registered during the interglacials and glacials.

Every year European herbivores, including horses, were forced to move on and search for new pastures when the ice and cold caused the grass to die back in their spring and summer habitats, to which they would return the following year. This rotation did not occur to the same geographical extent within Iberia. On the contrary, the Peninsula has been a refuge never voluntarily abandoned by any living creature, with the exception of the reindeer family and other cold–climate animals. To leave, animals would be forced to cross the Pyrenees and head north to less friendly

8.1 Panoramic view of the Côa Valley (Foz Côa), Portugal, where some of the oldest rock art engravings in Europe have been discovered. Dating back to c. 32,000 BC, they depict Przewalski-type horses.

environments. It is most likely that the opposite happened, however: animals, including horses, strayed into Iberian territory from the north during these annual migrations.

There is no archaeological register of equines older than the wild horses depicted in the cave and rock art of Iberia. This horse must have cross-bred with other equines, such as the horse from Solutré which roamed the south of France, and other indigenous ones living in southern Iberia. It is interesting to note that the types represented in the Altamira caves (the *garrano*) and the ones depicted in the Escoural Cave (closer to the Lusitano we know today – Fig. 8.2) indicate different natural evolutions and consequently also different crosses (see Chapter 3).

As we saw in Chapter 1, Uerpmann classified Eurasian wild horses into four geographically separated subspecies: (1) *Equus ferus ferus,* the steppe horse; (2) *Equus ferus sylvestris,* the northern European forest horse; (3) *Equus ferus lusitanicus,* the Iberian horse; and (4) *Equus ferus scynthicus,* the horse from the Black Sea.[1] If this particular classification is accepted, it would place the Iberian wild horse as one of the primitive ancestral types.

8.2 Horse's head from the Escoural Cave, Portugal (15,000-12,000 BC). The sub-convex profile and slender neck and features indicate a 'quality horse'.

The inclusion of Iberia in the phenomenon of horse extinctions in the Mesolithic, as a result of the advance of the forests forcing them to migrate *en masse* to Eastern Europe and the Asiatic steppes, is a questionable generalization. Because its 'closed' territory and favourable climatic conditions made Iberia a separate area with its own ecology, different from the prevailing environment of the rest of Europe, those who include the Peninsula in the same cycles of climatic change that occurred north of the Pyrenees make a grave mistake.

There is much discussion about the trajectory followed by the genus *Equus* between leaving America and reaching Iberia; did it come through

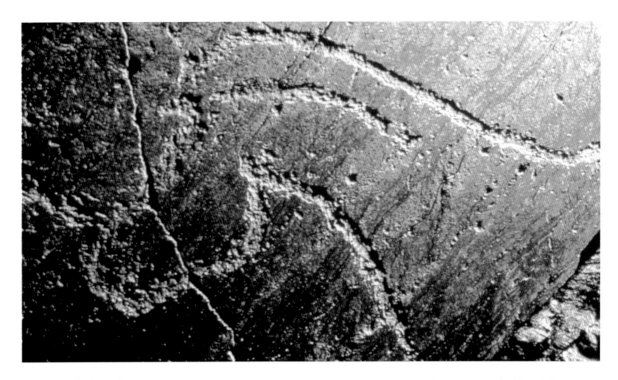

8.3 Head of a heavy horse from the Canada do Inferno, Côa Valley, Portugal.

Africa, crossing the Strait of Gibraltar, or, much more probably, did it cross the whole of continental Europe and enter via the Pyrenees?

There is no evidence that horses lived in Africa in prehistoric times. Neither is there any evidence of wild or domesticated horses in Africa before the second millennium BC. Many books written before the first half of the twentieth century, when most of the information now available was still unknown, accepted the erroneous theory that primitive ancestral horses of the Miocene came to the Iberian Peninsula by way of North Africa, crossing the Strait of Gibraltar. The myth of horses crossing the Strait of Gibraltar in prehistoric times, in either direction, persists today in some equestrian literature, especially when authors writing about other subjects take the previous literature for granted without further investigation. The myth can, however, easily be destroyed. Europe has not been connected by land to Africa during the period of the horse's evolution, even at the peak of the glaciations, and no water passages narrow or shallow enough ever allowed that transhumance. In fact, while in other parts of Europe ice covered the sea above the continental shelf, extending the shoreline to areas previously covered by the ocean, the Strait of Gibraltar remained ice free, maintaining its present width of approximately 13 km with water flowing unimpeded in and out of the Mediterranean in the

8.4 Horse's head
from the upper
Palaeolithic (Panel 3,
Ribeira de Piscos, Côa
Valley, Portugal.

8.5 Horses and goats (Penascosa, Côa Valley, Portugal).

same volume as it does today. The level of the Mediterranean Sea is about 10–50 cm lower than the Atlantic, a difference that accelerates the surface water current flowing from the latter into the former at an average speed of some 8 km per hour. The incoming cold ocean current is about 100 m deep and runs above the inverse warmer deep-ocean current that flows out of the Mediterranean into the Atlantic. These two currents have existed since the Mediterranean was formed, the only variation being that the water temperature at the surface was obviously much colder during the Ice Ages. Besides, the continental shelf at the Strait of Gibraltar rises to an approximate height of 400 m below sea level, forming a true wall that keeps the deeper Atlantic waters from penetrating into the Mediterranean, allowing only the warmer surface current to enter. This phenomenon is partly responsible for the warmer temperatures of the Mediterranean Sea. Not even the most radical and enthusiastic defender of the hypothesis that the European horse originated in Africa can sensibly postulate the theory that prehistoric horses swam the 13 km of icy water with a strong lateral current pushing them into the Mediterranean and away from their intended destination.

The only valid conclusion is that wild horses never passed from Africa into Europe or vice versa, which only leaves the possibility of them coming through continental Europe and crossing the Pyrenees.

Chariots were not part of Iberian culture, neither were they present in Western Europe, except in Britain, to Julius Caesar's great surprise. Mc-Neill observes:

> To be sure, the Indo-European conquest of the European Far West proceeded without benefit of chariots. The tribesmen from the steppe who subdued the peaceable villages and weak hunting tribes of the European peninsula had no need of the latest and best techniques of warfare. In any case, they probably lacked artisans sufficiently skilled to make spoked wheels, harnesses, and the other accoutrements needed for chariot fighting. In the course of time, the new superweapon did filter into Europe, but more as a ceremonial and symbolic device to show the dignity and greatness of its possessor than as a practicable instrument of the battlefield. Chariot tactics based on archery required open ground; and such ground was rare in the heavily forested regions of western and northern Europe.[2]

The war chariot was never used in Iberia, not only because of unfavourable topographical conditions but also because cultural influences from Asia Minor and Greece only arrived with the 'Sea Peoples', after the decline of the chariot as a war machine. Greek and Phoenician colonizers found in Iberia societies based on the use of the horse, and a type of horse several thousand years old. Not being horse peoples themselves, these colonizers, having no sources to supply horses from nearby, would not have attempted to negotiate in this live commodity which was so abundant locally. But they surely took advantage of their encounters with groups of horsemen to sell prestige chariots, a vehicle which they had manufactured for millennia and which was both unknown locally and had a vast population of domesticated horses ready to pull it for the delight of the local aristocracies.

The prehistoric peoples of Iberia were skilled horsemen, who had known how to ride and use the horse in combat from at least the third millennium. This could only have been possible if large indigenous horse populations of good quality were available. These Iberian horses were probably the foundation of the Barb, having been transported to North Africa by the 'Bell Beaker' navigators in the Bronze Age. Our discussion in Chapter 7 shows that horse transport implies domestication, which must therefore date from either the later Mesolithic or the early Neolithic.

As we shall see, when the Phoenicians arrived in Spain, there were no horses of any quality in North Africa, to the extent that the first mention of African stock-breeding comes from the Greek Classics and refers to the foundation of Cyrene in 630 BC, more or less contemporaneous with the establishment of the Iberian 'factories' and 'emporia'. A more detailed discussion of the North African scene is given in Chapter 9 below.

The archaeological spoils from Iberia show chariots engraved on stelae, a fact that confirms that they were only prestige vehicles owned by local chiefs (Fig. 8.6). We only learn about the full force of the Iberian horse and its horsemen, however, during the Roman period. This does not mean that these warriors were not there before the Roman conquest, but only that little was written or is known about the prehistoric populations of Iberia. Another point to remember is that it is impossible to form in a few centuries a cavalry as good and hard fighting as the Iberian. The fact that it existed proves the use of ridden horses for many centuries previously, not very different from what happened, for instance, in North Africa, where only the tribes of the Maghrib, which were influenced by Iberia over many centuries, were able to form top-class cavalry in ancient times.

8.6 Stela from a warrior's tomb (Solana de Cabañas, Logrosan, Spain), with engravings of a chariot (bottom) and a round Iberian shield (top).

Another important point that should not go unnoticed is the resistance of local populations to foreign cultural and military invasions. As was noted above, the populations most remote from the Pontic-Caspian focus were only marginally affected by the diffusion of the 'Agricultural Package', absorbing only selected items. Iberia is one such case, not only distant but a true *finis terra,* protected from all sides and not, as was the case with the areas fully taken over by the 'package', at the crossroads of practically every migration, constantly traversed in all directions by invading peoples. This enclosure makes the conditions that existed in Iberia and Mongolia, the two geographical extremes of this story, very similar, allowing indigenous cultural values to be developed and preserved, or eventually only partially imported. The ecological conditions of Mongolia caused the pony to be the indigenous equine, whereas the more favourable conditions of Iberia offered the ideal environment for all equines, including 'quality horses' like the Iberian and its ancestor the Sorraia (see Chapter 2).

8.7 Portuguese sculpture showing a typical Iberian horse. The horse is branded with a sun on the right hip, a practice still carried out in Portugal today. Part of a house frieze, c. 300–200 BC.

The very special conditions of the Iberian environment determined not only the type of indigenous horse but also the way in which the horse was used and the cavalry tactics developed locally: single combat instead of the confrontation of whole cavalry corps. This Iberian way of fighting became universally known as the *gineta*.

THE *GINETA*

Dr Ruy d'Andrade writes that even in a country as sparsely populated as Neolithic Iberia, fighting between neighbours was frequent. However, the irregular topography did not allow the formation of large groups of horsemen, but always involved small groups of warriors, contrary to the case in the Orient. In this environment, 'it is logical that individual combat was developed as a necessity'. This type of fighting was the origin of the so-called '*gineta*', a form of combat 'that depended on the quality of the horses, so much perfected over many years that it gave the peninsular horses the character that made them unique over such a long period of time right up until today'.[3] D'Andrade gives what is probably the best

181

description of the Iberian art of warfare, not previously available in English and therefore quoted at length here:

> What was the *gineta* in reality? It seems to me that a fair answer is: 'The ancient peninsular method of fighting on horseback.'
>
> The long spear, the *borrenes* saddle, fixed reins, the crowbar and *gineta* bits (the latter from the Roman period), spurs, chest protection for the horse, and the round, manoeuvrable shield are very old peninsular artefacts, made for single combat with spears. We have learned about this mode of fighting from Xenophon's writings on the presence of Iberian warriors in the Peloponnesian War in the fourth century BC [369]; from the battles that Polibius, Livy and Appian described in Spain and Capua; from Scipio himself about his wars with the Iberian kings; from Pompey in Spain and others and from the games or tactical exercises of the Celtiberians described by Arrian in his *Ars tactica*.
>
> I repeat: in a country where the population was not dense, where the terrain did not permit the use of war chariots, where the ancient horses were relatively big and very manoeuvrable, and the men light, agile and *gimnetes* [see section on Tartessus below], where the use of the bow and arrow was rare and arrived late, combat in a loose order was advantageous. For this reason, equitation consisting of manoeuvres and turns as described in the wars against the Carthaginians and the Romans, and in the Viriato and Sertorius Wars and so on, was born here.[4]

Dr Ruy d' Andrade then explains the tactics adopted by the *gineta* horsemen:

> In the historic period, we know that in order to protect the horse a neck defence was used, but later, when it was considered dishonourable to hit the enemy's horse, the horseman always had to use a shield – round to begin with and manoeuvrable and almost rectangular later – to protect himself. It was important to protect the left side, which without the shield would become exposed, the right side being defended by the spear which made the offensive strike. It was essential never to give the flank (the right) or turn the back.[5]
>
> ... Thus the duel on horseback becomes very interesting.
>
> As the left side is covered, the enemy horseman tries to win by riding around and attacking the right or weapon arm of his opponent; the horseman under attack will have to move less if he remains at the centre of this circle and so will have the advantage. The attacker will then break away and if his horse is faster than his enemy's will force a pursuit and try to reach the enemy's side as he defends himself with his spear. If he gains distance, he will turn around at the

right moment to hit the unprotected side of his enemy, who in self-defence will offer his left side, protected by the shield, and strike with his spear....[6]

If necessary, a horseman riding bareback without armour, not having the protection of a shield, would hide himself behind the horse's neck. He would even drop to the ground to escape from highly dangerous blows to his legs or abdomen, which due to the shape of the shield were the least defensible parts of the body.

Later on the Iberian horseman protected his horse with strong folded linen armour, maybe intertwined with wicker or animal sinews, that reached from chest to neck, and a rug that was used both as a saddle and as body protection, as can be seen in drawings from Liria.[7]

From there to a real saddle is a short distance, and as early as between the second and fourth centuries BC the Spanish had saddles with ... a front fold or pomo that was used to pass short reins around. These reins worked like modern side reins, keeping the horse's head low and making him concentrate, inasmuch as most bits were mere strips (filets) which would easily cause the horse to raise his head. From the time of Hannibal (second century BC) Iberian horses were already frenati (bitted) and some bits were severe, with sharp points on the mouthpiece called lupati (like wolf's teeth). We know this because Livy made the distinction between the horses of the Iberians and those of the Numidians that did not use bits. ...[8]

8.8 *Gineta* combat, according to Dr Ruy d'Andrade. Two stirrupless horsemen with round shields and spears locked in combat *à la gineta*.

Many people think that the sword was the weapon of equestrian combat: no! The sword and the club or the axe are weapons that were used only by the heavy horsemen of the cavalry, who due to the lack of mobility of their horses had to attack the strong armour of their enemies almost from a standstill, or who used these weapons against infantry as they were withdrawing. On the contrary, the weapon that the *ginetes* always used was the mobile spear, not the fixed lance. At most they would have two throwing spears to hit the enemy's infantry from a distance, and a runner would carry spare ones for them.[9]

D'Andrade ends by showing how the *gineta* has evolved since the Middle Ages, when the stirrup was in use in Europe:[10]

The horseman under attack would defend himself by using his shield to take the blow of his enemy or to hide behind, using his spear to deflect the enemy's weapon. He would attack the enemy if he felt he was the stronger or was defended by better armour or had a longer spear, as some did; all advantages would be used in war, although this one would demand a stronger arm.

However, the most usual combat tactic was to circle around waiting for the opportunity to strike. It could happen that during these movements the horseman under attack would 'give' his flank, i.e. to become exposed, which was the most dangerous situation. Unable to run away, his options were to use his own spear to deflect or hit his opponent's, or to confront the enemy face to face as one does with the sword, dodging or even turning away, using the inverted shield or the back of the shield as protection, and as a last dangerous recourse fleeing, which if done alongside the adversary's horse, with the head of the spear protected from the enemy, gave an advantage to the fugitive, especially if his horse was fleet because the enemy had to turn around to pursue him.

It is very difficult to protect one's back if one cannot soon gain a good distance, because turning back is always dangerous for the pursued as it shortens the distances between the two horsemen. For this reason it was important to have perfect command of the horse and make him turn around the left hand, which is the side with the shield. …

If during the escape the enemy could get close enough with his spear, it was necessary to resort to a violent blow or feint to deflect the head of the spear.

It must not be forgotten that persistent circling and attacking a well-protected enemy would very much tire out the horse. Consequently it was to be avoided as the attacker's horse had to cover a lot of ground while the opposing horse had much less to cover.

The quick exit with an element of surprise was very useful for gaining ground or position, and all the ways of avoiding blows were very carefully used. …

The spear could be used in the resting position or under the arm when attacking, but normally it was convenient to carry it high or low, moving it rapidly, because as the position of one's own horse and that of the enemy were changing at every moment, all directions of attack and all targets were valid; not just strikes from the front but also oblique, inverted or backwards. For this reason, some warriors used a spear with a head at each end of the shaft – although this weapon was dangerous to use in group formation.

Besides blows made with the arm raised above the head or with the spear in the resting position, this weapon was also used to strike from the left side of the horse over the saddle when the horseman was riding crosswise. Flanking or oblique blows were also used when the relative position of the opposing horsemen demanded or permitted them.[11]

The use of this equestrian weapon lasted until the end of the seventeenth century in Spain and was only dethroned by the modern *brida* equitation, spread by the French with the Bourbon domination in the eighteenth century and which later became the academic school of equitation.[12]

… The *gineta,* which as I say was the Iberian form of warfare since antiquity, lost its importance with the preponderance of infantry, against whom heavy cavalry was required to produce the power to break them apart, and with the introduction of firearms, especially the pistol, all fencing turns became useless, as shot took the place of the spear and against it the subtlety of fencing was lost.[13]

The *gineta* horse

Ruy d'Andrade writes about the unique characteristics of the Iberian Horse used for *gineta* combat in several paragraphs of the above-mentioned work, for example:

The horse, which reached 1.47 cm [14.2 hands] in height, was a big animal for that time and, as he was bred in a wild environment, was strong, fleet and tough. He was normally bred on rough terrain, with poor access, was used for grain threshing, and had balanced collection and high action (movements), and so was smooth and surefooted. He was admired for his generous and noble character, and by training became a horse that was *bien revuelto* (easy to turn), as the Spanish say. As a consequence he was the ideal fighting horse, so much so

8.9 The Tourada. Bullfighting on horseback reproduces *gineta* movements. It was probably developed as a drill for both the *gineta* horsemen and their horses. Shown in the pictures here, and on the following page, the bullfighters Paulo Caetano and João Moura show the continued tradition.

that the breeding process fixed the very special quality of extreme courage; when hurt he did not give up and because of his nobility he could be used as an entire, a quality that made him even more noble and valiant.

The technique of single combat rather than fighting in groups or in great numbers refined the equitation required. ...[14]

The horse had to be very flexible, quick of movement and obedient, and have great courage so as not to be afraid of blows and wounds. He had to have a fighting spirit so as to be not afraid of battle, but on the contrary he should long for a fight, as often happened.

It has been proved in many instances that the horse took the initiative in fighting, and assaulted enemy horses even when the latter were without riders. Even today, our good horses retain this combat-loving spirit and this is one reason they had to be kept entire. Nowadays some of our horses when restrained from attacking other horses bite themselves on the chest.

8.10 These pictures, and those on the following page, show Lusitano colts playing war games. The natural aptitude of the Lusitano for gineta combat is a genetic trait, improved after centuries of selection.

The interest these horses take in the fray is such that they spontaneously intervene and take the initiative in combat. It was thus not too far off the truth when the ancients said that the horse fought by himself.

In this respect our excellent horses shine above any other of any type or origin.

Horses that were not very obedient, that resisted, fought other friendly horses, pranced, ran away, shook their head or resisted the bridle (a reason why a good mouth was required), or that defended themselves in any way were very dangerous in battle. If they kept swishing their tail it might eventually get entangled with the spear, a reason why Iberian horses had to carry the tail close to the body rather than raising it, or even better tucking it under the body as in a capriole, so as to avoid swishing the tail when touched by the stick or the spurs. Similarly they always had to keep the head down so as not to obstruct the passage of the spear above it. Thus the requirements of a good mouth, keeping the head down, not raising the tail, and not ceasing to move when held on the spot, were the reasons that kept the Arabian horse out of the Peninsula while spear fighting was dominant there.

Kicking back as in a capriole could be useful, especially when the enemy was at a short distance.

The attributes in the horse of docility, bearing shocks with courage, indifference to wounds, agility, power in the loins and legs, toughness and manoeuvrability gave the horseman efficacy in combat. It was combat that forged the model and the character of the Iberian horse, which was considered the most courageous among warhorses.[15]

D'Andrade finishes in magisterial form with the words already quoted in Chapter 1: 'It was the Iberian warrior with the Iberian horse who created the *gineta,* and it was the *gineta* in turn that created the Iberian horse'.[16]

When and how the horse was domesticated in the Iberian Peninsula is still a controversial subject, but there is no doubt that the ridden horse was known there since at least the third millennium. As we have seen, several respected authors, among others Piggott and Uerpmann,[17] consider that equitation may have been born in Portugal and spread from there to the rest of Europe with the 'Bell Beakers'. According to Ruy d'Andrade, equitation was known in Iberia since the Neolithic, and proof of this is provided by the halberd:

At the end of the Neolithic a very strange weapon appeared which may, from its age, be linked to the megalithic monuments in our Peninsula.

I refer to the halberd, which is formed by a long, broad flint plate attached to

8.11 The Lusitano stallion Yacht (SA), showing the power and courage of the Iberian horse.

a long shaft [see Figs. 4.6 and 8.13]. This form continues to be found in the Bronze and Copper ages, when halberds were made of the relevant metals, so that the flint weapon preceding them indicates that the weapons were already in use for a similar purpose in previous times.

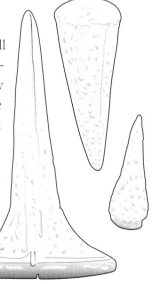

The halberd [Fig. 8.13] is not a weapon for administering blows like the axe, as it would be inadequate for that purpose due to the weak connection to the long and fragile shaft; it is a weapon to pull an enemy towards one, as is seen with the medieval halberd which had similar forms and methods of use.

8.12 Horseman from Osuna, Iberia (4th century BC sculpture). The position of the legs is only possible with stirrups.

Thus halberds were weapons that infantrymen used to unseat horsemen, the same way as the German lansquenet (*landsknecht*) did later. This indicates that since the Neolithic, there must have been warriors on horseback whom foot soldiers wanted to pull down to the ground.

The Neolithic halberd began to be used in an age that dates back to thirty or forty centuries before our Christian Age, and it appeared in the same regions where dolmen civilization developed, i.e. along the Atlantic coast and even in central Europe.[18]

D'Andrade concludes:

8.13 Neolithic halberd from Portugal, 3rd millennium BC. A weapon used to unseat horsemen.

It seems to me that it is not too daring to say that the use of the mounted horse in the Peninsula dates back to a period before the third millennium or maybe even earlier, because if the Neolithic halberd is an anti-horseman weapon, then we would be going back to the fifth or sixth millennium.

Another possibility for the spread of equitation, other than the 'Bell Beakers', is that the so-called 'Sea Peoples' who destroyed the ancient civilizations of Asia Minor might have gone westwards as far as Iberia. Many authors suggest that these peoples also introduced agriculture and the ridden horse into the Peninsula, many centuries before the Greek and Phoenician colonization.

A simple and superficial examination of the facts given above – the widely documented proof of the age-old use of the ridden horse and of the invention of typical cavalry warfare tactics – is more than sufficient to demonstrate even to the most sceptical reader that the use of both horse and equitation must have been practices imbued in the local culture, transmitted from generation to generation. The sheer force of all this historical evidence destroys any argument in favour of the arrival of horses and equitation in the Peninsula as recently as the third millennium, and significantly reinforces the alternative hypothesis of local domestication during the Mesolithic.

INFLUENTIAL CULTURES AND INVASIONS

We must now investigate the Peninsular cultures that existed in Iberia in the first millennium BC, before the Phoenicians and Greeks arrived there: the Cynesians, the Tartessians and the Celtiberians. The dearth of trust-worthy information regarding Iberian protohistory is a serious limiting factor in any analysis of this period. Some ancient Classical texts can be of some help, among them the *Ora Maritima* of Avienus and texts by Hecataeus of Miletus, Homer and Herodotus. It is interesting to note that many of these literary works contain references to the horses of Iberia, mainly in what is today southern Portugal and Andalusia in Spain, for ex-ample the famous 'Sons of the Wind' in *The Iliad:*

> For him then Automedon led beneath the yoke the fleet horses Xanthus and Balius, that flew swift as the winds, horses that the Harpy Podarge conceived to the West Wind as she grazed on the meadow beside the stream of Oceanus.[19]

Oceanus was the Greek name for the Atlantic, which started at the Pillars of Hercules (Heracles), i.e. the Strait of Gibraltar.

Tartessus

The first written reference to Tartessus is from the Greek poet Stesichorus, who described one of Heracles' labours against Gerion: 'beyond the silvery inexhaustible waters of the Tartessus river ...'. In his *Histories* Herodotus gives more information about Tartessus:

> The Phocaeans were the earliest Greeks to make long voyages by sea; they opened up the Adriatic, Tyrrhenia, Iberia and Tartessus. The ships they used for these voyages were penteconters[20] rather than round-bodied ships. When they reached Tartessus they became friendly with the Tartessian king, whose name was Arganthonius. He had ruled Tartessus for eighty years, and lived to be 120 altogether. The Phocaeans got to be on such very good terms with him that he

8.14 A typical modern Lusitano horse, from Interagro, Brazil. The modern descendants of the wild Iberian horse now formalized into the Lusitano (Portugal) and Spanish (or Andalusian) are currently bred world-wide.

8.15 (below) Indiano XVIII, a modern Spanish (or Andalusian) horse from California.

initially suggested that they leave Ionia and settle wherever they liked within his kingdom. The Phocaeans did not want to do that, however, so next – because they had told him about the growth of the Persian Empire – he gave them money to build a wall around their town. The amount he gave was extremely generous, because the wall makes a circuit of quite a few stades, and all of it is constructed out of hinge blocks of stone which fit closely together.[21]

Current knowledge about Tartessus is heavily influenced by the book *Tartessos,* written by the German scholar A. Schulten and published in 1922. This work cultivates the mythical and heroic legends associated with this culture in the romantic days of the nineteenth century.

Tartessus was the first known civilization in the Iberian Peninsula. Its origins are still nebulous; according to some authors it developed out of a pre-existing indigenous cultural substratum, invasions or colonization being totally absent; according to others, it came into being with the arrival of a group of the 'Sea Peoples' and later on attracted other immigrants from Greece, Rhodes, Mycenae and Cyprus. These incoming groups found an indigenous Middle-Bronze culture already in place in Iberia. Bendala Galán formulates this second theory:

> A more or less homogeneous group of peoples, ruled by a military caste, immigrated to the extreme west searching for new sources of wealth, far away from the difficult environment where they lived. They followed a route already known for many years; and, as indicated by the Algar culture, of clear Mycenaean influence, recent contacts had surely provided them with definite information about the treasures that existed in the peninsula. There, thanks to their military supremacy, they could integrate with the local indigenous population and became the dominant caste depicted in the *stelae*. Their princelings became the kings of these new dominions and Arganthonius may be one of their descendants.[22]

This absorption of eastern values was initiated between the second and first millennia, before the Phoenician colonization and the so-called 'orientalizing' period. According to several authors, such as Almagro-Gorbea and others, these contacts between the locals and the eastern Mediterranean peoples began with commercial transactions and resulted in the adoption, by the indigenous population, of objects and symbols of power and prestige from Asia Minor, for example brooches, ceramics, weapons and chariots.

Although the Phoenician influence is more evident in archaeological terms, one cannot deny the importance of the Greek presence reported in Classical literature, which is practically the only source of information we have about the people of Iberia before Roman times.

From Classical sources we become acquainted with other Tartessian tribes and other peoples or cultures. The Classics inform us of the existence of other peoples, some maybe older than the Tartessians, like the Cynetes, Gimnetes, Mastienans, Iberians, Ileateans etc., all from southern Iberia. The first two give credence to the story that horses were ridden in the area as early as the second millennium BC or even before, their names being derived from the Greek root *gymnétes,* from which comes the Spanish *jinete* and Portuguese *ginete* (horse rider). Herodotus twice speaks of the Cynesians, placing them precisely in the south of Portugal:

> The Ister [the Danube] rises in the land of the Celts, at the city of Pyrene (the Celts live beyond the Pillars of Heracles and are neighbours of the Cynesians who are the westernmost European people) …

> The Ister flows through the whole of Europe. It rises in the land of the Celts, who live beyond the Cynesians, further west in Europe than any other race, and then flows through the whole of Europe before entering Scythia from the side.[23]

Although Herodotus' geography was incorrect in that the Danube does not rise in Iberia, other authors confirm the information about the Cynetes, making it more credible. The report given by Herodotus about the journey of the Greek Colaeus (or Kolaios) is also very important:

> But then a Samian ship, captained by Colaeus, was blown off course on its way to Egypt and fetched up at Platea … Then they put to sea from the island with the intention of sailing to Egypt, but they were again driven off course by an adverse east wind. The wind was relentless and drove them through the Pillars of Heracles until, providentially, they reached Tartessus. This trading-centre was virgin territory at the time, and consequently they came home with the biggest profit any Greek trader we have reliable information about has ever made from his cargo…[24]

As already discussed in Chapter 2, the Greek colony of Cyrene, founded in about 630 BC on the isle of Platea, Libya, was a famous horse-breeding centre. It is intriguing to read from the ancient Classics that commercial contacts were established between Cyrenaicans and Tartessians during the first millennium. Were horses and chariots involved in these commercial exchanges?

When the Phoenicians arrived around 800 BC (1100 BC according to some), they met peoples with advanced knowledge of metallurgy and control of rich deposits of silver, lead, tin and mercury that could be reached by the rivers Tinto, Guadalquivir, Guadiana and Odiel. According to Arturo Ruiz Rodriguez, the vast quantities of Greek ceramics found in and around Huelva and dated to between 640 and 530 BC:

> support the written testimony of the excellent relations that existed between the Tartessian aristocracy (the mythical king Argantonios) and the Phoenician Greeks and by implication, therefore, the negative effects that these might have had on the existing colonial links between the Phoenicians and the Tartessians, as well as on those between the Tartessians and their indigenous periphery.[25]

There is no doubt about the warlike character of Tartessian culture and the knowledge these peoples had of horses and driving, the latter being with prestige vehicles probably introduced from the Orient through the commercial relations already mentioned. In a grave in Huelva, a war chariot with hubcaps decorated with lion heads, very similar to another unearthed in Cyprus, was found (Fig. 8.17). This vehicle apparently had four wheels, being similar to the chariots engraved on the funerary stelae of the region, as for example those of Logrosan, Cabeza del Buey, Torrejon el Rubio, Ategua and others. The weapons used by the Tartessian chiefs were also very typically Phoenician, indicating not only a Semitic influence but also a technological evolution, with the absorption of more sophisticated and better quality processes by the natives.

The decline of Tartessus

Many different hypotheses have been formulated to explain the decline and end of the Tartessian culture some time about 520 BC. The majority of theories favour the idea of sudden and violent destruction caused by external invasions. The first author to put forward this thesis was the German A. Schulten, according to whom the Punics (Phoenicians of Carthage), enemies of the Greeks and consequently jealous and afraid of the friendly relations between the latter and the Tartessians, were responsible for this catastrophe:

> Failing continually in their efforts to cut the communications between the Phocaeans and the Tartessian market, the Punics did not hesitate to destroy

8.16 (*facing*) Miniature cart in bronze, 2nd–1st century BC.

first Mainake and soon after the city of Tartessus, thinking, without any doubt, that it was better to establish a monopoly of silver and tin under their absolute control than to buy these metals from the Tartessians.[26]

The other current of opinion believes that internal decline was the sole cause of the disappearance of the Tartessian culture. This process would have been provoked by the over-production and exhaustion of metal ore quarries at a time when the technology for underground extraction was not yet known. Along the same line of thought, other authors believe that rather than the reduction in metal production it was the fall of their mother cities of Tyre and Sidon, conquered by the Assyrians, that engendered a lack of interest by the Phoenicians in the metal market and the consequent problem of the Tartessians. Another possible explanation for the Tartessian decline was the opening of new trade routes through Massilia (Marseilles), Narbonne and the Loire river, connecting the Mediter-

8.17 Iberian chariot wheels from a tomb of La Joya, Huelva, Spain (650–600 BC). Phoenician in origin, with hub caps ornamented with lions.

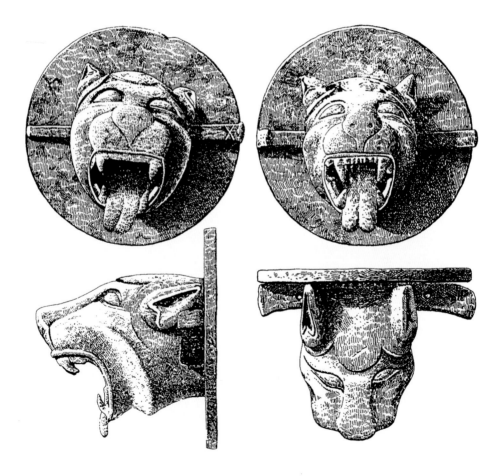

ranean to Brittany and the British Isles, rich in metals, that caused the abandonment of the already over-exploited Iberian mines. Finally, a recent school of thought tries to explain the phenomenon as the result of a combination of all the above-mentioned causes, i.e. the exhaustion of the superficial deposits causing a fall in production and income of the local population, who then turned against the colonizers to obtain by force of arms compensation for the lost profits, starting a conflict which ended with their defeat and total annihilation.

Iberians

Iberian culture occupied the area that starts, where Tartessus ended, on the Jucar river and stretches as far as the south of France. Iberian culture probably originated from Tartessian, and was an Iron Age culture appearing during the 'orientalizing' period (eighth to sixth centuries BC), when the Phoenician presence on the Mediterranean coast of Spain was already well established and when the first signs of decadence of Tartessus become visible (sixth century BC), with the abandonment or destruction of fortified villages, well documented by archaeological sites. It was in this atmosphere of crisis that the Iberian culture was born, to survive until the Romans arrived. Tartessian and Iberian graves reveal warlike and organized societies.

The Iberians developed active trade relations with northern Europe and the Mediterranean, being exporters of metals, salted fish and wines, and importers of ceramics and luxury goods, with the Greeks and the Phoenicians as their most important business partners.

From the fourth century BC onwards, fights between different aristocratic groups multiplied and the Classical texts speak about the many Iberian peoples such as the Oretani, the Bastetani and the Turduli, who were eventually dominated by the Romans.

Celtiberians

The Tartessians and Iberians were not Indo-Europeans. The earliest indications of Celtic cultural influences in Iberia only appeared around 500 BC, a fact that has been taken as a sure indication of the absence of Indo-Europeans in Spain and Portugal prior to that date. Basque, the only surviving non-Indo-European language in Europe, was spoken not only in northern

Spain but also in large areas of southern France, indicating the already-mentioned resistance of indigenous populations to cultural invasion.

The Celtic presence in Iberia has not yet been fully understood; the absence of substantial La Tène influences has reinforced the opinion that Celtic cultural values must have entered the Peninsula between 1000 and 500 BC, when evidence of associations with Hallstatt and Urnfield cultures, ancestors of La Tène, is abundant.

The Celtiberians, the result of the association of Celtic invaders with local Iberians or, alternatively, of the absorption of Celtic cultural values by indigenous Iberian populations, are a product of the sixth century BC. These pastoral warrior groups lived on the Meseta plateau and dominated iron metallurgy, which made possible the manufacture of weapons which, associated with mastery of the techniques of horse riding, led to territorial expansion and future confrontation with the Romans.

8.18 Sculpture of Iberian horse and rider, from Los Villares, Spain (c. 410 BC).

By the end of the Middle Bronze Age (1330–1200 BC), before the arrival of the Phoenicians, some signs of Celtic invasions or influences, such as ceramics and weapons of different styles, appeared near the Pyrenees. Of special interest is the La Polada culture, which extended from northern Italy to Iberia, embracing most of southern France. These are important testimonies of the active and intense relations that existed, since remote times, between peoples from both sides of the Pyrenees, and the probable immigration of peoples coming from France into Iberia.

As mentioned above, the arrival of the Celts or Celtic values in Iberia is a much-debated subject. Today, the predominant opinion amongst Spanish authors favours cultural diffusion, as opposed to the formerly accepted 'invasionist' hypothesis. According to the former, local Atlantic Bronze Age populations, who already had some cultural traits associated with Urnfield, Hallstatt or even La Tène cultures, selectively absorbed Celtic cultural elements, such as names beginning with the letter 'P' (which are intimately connected with the later Lusitanians) and circular houses. This proto-Celtic base would have progressively evolved, incorporating Mediterranean influences and transforming itself into the Celtiberian culture, initially located on the Meseta, the central plateau of Spain. Following the same process, this original cultural group would have expanded through the north and west of the Peninsula, except in the northern area occupied by the *castro* culture (fortified settlements), which was never affected by any Celtic influence. These theories, however, no matter how plausible they are, do not exclude military invasion by La Tène groups.

According to many authors, it was through these Indo-European movements (invasions or cultural diffusion) that equitation and traction arrived in central and western Europe and, so they say, in the Iberian Peninsula. Or, alternatively, these peoples found domesticated horses in Iberia, and crossed them with their own mounts, which were eventually totally absorbed. (See the wider discussion of this subject in Chapter 6.)

The Celtiberians were skilled horsemen who were employed by the Romans and Carthaginians during the Punic Wars. One of their peoples, the Lusitanians, were terrible adversaries of the Romans, as will be described in the second volume of this work.

8.19 Iberian horseman in bronze. Note the position of the rider, possible only with stirrups.

Phoenicians and Greeks

The commercial network established on the Atlantic coast since Neolithic times was the main source of supply of metals such as copper, tin and gold to the great civilizations of Asia Minor, who had the virtual monopoly of this trade. By the end of the second millennium, after the Great Catastrophe, these activities passed to the control of the Greeks and Phoenicians, who discovered or opened new supply sources in Iberia.

Some authors believe that the Phoenicians were already established in Spain around 1100 BC, and in North Africa, where they had Utica and later founded Carthage in 814 BC. The Greeks went first to Naples and later to Sicily, which became known as 'Magna Graecia'. The Etruscans, up to then greatly ignored in history, profited from these contacts and cultural influences and developed trade routes through the Alps and the Apennines, linking the Mediterranean with the Hallstatt populations of Germany.

Some writers, for instance Strabo, mention Greek colonies in the Iberian Peninsula since the eighth century BC, although it is only possible to prove their existence from the end of the seventh century, when the

8.20 Phoenician sea-commerce routes. The Phoenicians reached Iberia in 800 BC, founded colonies and traded actively with the Tartessians. Their influence gave birth to the 'orientalizing period' in southern Iberia.

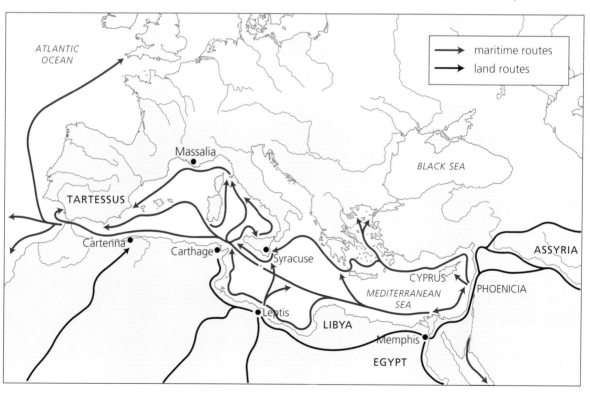

Phocaeans arrived there. The Greeks from Phocaea could not assemble large enough detachments to occupy the commercial outposts they founded in the Mediterranean, and so chose to locate them in small fortified villages – 'emporia' – whose survival depended on good relations with the natives.

The Phoenician presence in Iberia is well documented in their most ancient colonies, from the eighth century, situated in the bay of Cadiz and in Malaga, which predate the Greek ones of Emporium and Rhode. With the arrival of the Phoenician colonizers, the local populations retreated to fortified villages which were the predominant settlements of the Bronze Age. Stone stelae with engravings of warriors, chariots, brooches and weapons indicate the first signs of enrichment resulting from contact between the local aristocracy and the colonizers, and mark the beginning of the so-called 'orientalizing' period. These contacts and influences created a cultural exchange, with the absorption of foreign values and new technologies, such as writing and art, as well as better social and economic organization, all elements that characterize the rise from a prehistoric society to civilized status.

Archaeological spoils from the seventh century BC onwards have yielded iron instruments and potter's wheels, and the architectural design of houses changed from circular to rectangular buildings with internal divisions. These changes plus the rise of cemeteries indicate consolidation of power in the hands of an aristocracy with clear social differentiation. At the same time, the Phoenician 'factories' on the Mediterranean shores reinforced their defences, an indication of increasing hostilities between North Africans and the local Tartessian population. Occupying a strategic geographical position at the confluence of all the river, land and sea routes through which the metals from Iberia flowed to the rich markets of the East, Cadiz became the great Punic city of the Peninsula.

According to W. Culican, two commodities justified the Phoenicians' interest in the Portuguese Atlantic coast: in the south, from the Algarve to Alcacer do Sal, the rivers Sado and Arade 'were noted for their access to excellent timber' for the construction of boats; further north, the Tagus, the Mondego and the Douro gave access to tin and gold deposits, the Galicians being famous for their gold-work since the end of prehistory.[27]

The use of Iberian mercenary cavalry by these eastern colonizers is well documented by historical texts, as for example the description given by Diodorus Siculus about the defeat suffered by the Carthaginians in

8.21 (*above*) An Iberian funerary vase dating from c. 500 BC, illustrated with depictions of 'quality' horses. One head can be seen in the top centre of the vase. See also Figs. 1.9 and 1.10.

8.22 (*above right*) Detail from Iberian funerary vase of c. 500 BC, showing 'quality' horse with rider.

8.23 (*facing*) Detail from Iberian funerary vase of c. 500 BC, showing the head of a 'quality' horse.

Siracuse: 'Some Iberians alone massed together with their arms and dispatched a herald to treat about taking service with him. Dionysius made peace with the Iberians and enrolled them in his mercenaries ...'[28]

These Iberian mercenaries were then sent by Dionysius himself to help the Lacedaemonians in 369 BC:

From Sicily, Celts and Iberians to the number of two thousand sailed to Corinth, for they had been sent by the tyrant Dionysius to fight in alliance with the Lacedaemonians ...[29]

This fact is confirmed by Xenophon: 'These Iberians turn out later among the troops sent by Dionysius to aid the Lacedaemonians in 369 BC.'[30]

Greeks and Phoenicians, although not horse-peoples, had extensive contact with chariots and equitation. In their commercial relations with

the peoples of Iberia, they introduced prestige vehicles at a time when, as we have discussed previously, the chariot was already an anachronistic, obsolete weapon. According to Jose Maria Blázquez:

> The Phoenician presence on the Spanish coast is due to a series of cultural elements of the highest interest for the future of the Turdetanians and Iberian peoples, such as …
>
> … The arrival of new weapons, as for example shields, spears, chariots etc., represented in the so-called *stelae* Extremeñas, as they first appeared in that region, although they can also be found in the central part of the country, in the present province of Ciudad Real and as far as Aragón. The chariots, the shields, the lyre and the horn helmets presuppose the introduction of Oriental types of weaponry into the Occident. The Phoenicians probably gave these weapons as a gift to the local princelings of the open-cast tin-producing regions, which included all of the Portuguese and Spanish Extremadura, that is the region which, centuries later during the Roman conquest, was called Lusitania.[31]

CONCLUSION

Horses have lived in Iberia since the most distant prehistoric times, and never ceased to exist there, even during the Mesolithic when horses became extinct north of the Pyrenees. The still accepted picture of primitive horses arriving from Africa by swimming across the Strait of Gibraltar is a fantasy. Indeed, Iberian horses most probably formed the foundation stock of the Barb, having been transported to North Africa as domesticated animals by 'Bell Beaker' navigators.

The Iberian peoples practised the art of riding since at least the third millennium BC. Equitation may have been born in Portugal and spread from there to the rest of Europe with the 'Bell Beakers', or it might have come with the 'Sea Peoples' in the second millennium BC. The war chariot was never used in Iberia, not only because of unfavourable topographical conditions but also because cultural influences from Asia Minor and Greece only arrived with the 'Sea Peoples', after the decline of these war machines.

The ecological conditions of the Iberian Peninsula offered the ideal environment for all equines, including a 'quality horse' like the Iberian and its ancestor the Sorraia, one of the wild horses of Europe.

8.24 (facing) Celtiberian horseman (4th–2nd century BC).

External influences on the Iberian horse and equitation before the Christian Age were not significant. The three possible gateways for such influences are the Mediterranean (Greeks, Phoenicians, Punics and 'Sea Peoples'), the Pyrenees (Celts and other Indo-Europeans) and, according to theories relating to the arrival of the 'Bell Beakers' and other navigators, the Atlantic coast.

Chronologically the first candidates for entering the area would be the Indo-European invaders coming in by the Atlantic. Among these the only ones deserving any credibility are the 'Bell Beakers'. We have already met the two opposing hypotheses about this chapter of Iberian prehistory: either the 'Bell Beakers' are of Portuguese origin, having started their northbound journey from Portugal on horseback and returning later in the so-called 'reflux', as suggested by Piggott, Uerpmann and others;[32] or, as argued by Sherratt[33] and others (see Chapter 6), the movement was in the opposite direction, and they were peoples from the north who arrived in Iberia in the third millennium, bringing with them horses and equitation.

Regarding entry through the first possible gateway (by the Greeks, Phoenicians, Punics), the sole indications found at archaeological sites were chariot remains and representations of vehicles on stelae and other funereal monuments. What they indicate is only the arrival in the Peninsula of a luxury article, brought in by eastern invaders to please and exploit the local aristocracies. In other words, chariots were a superfluous commercial item, not war equipment introduced in great quantities by conquering armies. Only the vehicles would have been imported, and because horses existed locally these items did not cause any genetic alteration to the indigenous equine population, as would have been the case with a military invasion: one cannot imagine an invading army with chariots but without horses. As this invasion did not occur, the suggestion of a cross with Oriental horse breeds can be categorically abandoned. The second possible gateway, via the Mediterranean, relates to commercial relations between Iberia and North Africa involving horses. All the evidence suggests that at the time of the Greek and Phoenician invasions (see Chapter 9) both the south and north shores of the Mediterranean already had indigenous horse breeds, with large and well-used domestic herds. Considering their abundance on both sides of the internal sea, these horses probably did not have great value but were very expensive to transport across the sea, a fact which most certainly would depreciate them compared to articles such as metals, wines, salted fish, olive oil, weapons, chariots and other items whose commerce was intense, as we learn from Classical texts, which do not contain any mention of horse dealings. On the contrary, horse transit between Africa and Iberia is only mentioned at the dawn of the Christian Era, especially during the Punic Wars.

There is also no record or evidence to corroborate use of the final gateway – Celts coming via the Pyrenees. We do know, however, from other sources, that Celtic horses were of poor quality. Julius Caesar, for example, wrote:

> On their arrival he found that the horses they were using were unsuitable, and therefore he took the horses from the military tribunes and the rest of the Roman knights and the re-enlisted veterans, and distributed them among the Germans.
>
> Here [the Loire] Caesar had concentrated all the hostages of Gaul, the corn, the state chest, and great part of his own and the army's baggage; hither he had sent a great number of horses purchased for this war in Italy and Spain.[34]

We know from the writings of authorities on the Celtic influence in Iberia that it is far more probable that this influence was caused by cultural diffusion and not by war, and so did not involve the traffic of horses, as would have been the case with military conquests. It is not credible, then, that any influence on the Iberian horse might have been exerted by the Celts, not only due to the lack of numbers but also due to the bad quality of their mounts. Who would be interested in horses of bad quality in a country that already fought on horseback and had a large supply of equines of both excellent and poor (*garrano*) quality?

By exclusion, we are led to accept the only rational hypothesis, that of the existence of an age-old breed of horse with no significant external influence. This hypothesis is greatly reinforced by historic evidence, which indicates the existence of domestic horses in Iberia since the end of the Mesolithic; by the local development of a military tactic of fighting on horseback, the *gineta*; by the numerous 'horses of quality' supplied with or without mercenary soldiers to the Roman, Greek and Punic armies; not to mention the hard-fighting Iberian cavalries that fought with such bravery and ardour against foreign invaders during the final centuries BC.

8.25 Celtiberian horseman in bronze (3rd–2nd century BC).

Iberia offered the ideal environment for all equines, including for the development of a 'quality horse' like the Iberian and its ancestor the Sorraia. The Iberian horse was selected for the warring activities of the many indigenous tribes that lived in the Peninsula. This typical Iberian cavalry tactic is universally known as the *gineta,* and had almost complete control over the Iberian breed selection processes, being responsible for the Iberian horse as we know it today.

Chapter Nine

AFRICA

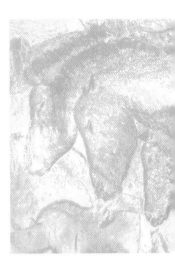

GENERAL VIEW

Little is known about western North Africa before the second millennium BC, although the African continent, like prehistoric Europe, has produced many interesting rock-art sites that have thrown some light on this mysterious past.

At the end of the eighth millennium, at the beginning of the Neolithic, the Sahara was not the desert it is today. On the contrary, it was part of the long, continuous tract of fertile soil that stretched with little or no interruption from the Atlantic coast of Africa to the Indus River, through Asia Minor and Central Asia, joining together all these regions that are today covered by desert or steppe. Up to the third millennium, when desiccation began, the Saharan region was watered by large lakes and permanent rivers, which made agriculture and cattle breeding possible.

The *General History of Africa* gives an overview of the different Neolithic art styles of Africa:

> African rock art dates from the Neolithic, a period which research is tending to set further and further back in Africa – to between 4000 and 10 000 years before the Christian era, depending on the region.
>
> A distinction has often been made between four main series of rock art, named after the type of animal most commonly represented. They are known respectively as the ages of the *Bubalus,* the Ox, the Horse and the Camel. The *Bubalus* was a kind of enormous buffalo, which appears in the earliest

specimens of rock art about 9000 years B.P. Elephants and rhinoceros were also depicted in the same period, and all these species are indicative of a thickly wooded environment. From about 6000 years B.P., the ox starts to be represented, in two forms: the *Bos ibericus,* with short, thick horns, and the *Bos africanus,* with long widely-spaced horns. The horse made its appearance in about 3500 years B.P. and is sometimes depicted in the 'flying gallop' style, with its four legs splayed out. By this time, which already comes within the historical era, the hippopotamus had disappeared from rock paintings, suggesting that there were no longer any permanent water courses or lakes. The camel was introduced into Egypt by the Persian invasion in about 500 before the Christian era and belongs exclusively to the historical period.[1]

9.1 Rock art of the Bovidean period, about 4000 BC, from Enneri Blaka, Djado, North Africa. Shows a man riding a bull of the *Bos ibericus* type.

The main theme of Ox or Bovine art, as the name indicates, was cattle, often shown in profile. Human beings were also depicted, generally Mediterranean Caucasoid types. The most numerous and important sites of this style are dated to around 3500 BC and are situated in the Tassili mountains. In its last phase, the Bovidians depict cattle harnessed to chariots (Fig. 9.3). The Bovidians were replaced at the end of the second millennium by the Equidians, peoples whose art-style was quite different, having as it main theme horses harnessed to two-wheeled chariots and later ridden.

The Bovidian style ended when the advance of the desert forced the cattle breeders to move out of the Sahara. The animalistic works like those of the Bovidians and Equidians are not the first nor the only manifestation of African prehistoric artists. As Henri Lhote points out:

> This phase is the most recent of the sixteen to which I have alluded, since the representations of oxen are often superposed upon the paintings of other epochs, but the 'Bovidian' phase is, all the same, earlier than that with pictures of horses for these latter are not prehistoric at all.[2]

9.2 Rock art of the Bovidean period, from the Tassili N'Ajjer, North Africa. Men riding bulls of the *Bos africanus* type.

215

The Capsian tradition in the north-eastern Sahara and the Saharan-Sudanese in the southern Sahara are also important Neolithic art cultures. The Mediterranean Neolithic, however, which includes the Bovidian and later the Equidian styles, is very different from all the others. The latter is significantly more important to us, as it is the best testimony of the introduction of the domestic horse in North Africa. As pointed out by Gabriel Camps, African art is closely related to Europe:

> It belongs to an essentially Mediterranean family covering the south of France, the Iberian peninsula, Italy and the islands. It is, therefore, not possible to overstate its maritime character. As early as the end of the seventh millennium, the first pottery-makers, by means of coastal trade and also by successful forays as far as the larger islands, had little by little won all the Mediterranean coast; the coasts of Tunisia, Algeria and Morocco were no exceptions.[3]

In previous chapters we have discussed at length the presence of the 'Bell Beakers' in Iberia and the vestiges of their culture in North Africa. If Uerpmann's theory of the Beaker's spread from Portugal is correct, then it must be possible that when they visited Africa and introduced their pottery and other cultural artefacts, they may also have introduced the ridden horse. In this case, the role of the Iberian horse as one of the foundations of the Barb is beyond contention.

THE INTRODUCTION OF HORSES INTO NORTH AFRICA

The introduction of the horse into North Africa is still surrounded by much debate. We can conclude from the paragraphs above that the earliest date for the appearance of the horse in Neolithic Africa is around 3500 BC[4] or, more probably, the late second millennium,[5] and that it came in as a domesticated animal. Who was the introductory agent? At least four different hypotheses can be considered: (a) the introduction from the Iberian Peninsula, by the Beaker or other prehistoric people; (b) the introduction by the Hyksos, around 1700 BC; (c) the introduction by the 'Sea Peoples' in Libya in 1200 BC, or much later, in 630 BC, by the Therans in Cyrenaica; and (d) a step-by-step introduction from more than one origin. These alternatives, which will be discussed below, are generally accepted as the most probable menu of possible answers to the question posed. Jean-Loïc Le Quellec puts them in very elegant and precise terms as follows:

9.3 (*facing*) Rock art of the Bovidean period, from Aïr, North Africa. Painting with giraffes, rhinoceros and a cart without a platform pulled by two oxen.

217

The North African and Saharan horses have those from the Asiatic steppes as their remote origin, and their introduction may have occurred through the Strait of Gibraltar or from Egypt, either following conquests or, more probably, by a step by step diffusion.

The introduction of the horse and chariot from Egypt is generally preferred by authors that consider the Hyksos as their probable vector, but it is convenient to observe that none of the Berber roots for the words designating the horse (*YS, GMR, I'LL*) has any correspondent in Egyptian, while the etymology of the pan-Berberian root */YS/* (cf. the Tuareg *ayis/iysan,* 'the horse') may indicate an Indo-European origin, maybe through the Greeks from Cyrene. In reality, the morphology of the Berber *ayis,* specially the suffix *an* of its plural form, indicates the former presence of a third consonant root, now disappeared, and ayes may come from *ekwos according to the following evolutionary scheme: *YS < *YWS < *KWS? < *ekwos.*[6]

9.4 Painted horse from the Tassili N'Ajjer, North Africa. Note the long slender neck and sub-convex head profile, typical of the Iberian horse.

Before exploring these alternatives more thoroughly, it is necessary first to address the topic from its very beginning. There is no evidence at all of horses living in Africa in prehistoric times. Neither is there any evidence

whatsoever of wild or domesticated horses in Africa before the second millennium BC. We have seen in previous chapters that horses did not exist in Mesopotamia or southern Asia Minor before the third millennium when domesticated horses arrived – brought by invading nomad charioteers (see Chapter 7) – from the Pontic-Caspian steppes. From there they spread to the rest of the Middle East and Africa. We may now return to the main question: how, when and by whom were horses introduced into North Africa? Gabriel Camps says that:

> The horse – which was not yet used for riding – was introduced into the Sahara at the same time as the light chariot of which there are many examples in the rock art from the Fezzan to Mauritania and the Saharan Atlas to Adrar des Iforas.[7]

This opinion is shared by Le Quellec, among others:

> One can conclude from this small 'dossier' that real horses are latecomers to the Sahara, where it is not possible to imagine their presence before the middle of the second millennium before our era, contrary to what was supposed by Henri Lhote.[8]

Let us now examine the different hypotheses.

Hyksos

The Hyksos, a Semitic people from Asia Minor, invaded and conquered Egypt with their war chariots, against which the Egyptians had no effective defence. They established themselves in the Nile Delta from where they ruled during the XIII to the XVII Dynasties (1785–1633 BC), until being beaten and expelled by the Egyptians circa 1567 BC. There is no doubt that the horse was unknown in Egypt before the Hyksos' invasion, a fact that authorizes the assumption that it did not exist until then in neighbouring countries of North Africa, such as Libya, Tunisia and Morocco. Many authors think that it was therefore the Hyksos who introduced the horse into North Africa:

> The use of the horse, which can be regarded as being one of the 'driving forces' of history, is recorded in Egypt at the time of the Hyksos invasion (1600 before the Christian era). Horses were used in Libya and Nubia in the early years of the first millennium before the Christian era, but only penetrated south of the Sahara in the 'Middle Ages', and at first only at the royal courts, as witnessed by Ibn Battuta's description of the court of the Emperor of Mali.[9]

Egypt was at that time separated from Libya, as explained by Brett and Fentress:

> The break between them [Berber languages] and old Egyptian (related to modern Coptic) could be explained by the physical barrier of the eastern desert, which became more and more impassable as the Sahara dried out. Again, this would suggest that the separation of the two had taken place *before* the definitive drying out of the Sahara between 2,500 and 2,000 BC.[10]

It is thus possible that the charioteers' horses remained in the Nile valley for a long time before entering Libya, the Maghrib and other western parts of North Africa. Their contribution to the development of the Barb is then questionable. The best one can reasonably suggest is that some cross-breeding might have occurred, but after the Berber was already an established strain.

Cyrenaica

Some authorities in North African history think that the introduction of the horse and chariot complex into the Sahara was made by the Equidians, probably the peoples known as the Garamantes and the Getules. These Caucasoid nomad horsemen from the Mediterranean gradually dominated the Bovidians and occupied the Sahara.

Some authors, such as Lhote, go as far as to say that these peoples got the horse from the Theran Greek colonizers of Cyrenaica, a subject discussed earlier:

> Indeed, the discovery of the first chariots provoked much excited discussion among archaeologists. Who could have drawn such things and what did they signify? Was it possible that once upon a time chariots had been driven through the Sahara? Herodotus mentions a people belonging to the great Libyan nation, the Garamantes (whose land lay in what is now the Fezzan), and they used in war two-wheeled chariots drawn by two or four horses. With these vehicles the Garamantes pursued another Saharan people, the 'Troglodytes', who lived in caverns and rock-shelters. As Herodotus died about 425 B.C. the events he related would have occurred, then, in the fifth century before our era.
>
> The Saharan chariot-pictures were thus, first of all, attributed to the Garamantes of Herodotus, but a careful examination of the paintings was made by such experts as Dussaud and Salomon Reinach, who concluded that the very

peculiar style of the horses galloping with outstretched legs was one clearly related to the 'flying gallop' convention in the Mycenaean art of Crete [Figs. 9.5, 9.6, 9.7 and 9.8].

Now, it is certain that, about 1200 B.C., immigrants from Crete[11] landed in Cyrenaica with the object of conquering Egypt and that these people mingled with the Libyans. So it appeared that the Saharan chariots must be more ancient than had at first been supposed and that they confirmed what historians had called (borrowing the words of the ancient Egyptian texts) an invasion by the 'Peoples of the Sea'. It might well be that after the failure of their campaigns against Egypt these invaders of Cretan origin retired towards the Saharan regions, where, sooner or later, the 'Peoples of the Sea' became assimilated with their Libyan allies.[12]

A similar but somewhat different angle is proposed by Camps:

Although, as is evident from excavations in Nubia, the horse was introduced into Africa some time before the Hyksos, it is difficult to believe that it can have spread as far as the Tassili n'Ajjer and the Ahaggar before the middle of the second millennium BC. ...

In the Fezzan and Tassili n'Ajjer the Equidians of protohistoric and ancient times can be identified with the Garamantes whose rule lasted up to the Roman Empire. In the west, however, that is to say south of the Atlas Mountains and in the neighbouring steppes, these horsemen became the Getules, of whom ancient historians have left several descriptions. At the time when the last of the Bovidians in the south of Mauritania were learning to harness their pack-oxen to wheeled vehicles, the horse in the northern Sahara was becoming a riding animal. The Garamantes and the Getules, horsemen of Mediterranean physical type, gradually dominated the peoples of the Sahara while still preserving their own type of nomad life-style.[13]

He concludes:

Thus, in the second half of the second millennium and the first centuries of the first millennium BC peoples of Caucasoid, Mediterranean type, perhaps descended from the Neolithic people of Capsian Tradition from the eastern Sahara, introduced the horse to the country between the Nile Valley and Cyrenaica.[14]

The second possible Greek origin for those horses is the foundation of Cyrene in 630 BC, as described and commented on in Chapter 2 above.

9.5 Warriors and war chariot pulled by a pair of galloping horses in the 'flying gallop' style. From the Tassili N'Ajjer, North Africa.

9.6 (below) Two horses in the 'flying gallop' pulling a chariot. From the Fezzan, North Africa.

From that material we know that the horses from Cyrene, of Bactrian origin, were highly regarded by the Greeks and so certainly also desired by the local African chiefs. We have here all that it takes to recognize an important source of horses for the neighbouring countries in North Africa.

That the Cyrenian horse was a different breed from the Arab and may have been one of the foundations of the Barb are facts already mentioned in ancient texts, as for example, in Oppian:

The dappled breed of Moorish [North African] horses are far the best of all for extended courses and laborious toil. And next to these for accomplishing a long course come the Libyan horses, even those which dwell in many-pebbled

9.7 Two-wheeled chariot pulled by horses in the 'flying gallop'. From the Fezzan, North Africa.

Cyrene. Both are of similar type, save only that the strong Libyan horses are larger to look at; but these latter are long of body, having in their sides more space of broad rib than others, and hence are stouter to look at and superior in a charge and good at enduring the fiery force of the sun and the keen assault of noontide thirst.[15]

Strabo, writing about the Libyans, says:

the Libyans in general, dress alike and are similar in all other respects, using horses that are small but swift, and so ready to obey that they are governed with a small rod. The horses wear collars made of wood or of hair, to which the rein is fastened, though some follow even without being led, like dogs.[16]

He adds in the same text: 'Their horsemen fight mostly with a javelin, using bridles made of rush, and riding bareback; but they also carry daggers.'[17]

Iberian origins

It is clear from the preceding chapters that the horse, wild and domesticated, lived in Iberia much earlier that its first appearance in North Africa. It has also been proven that intense cultural and commercial exchanges existed between Iberia and North Africa in prehistoric times. It is thus not at all improbable that the horse may have come to western North Africa from the Iberian Peninsula at the same time or even before the 'Sea Peoples' brought them to Libya, the Hyksos to Egypt, or the Cretans to Cyrenaica.

In Morocco and to a lesser extent in western Algeria, Iberian cultural traits took root – metallurgy, Beaker ware and channelled pottery, tombs in the form of cists and silos. In the east, on the other hand, in Tunisia and eastern Algeria, other traits from the eastern Mediterranean via Italy and Sicily became dominant: the introduction of dolmens and *haouanet* tombs, painted pottery, the square house and pitched roofs. To the south in the steppes the nomad horsemen brought knowledge of new species of domesticated animals – the Barbary horse and sheep – and developed certain funeral practices …[18]

We have already discussed the hypothesis of equitation having spread from Iberia into Western Europe with the Bell Beakers and we have also seen that Beaker and Cardial ware of Iberian origin were found in North Africa, and that the Levantine rock-art from southern Spain has a strong African influence. Camps mentions that exchanges between Iberia and

North Africa were intense, involving not only ceramics but metal articles, including weapons:

> The weapons are halberds or battle-axes, very carefully portrayed even to the rivets and the central mid-rib; daggers with wide, mid-ribbed blades in every way comparable to those of the Middle Bronze Age in the south of France, and also lance-heads and arrows. These representations belong to an art that is very different from that of the Neolithic both in subject-matter and style. It is true that animals continue to be portrayed: bovids, canids and antelopes, but now man himself and his manufactured goods (chariots, weapons, jewellery) or his symbolism (variously ornamented roundels or circles) usually take pride of place.[19]

9.8 War chariot pulled by a pair of horses in the 'flying gallop'. Possibly a combat scene. From the Tassili N'Ajjer, North Africa.

As we saw in Chapter 8, Dr Ruy d'Andrade points out that halberds are weapons mostly used to unseat riders, and that finds of this weapon from archaeological sites indicate the existence of domestic equines. It is possible to speculate that both the ridden horse and the weapons associated with it – offensive or defensive – may have arrived in the same package, brought by the same agents; in this case the peoples from Iberia that already dominated these new technologies. It is interesting to see how Camps reinforces the likelihood of an Iberian cultural presence in North Africa:

> Although the western part of the Maghrib, near to Spain (an important diffusion centre for metal-working technology) has produced undeniable traces of Bronze Age preceded by a few Copper Age imports, and although the western Sahara itself had an indigenous copper-working industry, the central and eastern part of North Africa, east of the longitude of Algiers, has not yielded a single bronze weapon nor any indisputable representation of one in the rock art. This fact alone proves the Iberian origin of this trait.[20]

Lastly, the great morphological similarities between the Iberian and the Barb horses indicate a close blood relationship that may have started in very ancient times and been preserved for many centuries, establishing a genetic pool that has resisted all later infusions of blood. Only a strong and long-term blood kinship can explain that.

Step by step

The step-by-step hypothesis is no more than the admission that all or most of the incursions suggested by the previous hypotheses have occurred at different times, so that it is impossible to ascertain which one of them is the more or less important. It is undeniable that some cross-breeding occurred on several occasions, determined by the prestige or the imposition of invading conquerors or local rulers. Fashion was then, as it is now, a governing factor in breed selection. The similarities between the Barb and the Iberian horses, and the strong evidence for horses being brought from Iberia into Africa in prehistoric times and not at other times, points already discussed, are factors that reinforce the opinion that the Iberian strain was the one responsible for the development of the Berber breed. These exchanges of animals and cross-breeding between the two strains were obviously greatly reinforced during Roman times, making it very difficult today to discover what really happened in the prehistoric past.

From all these horse invasions, two African breeds have persisted until today: the Berber or Barb and the Dongola. Camps, our most important source of information, describes the two very similar breeds as follows:

> In profile, the head shape of both these types is convex; they are not at all grace-
> ful (particularly the Dongola), their heads are heavy, their hindquarters low and
> they are short in stature. But they are very resistant, hardy and full of courage
> and their adaptation is so good that they have survived and preserved their
> characteristics in the face of multiple introductions, in particular of the eastern,
> so-called Arab, horses. At the same time that the horsemen from the steppes
> were introducing this new animal (destined later to make the Numidians fa-
> mous) to the people of the Maghrib, they also brought a new type of sheep ...[21]

THE DEVELOPMENT OF THE BERBER HORSE

We have seen that by the end of the second millennium, the Equidians, Caucasoid peoples from the Mediterranean, introduced the horse into the Saharan region. These invading aristocrats were responsible for the flour-ishing of Berber civilization, a group of warriors that conquered the other Saharan peoples and ruled ancient Numidia during historical times. Their descendants, the Tuaregs, continue their traditions in modern times.

The Numidians developed a famous cavalry that occupies a central po-sition in the history of later centuries of the pre-Christian era and of the first ones of our times, when it was either employed as a mercenary force or fought against the Romans and Carthaginians. Classical sources say that the Numidians rode their horses bareback and used no bits to control their mounts.

According to Strabo: 'Horse-breeding is followed with such exceptional interest by the kings that the number of colts every year amounts to one hundred thousand.'[22] Aelian described Libyan horses thus:

> Concerning the Libyan Horse this is what I have learnt from accounts given by
> the Libyans. These Horses are exceedingly swift and know little or nothing of
> fatigue; they are slim and not well-fleshed but are fitted to endure the scanty at-
> tention paid to them by their masters. At any rate the masters devote no care to
> them: they neither rub them down nor roll them nor clean their hooves nor
> comb their manes nor plait their forelocks nor wash them when tired, but as
> soon as they have completed the journey they intended they dismount and turn

9.9 A modern example of the Spanish Barb.

the Horses loose to graze. Moreover the Libyans themselves are slim and dirty, like the Horses which they ride. The Persians on the other hand are proud and delicate, and what is more, their Horses are like them. One would say that both horse and master prided themselves on the size and beauty of their bodies and even on their finery and outward adornment.[23]

CHARIOTS

A last word must be said about the chariots of the Sahara. These light vehicles were always drawn by a pair of horses, and were so light and fragile that they could not possibly have been employed to carry goods or more than two persons, limitations that have led many authors to consider that they were purely prestige or hunting vehicles, used only by the elite. Other

more radical theories are that they were never used at all, the drawings found in the rock-art of the region being a mere representation of the prestige of the chiefs and rulers of prehistoric Sahara. This opinion is shared, among others, by John Reader, who wrote:

9.10 Chariot with two drivers and another man. A total of eight reins but only one horse is shown. From the Tassili N'Ajjer, North Africa.

> If carts did cross the Sahara (rather than just an artist's impression of them), logic demands that the traffic must have been very light. In fact, of the thousand or so of known sites of rock-drawings in the Sahara and its approaches, only about fifty have representations of wheeled transport – and they all look more like racing chariots than traders' carts. Furthermore, the images become more and more abstract as the distance from the Mediterranean increases.[24]

Lhote, commenting on the engraved chariot discovered in Adrar and other findings, developed his theory of the existence of a Roman highway cutting through the Sahara. We present below selections from his argument:

> The discovery was indeed an extraordinary one to make so far south. At once the idea crossed my mind that the chariot people may have driven right across the Sahara ... The geographical disposition of the painted chariots (which must be considered, as a whole, more ancient than the engraved chariots) shows that

the horse-riding populations, descended from the 'Peoples of the Sea' and the Libyans, must have reached the Niger by almost as early as 1000 B.C. ... One discovery leads to another and often allows us to lift the veil from things which have been obscure enough. What I want to mention now is Roman penetration into the Sahara ... It was, indeed, a great highway, cutting through the whole breadth of the Sahara from Phazania (that is, the Fezzan) to the Niger, and there were many indications that a track had been, in Roman times, a caravan route by which the products of the Sudan ... were sent to the commercial centres of the north ...[25]

This theory is vehemently opposed by Camps:

The so-called 'chariot routes' that have been arbitrarily marked on the map by joining the points where chariots are depicted in the art are nothing more than

9.11 Two-wheeled chariot pulled by a pair of horses. From the Tassili N'Ajjer, North Africa.

wishful thinking because chariots have been found portrayed in places where they could not possibly have been driven – in mountain screes or massifs where even mules or camels would have difficulty in getting through. All this leads to the conclusion that the Saharan chariot, far from being an utilitarian or economic vehicle, must have been a status symbol pertaining to a chief or nobleman.[26]

CONCLUSION

There were no native ancestral or wild horses in Africa. Equines were introduced into North Africa, probably around 3500 BC, from Iberia by the Bell Beaker peoples. Other possible agents for such introductions are the Hyksos (c. 1700 BC), the 'Sea Peoples' (c. 1200 BC) and the Greek col-onizers from Thera (c. 603 BC).

Chapter Ten

THE CIRCULATION OF HORSES IN HISTORIC TIMES

GENERAL VIEW

This book has discussed the prehistory of the European and in particular the Iberian horse. It will be followed by a second volume covering the historical period (from c. 500 BC to the end of the first 1500 years of the Christian era), a no less difficult area where theories and opinions are even more controversial and any possible consensus even more difficult to reach. However, in order not to leave this work open-ended and inconclusive, it is necessary to anticipate briefly some of the topics that will be treated in the next volume. We have discussed some of the important migrations of horses that took place in prehistoric times and the possible consequences of these movements for various indigenous Eurasian breeds. During the historic period, these movements increased and thus so did the exogenous impact suffered by local breeds of horse.

The second volume will try to demonstrate, using historical facts, the two main propositions postulated in this book, as follows:

1. Native 'quality horses' existed in Iberia, North Africa and in the Pontic-Caspian region, and these horses continued to exist throughout the historical period. They formed the basic pool of horses for all the important cavalry corps of antiquity and Classical, Roman and post-Roman periods, including those of the Carthaginian, Celtic, Germanic and Iberian peoples, as well as of the Romans themselves.

2. The contacts and possible interbreeding between the Iberian, Barb

and Pontic-Caspian horses as a result of prehistoric migrations of horses continued, now conducted by man's activities, with the main agent being war and cavalry combat. Central to all these actions was Rome and her wars. With respect to the Iberian Peninsula, the most important events chronologically were the Punic Wars, the ensuing Roman period, the barbarian invasions and, to a much lesser degree, Moorish domination. Other important historical events, the Crusades for instance, had little or no direct effect on the Iberian Peninsula and its horses. Rome was not a horse country and her cavalry – always less important than the legion – was formed with horses obtained elsewhere or by mercenary troops. Consequently the major role played by the empire was that of a transfer agent: Rome through her wars and domination distributed Iberian and Caspian horses all over Europe and Asia Minor. The same movement was continued later during the barbarian invasions. In other words, there was a very active 'circulation' of horses connecting the more important breeding countries, such as the Pontic-Caspian steppes, North Africa and Iberia, with each other and with intermediate and neighbouring areas such as Gaul, Italy, Macedonia and Greece. Although each episode involved a limited number – a few thousand animals – and thus had no lasting effect in

10.1 The modern Caspian pony, thought to be a direct descendant of the 'quality' Type IV horse of the Pontic region.

themselves, their repetition throughout millennia may have ended up by introducing notable blood relationships between the breeds.

The recognition of the Iberian and Pontic-Caspian horses as superior 'quality horses' coveted and much sought after by the Romans and their enemies is reported in many Classical texts, already quoted above. The authority Edward Gibbon also wrote about sources for the supply of horses to Rome: 'The horses were bred, for the most part, in Spain or Cappadocia.'[1]

At all the historical moments mentioned above, the Iberian horse played an important role as a war-horse, highly regarded and extensively used by the local populations, the invading armies and the colonizers. It is important to keep in mind that all through this process, the Iberian horse received an input of foreign blood brought in by the invading armies but also, in no lesser measure, exported the Iberian strain to the rest of Europe and North Africa in the same process.

The figures given by most Classical writers are in agreement, indicating a small number of animals involved in every case of invasion or migration. Polybius for example, writing about the Punic Wars, gives numbers for Hannibal's transference of horses and troops to Africa and back to Spain, and the size of the army which left Iberia and arrived in Italy, as reproduced in the next section. Writing about Cannae, he says:

> For of the six thousand cavalry, seventy escaped to Venusia with Terentius, and about three hundred of the allied horse reached different cities in scattered groups … Both on this occasion and on former ones their numerous cavalry had contributed most to the victory of the Carthaginians, and it demonstrated to posterity that in times of war it is better to give battle with half as many infantry as the enemy and an overwhelming force of cavalry than to be in all respects his equal.[2]

There is also this text from Livy:

> [Hannibal appointed his brother] Hasdrubal – an active, energetic man – and secured it with troops, for the most part African. Of infantry there were eleven thousand eight hundred and fifty Africans, three hundred Ligurians, and five hundred Baliares. To these infantry forces he added the following units of cavalry: four hundred and fifty Libyphoenicians – a race of mixed Punic and African blood – and some eight hundred Numidians and Moors, who dwell near the ocean, and a little company of three hundred Spanish Ilergetes. Finally, that no sort of land force might be lacking, there were twenty-one elephants.[3]

Similarly, Plutarch states:

> For with the twenty-six hundred men whom he called Romans, and a motley band of seven hundred Libyans who crossed over into Lusitania with him, to whom he added four thousand Lusitanian targeteers and seven hundred horsemen, he waged war with four Roman generals, under whom were a hundred and twenty thousand footmen, six thousand horsemen, two thousand bowmen and slingers, and an untold number of cities, while he himself had at first only twenty all told.[4]

The rest of this chapter considers the four periods which had a particular impact on the Iberian Peninsula.

THE PUNIC WARS (264-202 BC)

The wars between Rome and Carthage lasted from 264 to 202 BC and embraced the whole of the western Mediterranean including Italy, North Africa and Iberia. The first Punic War, fought in Sicily and Africa, needs mentioning because it supports the theory put forward here of an active traffic in horses connecting the Pontic-Caspian to Iberia and North Africa. Sicily was not, initially, a horse country. Up to the first millennium BC, all local equines originated from Asia Minor and North Africa. Carthage always operated an efficient and numerous fleet and, as reported by Classical authors, deployed elephants and cavalry corps – mainly mercenary Numidians – in all her foreign and local wars. The Pontic-Caspian supply source was extensively discussed in previous chapters: as we saw, Cyrene was founded in 630 BC and the Greeks were familiar with horse transportation aboard merchant and war ships. It is probable that the Sicilian horses were mostly Berbers and crosses between the latter and equines descended from Asian ancestors. These Italian horses were in their turn also taken to Africa, as described by Appian:

> In the meantime Scipio, having completed his preparation in Sicily,… set sail for Africa [204 BC] with fifty-two warships and 400 transports, with a great number of smaller craft following behind. His army consisted of 16,000 foot and 1600 horse.[5]

It is important to remember that Sicily at that time already had a large and respectable horse population, formed by the Greeks and Carthaginians when these ancient civilizations founded colonies on the island. It is interesting to mention here the great Athenian fiasco; their attempt to conquer Syracuse (415 BC) failed due to their lack of cavalry, a weapon used in a masterly fashion by the Syracusans.

In Spain, the war started in 220 BC with Hamilcar Barca, who died in the campaign and was replaced as commander by Hannibal, the most famous of all Punic generals. Hannibal and his countrymen were true horsemen, as explained by Theodore Ayrault Dodge, the best of Hannibal's biographers: Hannibal 'returned to Spain in B.C. 224, at the age of twenty-five, called thither by Hasdrubal, and in the next three years received his maturer military training in the field, as commandant of Hasdrubal's cavalry'.[6]

In 221 BC, Hannibal broke the treaty with Rome by crossing the Ebro river, and from Spain started the series of campaigns that made him one of the most capable and admired military commanders in history. During the winter, in preparation for the coming campaigns Hannibal took quarters at Cartagena, transferred the command in Spain to his brother-in-law Hasdrubal, and took measures to guarantee his rearguard. The movements of horses all over the theatre of war is recorded by Classical writers, specially by Polybius:

> Hannibal, who was wintering in New Carthage, in the first place dismissed the Iberians to their own cities hoping thus to make them readily disposed to help in the future; next he instructed his brother Hasdrubal how to manage the government of Spain and prepare to resist the Romans if he himself happened to be absent; in the third place he took precautions for the security of Africa, adopting the very sensible and wise policy of sending soldiers from Africa to Spain, and *vice versa,* binding by this measure the two provinces to reciprocal loyalty. The troops who crossed to Africa … numbered twelve hundred horse and thirteen thousand eight hundred and fifty foot … He also gave him [Hasdrubal] as cavalry Liby-Phoenicians and Libyans to the number of four hundred and fifty, three hundred Ilergetes and eighteen hundred Numidians … and Maurusi, who dwell by the ocean …[7]

After taking these precautions, Hannibal initiated his march to Italy. According to Polybius: 'Having thus assured the security of Africa and Spain, he advanced on the day he had fixed with an army of about ninety thousand foot and twelve thousand horse.'[8] This army was soon reduced:

> He assigned to Hanno out of his own army ten thousand foot and one thousand horse, and he left with him all the heavy baggage of the expeditionary force … With the rest of his force … consisting now of fifty thousand foot and

about nine thousand horse, he advanced through the Pyrenees towards crossing the Rhone, having now an army not so strong in number as serviceable and highly trained owing to the unbroken series of wars in Spain.[9]

Hannibal's long march from Cartagena to the Po valley in Italy took five months, the crossing of the Alps alone consuming fifteen days. Only about fifty per cent of his original troops arrived in Italy, twenty thousand foot – of which twelve thousand were Carthaginians and eight thousand Iberians – and not more than six thousand horse. It is interesting to point out that Hannibal considered his cavalry his most important weapon and had very special care to preserve it in good condition, as related by Polybius:

> Hannibal now shifting his camp from time to time continued to remain in the country near the Adriatic, and by bathing his horses with old wine, of which there was abundance, he thoroughly set right their mangy condition. ...

> ... after some days he was compelled to tell off a portion to pasture the animals, and send others to forage for corn, as he was anxious, according to his original plan, to avoid loss in the live stock he had captured and to collect as much corn as possible, so that for the whole winter there should be plenty of everything both for his men and also for the horses and pack-animals; for it was on *his cavalry above all that he placed reliance* [my emphasis].[10]

The selected texts reproduced above give an idea of the considerable circulation of horses that existed in Africa and Europe during the Punic Wars. It also shows, as mentioned before, that it basically consisted of not very numerous cavalry groups. The main flow, at that time, was outbound from Spain, taking Iberian and Berber horses to foreign destinations. On the other hand, the most important influx consisted of Berber horses from North Africa. This vast topic and its consequences will be fully addressed in the second volume.

THE PERIOD OF ROMAN DOMINATION (206 BC–AD 409)

The Romans were not good cavalrymen. Their efficient and unequalled weapon was the famous legion, an infantry army supported by small cavalry groups. Theodore A. Dodge writes on this subject:

> The cavalry was by no means as good. This arm had never been a favorite with the Romans. It was considered as a mere auxiliary to the foot ... Even at the be-

ginning of the Punic wars the horsemen had no armor, only leather shields which the rain weakened, poor swords, and lances far from stout enough. [11]

In 210 BC, Rome sent the young Cornelius Scipio, the future 'Africanus', to attack the Carthaginians in Spain. From then on, until the barbarian invasions, Spain was dominated by the Romans and, during that period, horses were taken from Iberia to Italy and many other imperial provinces, and vice versa.

> Scipio Africanus was the first to introduce good cavalry tactics, which he did in Spain. Polybius gives us interesting details of these. The individual was well drilled, alone and in squads, and the turma was practiced in wheeling to the right, left and rear; in forming column to the right or left or forward from the centre; in forming lines with intervals or without; in deploying into column or more or less files, and in marching to the front or by the rear rank, with many other exercises. All these exercises were practiced at every speed. [12]

Scipio's experience, however, was not widely accepted or adopted by the Romans, who continued to use the legion as their main weapon. It is interesting to see that the two great Roman commanders who knew how to employ cavalry efficiently, Scipio and Caesar, had both lived in Spain where they probably acquired their expertise and experience of cavalry in battle.

The Romans conducted many hard-fought campaigns against the local Iberian peoples to maintain their constantly contested domination of the country. Amongst these ferocious enemies, one of the toughest was the Lusitanians. Appian writes about this confrontation (155 BC):

> At this time another of the autonomous nations of Spain, the Lusitanians, under Punicus as leader, were ravaging the fields of the Roman subjects and having put to flight their praetors, Manilius and Calpurnius Piso, killed 6000 Romans, and among them Terentius Varro, the quaestor. [13]

In 148 BC Viriathus, now the established leader of the Lusitanians, won the first great victory against the Romans, using his cavalry as the main weapon. In 150 BC, the Roman Galba massacred the Lusitanians, breaking the pledges he had made, thus avenging 'treachery with treachery, imitating barbarians in a way unworthy of a Roman. A few escaped, among them Viriathus, who not long afterward became the leader of the Lusitanians and killed many Romans and performed great exploits.' [14]

The quality of the Lusitanian horses is once again mentioned by Appian in the battle of Itucca (142 BC): 'But Viriathus continued to make frequent incursions by night or in the heat of the day, appearing at every unexpected time with his light-armed troops and his *swift horses* [my emphasis] to annoy the enemy, until he forced Servilianus back to Itucca.'[15]

The number of horses that left Iberia during this half millennium of Roman domination was considerable, as the region was one of the most important sources of good horses for the Roman and allied armies. The quantity of horses that entered Iberia during that same period was certainly considerably smaller, and at the turn of the millennium consisted mostly of Berbers, decreasing thereafter. These facts can be demonstrated by numerous historical references which will be presented in the second volume of this work.

In 61 BC Caesar arrived in Spain. During the Civil Wars, there were many battles between Caesar's and Pompeius' factions in Iberia. Caesar gives interesting information relating to our theme, for example:

> Afranius and Petreius and Varro, legates of Pompeius, of whom one held hither Spain with three legions, another further Spain … with two legions, the third the district of the Vettones from the Anas and also Lusitania with an equal number of legions, divide their tasks in such a way that Petreius should march from Lusitania through the Vettones with all his forces to join Afranius, while Varro should protect the whole of further Spain … When these arrangements were made Petreius requisitions cavalry and auxiliary troops from the whole of Lusitania, Afranius from Celtiberia, the Cantabri, and all the barbarous tribes that extend to the ocean. …
>
> There were … some heavy-armed [legions] from the hither province, others light-armed from further Spain, and about five thousand cavalry from each province. Caesar has sent forward six legions into Spain, five thousand auxiliary infantry and three thousand cavalry which he had with him during all his former wars, and an equal number from Gaul, which he had himself pacified …[16]

It will be remembered that Caesar also took animals from Spain and Italy to Gaul, as mentioned before and repeated here for convenience:

> Here [the Loire] Caesar had concentrated all the hostages of Gaul, the corn, the state chest, and great part of his own and the army's baggage; hither he had sent a great number of horses purchased for this war in Italy and Spain.[17]

The texts transcribed above prove the continuation of the age-old circulation of horses in the area here discussed, involving the 'quality horses' of Iberia, North Africa and the Pontic-Caspian.

BARBARIAN INVASIONS (AD 409–711)

The next important movement was the series of barbarian invasions that finally led to the fall of the Roman Empire in the West. This vast and complex subject cannot be fully discussed in the short space of this chapter, but a brief exploration of this period is indispensable to complete our story.

During the third and fourth centuries AD, the Goths arrived at the Black Sea, where they formed two separated nations, the Ostrogoths (Eastern Goths) and the Visigoths (Western Goths). At that time, some events that were to have terrible consequences for the future of the Roman Empire were brewing: on the one hand, the progressive and intense Germanization of the Roman Army, with German commanders assuming important positions and increasing the numbers of ethnic German troops, and on the other hand, the division of the Roman Empire into two independent halves, the Roman Empire of the West in Rome and the Roman Empire of the East in Constantinople. In the west, the army structure was modified with the two posts of command – the Master of Infantry (Magister Peditum) and the Master of Cavalry (Magister Equitum) – being unified into a single command, the Magister Equitum and Peditum, a new uncomfortable rival for the Emperor. Even worse were the consequences of the policy of withdrawing legions from the frontiers. They were replaced with centralized mobile light legions that could be called on when necessary to defend the limits of the Empire, now protected by local populations inside fortified cities who could only resist because the barbarians did not have siege equipment. The most disastrous modification brought about by these reforms was the change in the relation of horse to foot soldiers. Until then, the legions were formed by disciplined, trained Roman citizens, with a high sense of morality and patriotism, who had been practically invincible. Each legion was completed by a cavalry corps of 300 horsemen, divided into ten squadrons, which marched at the flanks of the legion, each one commanded by a decurion. This impressive and powerful body was only defeated by bad command or accidents, but even at such moments of disgrace inflicted heavy losses on the enemy. All these qualities were lost with the absence of Roman citizens and the increase of mercenary cavalry in the new mobile legions.

The Huns were the first Asian steppe people to appear in Europe, after their empire was destroyed by the Chinese forcing their withdrawal from

Mongolia to Turkestan. The Huns initially defeated the Ostrogoths and soon afterwards the Visigoths; the latter, completely demoralized and fearful, asked the Romans' permission to cross the Danube and establish themselves in a new home in Thracia. After a short deliberation the Romans authorized the first known migration in history of a whole nation – some 200,000 people according to some authors, 80,000 according to others – a decision that had enormous and ominous consequences for the future of Europe. The impossibility of finding enough food and arable land to settle this multitude of people caused the only foreseeable result: war and the catastrophic battle of Hadrianopolis (Adrianopolis), one of the most disastrous defeats in Roman history, where the Emperor Valens lost his life and his army. According to some authors, Hadrianople was a great cavalry battle which marked an irreversible change in the military use of the horse, with the end of light cavalry in favour of the heavy, armoured cavalry already largely employed in the Orient. According to J. B. Bury:

> Hitherto in warfare the Romans had always depended on their infantry. It was their main arm, and in regular battles the cavalry was always considered subsidiary and auxiliary to the legions. Other things being equal, the well-trained legions were almost invincible. In this battle the legions had the novel experience of being ridden down by the heavy cavalry of the German warriors. This was a lesson which showed what cavalry could do; and it had an influence on all subsequent warfare. Between the fourth and the sixth century there was a revolution in the character of the Roman armies and Roman warfare. In the fourth century infantry was the arm on which the Romans still mainly relied, and with which they won their victories in the open field; whereas in the sixth century infantry played a small part in their battles, and victories were won by cavalry.[18]

So from this point onwards cavalry assumed the prime position in warfare and horses became the most important asset, carrying the barbarians on their invasions, the dominant historic theme of the next 500 years. In the words of R. C. Blockley: 'After the death of Julian the western part of the empire faced attacks in many regions. Ammianus (XXVI.4.5) lists the invaders: Alamanni and Saxons in Gaul, Sarmatians and Quadi in Pannonia, Picts, Scots, Saxons and Attacotti in Britain, Moors in Africa.'[19]

In AD 401 the Visigoths, now under Alaric, made a strong comeback with several incursions into Greece and Italy, leading to the sack and burning down of Rome in AD 410. In the meantime other hordes of barbarians crossed the Rhine in 406. Among them were the Vandals and Suebi and the non-Germanic Alans.

In 409 Iberia was simultaneously occupied by the Vandals, Suebi, Alans and Visigoths, all of them fighting each other for geographical space. The Vandals had Baetica, the Alans had Lusitania, the Suebi and another Vandal faction occupied Galicia and the northern Douro. Only the Roman provinces of Terraconensis and Carthaginensis did not fall under barbarian domination, although constantly attacked. These barbarians were all sedentary horse-peoples who came to Iberia looking for a place to live permanently, bringing with them their families and all their possessions, including horses, cattle and carts. According to Norman Davies:

> Their raiding parties could easily cover a couple of thousand miles a month. Mounted on swift Mongolian ponies and armed with bows and arrows, they could ride deep into Europe or the Far East and return in the course of a single summer. Like all the true nomads, they generated a huge motive force on the agricultural or semi-nomadic peoples with whom they came into contact. In the second century AD their base shifted to the north of the Caspian Sea; in the fourth century it was shifting towards what is now Ukraine. There, in 375, they encountered the Ostrogoths, a Germanic people who, exceptionally, had been moving in the opposite direction. The resultant clash pushed the Ostrogoths, and the neighbouring Visigoths, into the Roman Empire. Within fifty years another of the associated tribes, the Alans, appeared in what is now southern Portugal – almost 3,000 miles away. The Huns did not attack the Empire themselves until 441. The rate of migration, of course, was extremely slow. The Alans, who crossed the Dnieper c. 375 and the Rhine in 406, and reached the Atlantic in the 420s, averaged perhaps 5 miles per year. The 'sudden irruption' of the Vandals, who shared part of the Alans' journey, maintained a mean speed of 2 km per week. Tribal columns weighed down with carts, livestock, and supplies could not hope to compete with the nomads.[20]

The descriptions above reveal that two different classes of invading barbarian horsemen can be distinguished: the nomadic tribes and the more sedentary agricultural peoples. The latter moved with their families and possessions, livestock and carts to occupy new homelands inside the borders of the Roman Empire. They came with horses and mares, most certainly in larger numbers than was the case during the Punic Wars, which were conflicts between opposing armies and not the migration of a whole tribe or people.

The numbers of barbarians in each invasion is mere historical guess-work; however, it is valid to transcribe opinions like that of Bernard F. Reilly:

> Combining the best estimates of the numbers of all of the German tribes who invaded the peninsula during the fifth and sixth centuries would not yield a total of more than 500,000 persons as against an indigenous population of perhaps 5,000,000, depending upon the time of their entry.[21]

It would not be very off the mark to assume that this proportion also applies to the horse population. A good visualization of the barbarian's wanderings with their horses and the influences that these animals may have exerted upon local breeds can be deduced from Fig. 10.2. A more detailed analysis of these movements and the possible number of horses involved will be presented in the second volume.

After more than twenty years of wandering, the Visigoths were finally granted a permanent home in Gaul by Honorius, for the time being

10.2 The barbarian invasions of the fifth century AD.

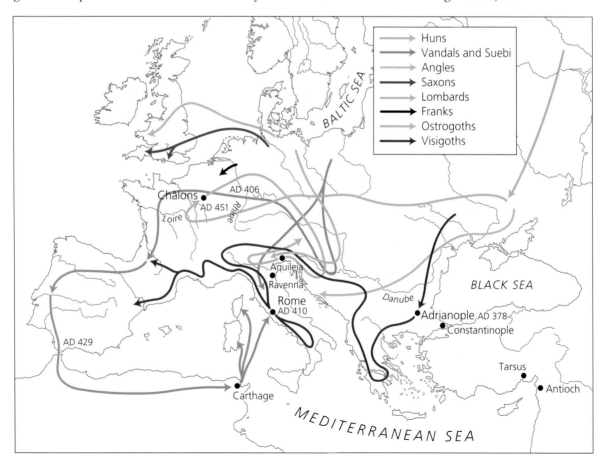

leaving the Iberian Peninsula which became a field of war between the Vandals and the Sueves. The Visigoths certainly moved out of Iberia riding Iberian horses, thus reinforcing the circulation of horses into Gaul. By the end of AD 423, Boniface, the Roman commanding officer in Africa, rebelled and invited the Vandals to come to his aid against Rome. In 429, 80,000 Vandals and Alans (15,000 according to some) crossed the Strait of Gibraltar and entered Africa with a large cavalry, always their main offensive weapon. J. B. Bury gives an interesting description of this invasion: 'The whole nation of the Vandals and Alans embarked in May A.D. 429, and crossed over to Africa. If the united peoples numbered, as is said, 80,000, the fighting force might have been about 15,000.'[22] These figures, if correct, greatly exceed the number of horses that came to Iberia with the Arab invasion in 711 BC.

While these events were unfolding in Africa, Rome had to face a new threat: the Huns, who so far had been fighting against the Roman Empire of the Orient, now under Attila turned their eyes and cupidity towards the west. In AD 451 Attila invaded the empire, being defeated near Challons by Aetius, who commanded a coalition of Romans, Franks and Ostrogoths. The respected author, Charles Oman, descibes the battle:

> The decisive battle was pre-eminently a cavalry engagement. On each side horse-archer and lancer faced horse-archer and lancer – Aetius and his Romans leagued with Theodoric's Visigothic cavalry – Attila's hordes of Hunnish light horse backed by the steadier troops of his German subjects … The victory was won not by superior tactics, but by sheer hard fighting, the decisive point having been the riding down of the native Huns by Theodoric's heavier Visigothic horsemen. It was certainly not the troops of the empire who had the main credit of the day.[23]

The consolidation of Germanic domination, not only in Spain but also in the rest of Europe, brought identical consequences everywhere: the progressive dissolution of central power, now substituted by local aristocracies. This was certainly the period of the greatest importation of horses into Iberia. The invading barbarians, all of them horse peoples, came from the east, following the routes shown in Fig. 10.2. These indicate the trajectory of the barbarians since Adrianople, mounted on Pontic-Caspian horses, all through Italy and France, arriving in Iberia around AD 406. The map also shows the exodus of horses from Iberia, with the Vandals' invasion of Africa. The Afro-Eurasian 'circulation' of horses thus continued unabated.

THE ARAB INVASION (AD 711)

The Arabs, already mentioned as being among the barbarian invaders of the Roman Empire, were not active or threatening in Iberia until the seventh century AD.

Exploratory raids

The first point to discuss is that the Muslims knew the southern Iberian territory they wished to invade reasonably well. Invasion was preceded by exploratory raids, the last one commanded by Tarik, the great Muslim leader. This event is mentioned briefly by some authors, for example:

> The first Muslim incursion took place in July 710 (Ramadan 91). Only four hundred men participated, of which one hundred were cavalry, under the orders of the Berber officer Tarif ibn Malluk. They used four ships furnished by [the Visigoth traitor] Count Julian and landed on the small island, very near the port, that became known as Tarifa (in Arabic, Djazirat Tarif) after their chief, Tarif. From there, the Muslim troops executed a series of profitable incursions on the shores of the Strait of Gibraltar.[24]

During these expeditions, it would have been possible for the Muslims to make a survey of Iberian territory near the Mediterranean shore and investigate the availability of horses and other important war supplies. Such an investigation – especially in Andalusia, the final destination of Tarik – would have revealed a vast population of horses of excellent quality. This fact, combined with the promised support of local Visigoth traitors with their cavalry, would make the transport of cavalry from North Africa unnecessary if not redundant.

The total collapse of Visigothic Spain and its conquest by the Moors, with practically no resistance, leaves us without the military chronicles that normally cover other great war campaigns. It also explains, together with the facts presented above, the absence of large Moorish cavalry corps, a weapon that would have been built up just after landing and during the campaign if necessary. In this case, the abrupt end of hostilities with the total capitulation of the Visigoths made these logistical decisions unnecessary; the Arabs obtained not only mounts for themselves but also Visigothic cavalry troops, who joined them from the very beginning of the conquest.

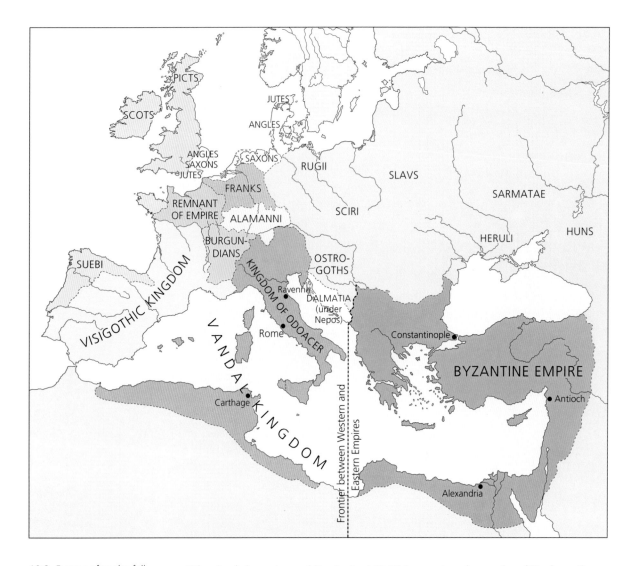

10.3 Europe after the fall of Rome (AD 476): the Byzantine Empire and the barbarian kingdoms of Europe.

The Arab invasion of Spain in AD 711 consisted mostly of Berbers from North Africa:

Although no quantitative data survives that would make it possible to know what percentage of the troops involved in the conquest of Spain in the period 711–720 was of Berber origin, it is notable that the crucial expedition of 711 was led by Tãrik ibn Ziyad, a Berber freedman and client of Mûsâ ibn Nusayr, the governor of Ifriqiya.[25]

Some numbers have been advanced by other authors, amongst whom E. Lévy-Provençal suggests: 'At the same time it seemed worth to him to demand reinforcements from Africa: he received some five thousand additional Berbers. This brought the total number of his army to twelve thousand warriors, almost all infantry ...'[26]

The success of Tarik's invasion made Musa very jealous, and he decided to go to Spain with another army to make his own conquests in an effort to keep down his subordinate. Musa raised an army of some eighteen thousand, this time mostly Arabs, and landed in Algeciras in June 712.

During the first five centuries of effective occupation by the Moors we have no evidence of Arabian horses being introduced to Iberia. On the contrary, all the scattered information indicates the continuation of the age-old traffic of horses between North Africa and Iberia. It is obvious that the Berbers and Arabs were acquainted with past history and knew the quality and quantity of horses they would find in Iberia, as well as having knowledge of the Iberian horse itself. Consequently they also knew that they did not have to look to Africa for supplies of horses for Spain. Horses are not an easy cargo to transport over water, even for short distances such as the Strait of Gibraltar, and the availability of boats for the invasion of Spain was very restricted, limited to ships supplied by the aforementioned Count Julian of Ceuta.

We are thus talking about a total invading army of approximately thirty thousand men, mostly infantry. Any cavalry that came with Tarik was certainly Berber. Musa's army was formed in North Africa, again mostly infantry, and his horses were probably also Berbers.

Internal divisions

The second point to consider is the internal divisions that existed among the Muslims, particularly the rivalry between the caliphate of Baghdad and the Moors of North Africa. This subject is described by Joseph F. O' Callaghan:

> The Umayyad dynasty which had ruled the Muslim world since 661 was overthrown in 750 by the Abbasids, who attempted to slaughter all their rivals. One Umayyad, Abd al-Rahman, a grandson of the Caliph Hisham, survived the destruction to restore the fortunes of his family in Spain.[27]

In January 929 Abd al-Rahman III assumed the title of Caliph:

> Until then the Umayyads of Córdoba, while maintaining their political independence in Spain, had recognized at least in theory the supremacy of the

Abbasid caliphs of Baghdad as the rightful successors of Muhammad and rulers of the Muslim community. Abd al-Rahman III elected to end this fiction, by reasserting the ancient rights of his family.[28]

In 909 the Fatimid caliphate was established in North Africa.

The rivalry of the Fatimids, Abbasids, and Umayyads probably induced Abd al-Rahman III to initiate diplomatic exchanges with the Byzantine Emperor Constantine VII Porphyrogenitus, the natural enemy of both eastern caliphates. [29]

These feuds caused the collapse of the Muslim dominions in Spain; by 1250 all of Spain, with the exception of Granada, had been repossessed by the Spaniards. They also kept Baghdad, North Africa and Spain politically and militarily separated. Under these circumstances, the movements of troops and horses between Asia Minor and the western parts of the Muslim world was never substantial; this is one of the explanations for the absence of Arabian horses in Iberia at that time.

Cavalry tactics

The third and final aspect to take into consideration is the battle tactics, mostly raids, which did not require large cavalry groups. The reasons for the military success of the 'Reconquista' are many, but certainly the most important is the cavalry tactics employed by the Christians against the Arabs. It is interesting to reproduce the conclusions of Bernard F. Reilly on this subject:

Moreover, the development of western military techniques in the direction of the superiority of a mounted, heavy cavalry reinforced the economic and social power of the new nobility in particular. ...

The sudden and catastrophic collapse of an independent Muslim Iberia between 1090 and 1100 was due to a multitude of factors, some quite old and others quite new. Among the latter was the rise of a new northern society which was able to support a strong force of heavy, mailed, shock cavalry out of very limited resources. Operating in raiding parties of between 50 and 300, with absolutely essential supplies travelling by muleback, they were very mobile, covering distances of thirty to forty kilometres per day. ...

Since the Muslim world continued to rely on essentially light cavalry, mounted archers in many cases, backed by infantry masses they had to depend on surprise, ambush, and on the invader hampering his own withdrawal by his un-willingness to abandon flocks and human chattels once seized. Those were difficult terms on which to fight an invader. Of course, when outright conquest became the object, then the northerner must stand and fight on defined ground. As Zalaca and Uclés attest, the superior number of the Muslims could then be brought to bear and victory often achieved. But even there, the heavy cavalry of the Christian world, when properly employed, remained without an adequate military answer from Islam in the west and the battle would often go to the smaller force as at Cuart de Poblet.[30]

The same points are mentioned in *The New Cambridge Medieval History:*

> The Muslims regularly took the offensive against the Christians in raids known as sawa'if (sing. sa'ifah). They were directed at all points of the Christian-held lands … These raids do not seem to have been an attempt to conquer Christian territory.[31]

The descriptions above bring to mind a curious paradox: the Iberians, for millennia, were the masters of *gineta* cavalry tactics, as we saw in much detail; suddenly, during the *Reconquista,* the northern Spaniards, influenced by the French with whom they had very close relations, adopted the heavy cavalry tactics then being used north of the Pyrenees, especially by the armies of the Crusades. This also raises the question of the differences between Spanish and Lusitanian horses, which may have started to develop at that time, as the cavalries from Andalusia (Muslim) and from Lusitania (Portuguese) continued to employ light cavalry and *gineta* tactics during the whole period under discussion (711– 1500). This very complex subject will be discussed in the second volume.

   In other words, the absence of large battles meant there was no need for reinforcements from the Arab world, of either men or horses. It is safe to assume that the co-existence of Moors and Christians, rich in clashes and fights, could always be maintained from local resources. It is also very important to remember that the minor influence of the Middle Eastern Arabs in Iberia was certainly caused not only by the political problems related above but also by their wars against Byzantium and by the Crusades. The latter, lasting from AD 1095 until the middle of the fifteenth century, and the former ending with the fall of Constantinople in 1453, were enormous drains on the resources of the Caliphate, especially of men and horses that had to be reserved for their Asian army facing fierce enemies in that continent. It is not difficult to see that, under those circumstances, it was practically impossible to send any reinforcements to the distant and secondary war theatre of the Iberian Peninsula. This is certainly one of the reasons why Arabian horses never entered Spain during the Moorish domination.

The picture outlined above makes the hypothesis of a non-existent or minimum importation of Arabian horses into the Iberian Peninsula extremely probable and credible. Any influence existing from AD 711 to 1500 would have been entirely concentrated on crosses between Iberian and Berber horses, and even that on a small scale. We will discuss this in detail in the second volume.

The two centuries from 1250 to the fall of Granada in 1492 saw the Arabs practically confined to Granada, and clashes with Christians were fought around that city, without any significant large battles. In the last centuries of Moorish presence in Iberia there was even less reason to bring horses from outside; they were simply not necessary.

LOOKING AHEAD

The only other large movement of horses since the events described above was the disastrous invasion of Africa by the king Don Sebastião in 1578. His army was routed and the king killed in the battle of Alcácer Quibir; the horses that survived, supposedly in great numbers, were captured by the Moors.

The breeds in Spain and Portugal suffered large losses in the wars fought between the two countries over the next two centuries. The first official acts with the objective of starting a rational selection of horses and control of horse breeding happened in Spain with the foundation of the Cordoba Royal Stud by Phillip II in 1571, and in Portugal by the foundation of the Alter Real Stud by the king Don João V in 1748.

CONCLUSION

This last chapter has rounded up the history of the Iberian horse, anticipating some of the main themes to be discussed in the second volume of this work. It is obvious that such an extensive period of time as the one to

10.4 The museum building at the Alter Real Stud, Portugal.

be dealt with in that volume cannot be exhaustively presented in the abridged form given above; the reader is asked to understand that this chapter is only a superficial outline of the complete work to follow, and so to excuse the many lapses and omissions that inevitably occur in such a condensed text.

It is important nevertheless to mention that the historical period to be discussed will be rich in evidence demonstrating the original thesis of the present work, namely that the intense 'circulation' of horses that existed in the prehistoric period continued unabated during antiquity and medieval times, and was responsible for the spread of equitation and equine types all over Eurasia. In particular, the Punic Wars, Roman domination, the barbarian invasions and lastly the Arabian Conquest were the four main historical events that kept an active circulation of horses during the period 200 BC to AD 1500, especially with regard to the horses of the Iberian peninsula.

NOTES

Chapter 1 Introduction

1. Hermann Ebhardt, a horse-breeder from Hamburg, devised his theory in the early twentieth century and his classifications are quoted widely. See for example Colin P. Groves, *Horses, Asses and Zebras in the Wild* (Newton Abbot, 1974), Hardy Oelke, *Born Survivors on the Eve of Extinction*.
2. H. P. Uerpmann, *Die Domestikation des Pferdes im Chalkolithikum West und Mittleuropas* (Madrider Mitteilungen, 1990).
3. J. P. Mallory, *In Search of the Indo-Europeans* (London, 1996). See also Chapter 5 below.
4. Ruy d'Andrade, *Alrededor del Caballo Espa–ol* (Lisbon, 1954), ch. 15.

Chapter 2 Horses – Ancestral, Wild and Domesticated: An Overview

1. Colin P. Groves, *Horses, Asses and Zebras in the Wild* (Newton Abbot, 1974), p. 169.
2. Hermann Ebhardt, 'Ponies und Pferde im Röntgenbild nebst einigen stammesgeschichtlichen Bemerkungen dazu', *Säugetierkundliche Mitteilungen,* 10 JHg, BLV, Munich.
3. Groves, *Horses, Asses and Zebras*, p. 169.
4. Equine Research Publications, *Equine Genetics and Selection Procedures* (Texas, 1978), p. 17.
5. Groves, *Horses, Asses and Zebras*, p. 170.
6. Sándor Bökönyi, *The Przevalsky Horse* (London, 1974), pp. 37–8.
7. Groves, *Horses, Asses and Zebras*, pp. 55–6.
8. Herodotus, *The Histories*, IV, 52, transl. Robin Waterfield (New York, 1998), p. 252.
9. Bökönyi, *Przevalsky Horse*, pp. 70–2.
10. Miklos Jankovich, *The Rode into Europe* (London, 1971), p. 36.
11. Bökönyi, *Przevalsky Horse*, p. 69.
12. In Ruy d'Andrade, *Alrededor del Caballo Espa–ol* (Lisbon, 1954).
13. *Ibid.*
14. *Ibid.*, pp. 644–5.
15. Strabo, *The Geography*, 3.4.15, transl. H. L. Jones (Loeb Classical Library, London/Cambridge MA, 1925), Vol. II, p. 107.
16. In Arsenio Raposo Cordeiro, *Cavalo Lusitano: O Filho do Vento* (Lisbon, 1989), p. 72.
17. D'Andrade, *Alrededor del Caballo Espa–ol*, pp. 645–9.
18. In Cordeiro, *Cavalo Lusitano*, p. 74.
19. D'Andrade, *Alrededor del Caballo Espa–ol*, p. 648.

20. Cordeiro, *Cavalo Lusitano*, p. 65.
21. *Ibid*.
22. Jankovich, *They Rode into Europe*, p. 36.
23. Richard Walsh (ed.), *The Adventures of Marco Polo* (New York, 1948), p. 28.
24. Jankovich, *They Rode into Europe*, p. 33.
25. John Clabby, *The Natural History of the Horse* (London, 1976), p. 53.
26. Jacques Gernet, *A History of Chinese Civilization*, transl. J. R. Foster and Charles Hartman (2nd edn, Cambridge, 1996), p. 51.
27. Stuart Piggott, *Wagon, Chariot and Carriage* (London/New York, 1992), p. 67.
28. *Ibid*., p. 66.
29. Sven Hedin, *The Silk Road* (London, 1938).
30. George Rawlinson, *The Five Great Monarchies*, 4 vols. (London, 1862–5), Vol. III, pp.14–15.
31. Jankovich, *They Rode into Europe*, p. 44, quoting Oppian, *Cynergetica* I, 280–329.
32. Herodotus, *Histories*, III, 106; p. 213.
33. *Ibid*., VII, 40; p. 422.
34. *Ibid*., VII, 196; pp. 473–4.
35. Arrian, *History of Alexander*, VII, 13, transl. P. A. Brunt (Loeb Classical Library, 1983), Vol. II.
36. Diodorus Siculus, *Library of History*, XVII, 110, 6, transl. C. Bradford Welles (Loeb Classical Library, London/Cambridge MA, 1989).
37. Strabo, *Geography*, 11.13.7, Vol. V (London, 1928), p. 311.
38. *Ibid*., 11.14.9.
39. Bökönyi, *Przevalsky Horse*, p. 88.
40. Herodotus, *Histories*, IV, 156–9; pp. 288–9.
41. *Ibid*., IV, 170; p. 293.
42. Jankovich, *They Rode into Europe*, p. 48.
43. G. Grote, *A History of Greece*, 10 vols. (London, 1872), Vol. 3, p. 263.
44. Herodotus, *Histories*, IV, 152; p. 286.
45. Sándor Bökönyi, 'Data on Iron Age horses of central and eastern Europe', Mecklenberg Collection, part I, *Bulletin of the American School of Prehistoric Research* 25 (1968), p. 6 .
46. Herodotus, *Histories*, IV, 6; IV, 9–12; pp. 237–9.
47. Bökönyi, 'Data on Iron Age horses' p. 43.
48. *Ibid*., p. 52.
49. *Ibid*., p. 46.
50. Stuart Piggott, *Ancient Europe* (Edinburgh/Chicago, 1963), p. 98; see also Chapter 8 below.

CHAPTER 3 The Palaeolithic

1. Paul Mellars, 'The Upper Palaeolithic revolution', in *The Oxford Illustrated History of Prehistoric Europe*, ed. Barry Cunliffe (Oxford, 1994, pp. 42–78), p. 53.
2. *Ibid*., p. 54.
3. Richard Rudgley, *The Lost Civilizations of the Stone Age* (New York, 1999), p. 158.
4. André Leroi-Gourhan, *Préhistoire de l'Art Occidental* (Paris, 1995).
5. Mila Simões de Abreu, 'O universo da arte rupestre: arte paleol'tica', pp. 31–46 in *História da Arte Portuguesa*, 3 vols., ed. Paulo Pereira, Vol. I (Lisbon, 1995).
6. Leroi-Gourhan, *Préhistoire de l'Art Occidental*, p. 582.
7. *Ibid*., p. 599.
8. Peter J. Ucko and Andrée Rosenfeld, *Palaeolithic Cave Art* (London, 1967).
9. *Ibid*., pp. 83–6.
10. Colin P. Groves, *Horses, Asses and Zebras in the Wild* (Newton Abbot, 1974), pp. 180–1.
11. Leroi-Gourhan, *Préhistoire de l'Art Occidental*, p. 174.
12. N. K. Sandars, *Prehistoric Art in Europe* (Harmondsworth, 1985), p. 116.
13. Miklos Jankovich, *They Rode into Europe* (London, 1971), p. 35.

Chapter 4 The Mesolithic

1. Paul Mellars, 'The Upper Palaeolithic revolution', pp. 42–78 in *The Oxford Illustrated History of Prehistoric Europe*, ed. Barry Cunliffe (Oxford, 1994), p. 76.
2. National Archaeological and Ethnological Museum of Lisbon, *Portugal das Origens à Época Romana*, ed. Francisco Alves (Lisbon, 1989), p. 27.
3. Steven J. Mithen, 'The Mesolithic Age', pp. 79–135 in Cunliffe (ed.), *The Oxford Illustrated History of Prehistoric Europe*, p. 106.
4. *Ibid.*, p. 105.
5. André Leroi-Gourhan, 'Histoire Universelle', *Encyclopédie de la Pléiade* (Paris, 1956).
6. G. Camps, *La Préhistoire: A la Recherche du Paradis Perdu* (Paris, 1982), p. 214.
7. N. K. Sandars, *Prehistoric Art in Europe* (Harmondsworth, 1985), p. 150.
8. *Ibid.*, p. 154.
9. Camps, *La Préhistoire*, p. 214.
10. Sandars, *Prehistoric Art*, p. 142.
11. Chris Scarre, *Exploring Prehistoric Europe* (Oxford/New York, 1998), p. 53.
12. Mithen, 'The Mesolithic Age', p. 86.
13. Jean-Georges Rozoy, 'The Mesolithic way of life', in *L'Europe des Derniers Chasseurs*, ed. André Thévenin (Paris, 1999).
14. Camps, *La Préhistoire*, pp. 234–5.
15. *Ibid.*, p. 239.
16. Colin Renfrew, *Archaeology and Language: The Puzzle of Indo-European Origins* (Cambridge, 1987), p. 151.
17. Ruy d'Andrade, *Alrededor del Caballo Espa–ol* (Lisbon, 1954), p. 673.
18. *Ibid.*

Chapter 5 The Neolithic

1. Colin Renfrew, *Archaeology and Language: The Puzzle of Indo-European Origins* (Cambridge, 1987), p. 156.
2. Andrew Sherratt, *Economy and Society in Prehistoric Europe* (Edinburgh, 1997), p. 335.
3. J. P. Mallory, *In Search of the Indo-Europeans* (London, 1996), p. 217.
4. *Ibid.*, p. 119.
5. *Ibid.*, pp. 162–3.
6. *Ibid.*, p. 162.
7. Bernard Sergent, *Les Indo-Européens: Histoire, Langues, Mythes* (Paris, 1995), p. 294.
8. Edgar Polomé, 'The impact of Marija Gimbutas on Indo-European Studies', pp. 102–7 in *From the Realm of the Ancestors: an Anthology in Honor of Marija Gimbutas*, ed. Joan Marler (Manchester CT, 1997), p. 102.
9. Renfrew, *Archaeology and Language*, p. 265.
10. *Ibid.*, p. 205.
11. L. Luca Cavalli-Sforza, 'Genetic evidence supporting Marija Gimbutas' work on the origin of Indo-European People', in *From the Realm of the Ancestors*, ed. Joan Marler (Manchester CT, 1997).
12. Polomé, 'The impact of Marija Gimbutas'.
13. Sergent, *Les Indo-Européens*, pp. 396–7.
14. Dumézil's three functions are, in hierarchical order, the priests, the warriors and the farmers/herders.
15. Mallory, *In Search of the Indo-Europeans*, p. 135.

Chapter 6 The Bronze and Iron Ages

1. Andrew Sherratt, 'The emergence of élites: earlier Bronze Age Europe 2500–1300 BC', pp. 244–76 in *The Oxford Illustrated History of Prehistoric Europe*, ed. Barry Cunliffe (Oxford, 1994), p. 256.

2. Stuart Piggott, *Ancient Europe* (Edinburgh/Chicago, 1965), p. 98.
3. H. P. Uerpmann, *Die Domestikation des Pferdes im Chalkolithikum West und Mittleeuropas* (Madrider Mitteilungen, 1990).
4. Sherratt, *Economy and Society in Prehistoric Europe: Changing Perspectives* (Edinburgh/Princeton, 1997), p. 219.
5. Stephen Shennan, 'Ideology, change and the European early bronze age', pp. 155–61 in *Symbolic and Structural Archaeology*, ed. I. Hodder (Cambridge, 1982), p. 159.
6. Colin Renfrew, *Archaeology and Language: The Puzzle of Indo-European Origins* (Cambridge, 1987), p. 90.
7. Herodotus, *The Histories*, IV. 11–12, transl. Robin Waterfield (New York, 1998), pp. 238–9.
8. Strabo, *The Geography*, 7.4.8, transl. H. L. Jones (Loeb Classical Library, London/Cambridge MA, 1924), Vol. III, p. 249.
9. Barry Cunliffe, *The Ancient Celts* (Oxford, 1997), p. 47.

CHAPTER 7 Chariots, Warfare and Domestication

1. Bernard Sergent, *Les Indo-Européens: histoire, langues, mythes* (Paris, 1995), p. 396.
2. H. P. Uerpmann, *Die Domestikation des Pferdes im Chalkolithikum West und Mittleeuropas* (Madrider Mitteilungen, 1990).
3. Edgar Polomé, 'The impact of Marija Gimbutas on Indo-European Studies', pp. 102–7 in *From the Realm of the Ancestors: an Anthology in Honor of Marija Gimbutas*, ed. Joan Marler (Manchester CT, 1997); Sergent, *Les Indo-Européens*, p. 294.
4. John Keegan, *A History of Warfare* (London, 1993), p. 177.
5. Jacques Gernet, *A History of Chinese Civilization*, transl. J. R. Foster and Charles Hartman (2nd edn, Cambridge, 1996), p. 71.
6. J. P. Mallory, *In Search of the Indo-Europeans* (London, 1996), p. 163.
7. Homer, *The Iliad*, III, 315; XVI, 506; transl. Robert Fagles (New York, 1990), pp. 137, 426.
8. William H. McNeill, *The Rise of the West* (Chicago, 1963), p. 104.
9. Keegan, *History of Warfare*, p. 159.
10. Mallory, *In Search of the Indo-Europeans*, p. 41.
11. Charles O. Hucker, *China's Imperial Past* (London, 1975), p. 28.
12. Homer, *The Iliad*, II, 927 (p. 125); III, 380 (p. 139); XVI, 156 (p. 416).
13. *Ibid.*, VIII, 498–501, 507–9 (p. 245); Homer, *The Odyssey*, IV, 45–9, transl. Robert Fagles (New York, 1996), p. 52.
14. Keegan, *History of Warfare*, p. 167.
15. Stuart Piggott, *Wagon, Chariot and Carriage: Symbol and Status in the History of Transport* (London/New York, 1992), pp. 45–6.
16. Robert Drews, *The End of the Bronze Age* (Princeton, 1993), p. 106.
17. McNeill, *The Rise of the West*, pp. 113–14.
18. Drews, *The End of the Bronze Age*, p. 145.
19. *Ibid.*, pp. 209–10.
20. Gernet, *History of Chinese Civilization*, p. 66.
21. Drews, *The End of the Bronze Age*, pp. 166–7.
22. McNeill, *The Rise of the West*, pp. 114–16.
23. Piggott, *Wagon, Chariot and Carriage*, p. 70.
24. Anthony Harding, 'Reformation in Barbarian Europe 1300–1600 BC', pp. 304–35 in *The Oxford Illustrated History of Prehistoric Europe*, ed. Barry Cunliffe (Oxford, 1994), p. 329.
25. John Clabby, *The Natural History of the Horse* (London, 1976), p. 49.
26. Mallory, *In Search of the Indo-Europeans*, pp. 40–1.
27. Homer, *The Iliad*, II, 866–70; p. 124.
28. *Ibid.*, XIII, 5–8; p. 341.
29. Keegan, *History of Warfare*, p. 177.
30. Amélie Kuhrt, *The Ancient Near East*, Vol. I (London, 1995), p. 343.

31. Florence Malbran-Labat, *L'Armée et L'Organisation Militaire de l'Assyrie* (Paris, 1982).
32. Piggott, *Wagon, Chariot and Carriage*, pp. 42–4.
33. Harding, 'Reformation in Barbarian Europe', p. 317.
34. Sergent, *Les Indo-Européens*, p. 396.
35. Keegan, *History of Warfare*, pp. 162–3.
36. Lionel Casson, *The Ancient Mariners* (Princeton, 1991), p. 103.
37. Fernand Braudel, *The Mediterranean in the Ancient World* (London, 2001), p. 215.
38. Homer, *The Iliad*, II, 464–7; p. 114, 549–52.
39. Casson, *The Ancient Mariners*, pp. 88, 91–2.

CHAPTER 8 The Iberian Peninsula

1. H. P. Uerpmann, *Die Domestikation des Pferdes im Chalkolithikum West und Mittleeuropas* (Madrider Mitteilungen, 1990).
2. William H. McNeill, *The Rise of the West* (Chicago, 1963), p. 106.
3. Ruy d'Andrade, *Alrededor del Caballo Espa–ol* (Lisbon, 1954)
4. *Ibid.*, p. 745.
5. *Ibid.*, p. 746.
6. *Ibid.*
7. *Ibid.*, p. 747.
8. *Ibid.*, p. 748.
9. *Ibid.*, p. 749.
10. *Ibid.*, p. 782.
11. *Ibid.*, p. 785.
12. *Ibid.*, p. 786.
13. *Ibid.*, p. 749.
14. *Ibid.*, pp. 745–6.
15. *Ibid.*, pp. 781–5.
16. *Ibid.*, p. 787.
17. Stuart Piggott, *Ancient Europe* (Edinburgh, 1965); Uerpmann, *Die Domestikation des Pferdes*.
18. Ruy d'Andrade, *Alrededor del Caballo Espa–ol*, pp. 202–3.
19. Homer, *The Iliad*, XVI, 130–50, transl. A. T. Murray (Loeb Classical Library, London/Cambridge MA, 1999), Vol. II, p. 173.
20. The penteconters were warships, with all space aboard being primarily reserved for the oarsmen, while the commercial boats were round-hulled sailing ships. This information from Herodotus indicates that the Phocaens were on a military or exploratory expedition to unknown or hostile countries.
21. Herodotus, *The Histories*, I, 163, transl. Robin Waterfield (Oxford/New York, 1998), p. 72.
22. Manuel Bendala Galán, 'La civilización tartésica', pp. 595–642 in *História General de Espa–a y América*, Vol. I.1 (Madrid, 1985), p. 611.
23. Herodotus, *Histories*, II, 33 (p. 108); IV, 49 (p. 251).
24. *Ibid.* IV, 152 (p. 286).
25. Arturo Ruiz Rodriguez in *The Archaeology of Iberia*, ed. Margarita Diaz-Andreu and Simon Keay (London, 1997), p. 180.
26. Adolf Schulten, *Tartessos: Ein Betrag zur ältesten Geschichte des Westens* (Hamburg, 1922), p. 46; translated from (Madrid, 1972) edition, p. 125.
27. W. Culican, 'Phoenicia and Phoenician colonization', pp. 461–546 in *The Cambridge Ancient History*, Vol. III.2 (Cambridge, 1991), pp. 533–40.
28. Diodorus Siculus, *Library of History*, XIV, 75, transl. C. H. Oldfather (Loeb Classical Library, London/Cambridge MA, 1954), Vol. VI, p. 217.
29. *Ibid.*, XV, 70, transl. C. L. Sherman (Loeb Classical Library, London/Cambridge MA,1952), Vol. VII, p. 145.
30. Xenephon, *Hellenics*, VII.1.20.

31. José Mar'a Blázquez, *Fen'cios, Griegos y Cartagineses en Occidente* (Madrid, 1992), pp. 69–70.
32. Piggott, *Ancient Europe*; Uerpmann, *Die Domestikation des Pferdes*.
33. Andrew Sherratt, *Economy and Society in Prehistoric Europe* (Princeton, 1977), p. 219.
34. Julius Ceasar, *The Gallic War*, VII, 65 and VII, 55, trans. H. J. Edwards (Loeb Classical Library, London/Cambridge MA, 1917), pp. 473, 459.

CHAPTER 9 Africa

1. UNESCO, *General History of Africa*, Vol. I, *Methodology and African Prehistory* (Abridged Edition, London/Berkely CA, 1990), p. 286.
2. Henri Lhote, *The Search for the Tassili Frescoes* (New York, 1959), p. 61.
3. G. Camps, 'Beginnings of pastoralism and cultivation in north-west Africa and the Sahara: origin of the Berbers', pp. 548-623 in *The Cambridge History of Africa*, Vol. I (Cambridge, 1982), p. 589.
4. UNESCO, *General History of Africa*, Vol. I, p. 286.
5. Lhote, *The Search for the Tassili Frescoes*.
6. Jean-Loïc Le Quellec, *Art Rupestre et Préhistoire du Sahara* (Paris, 1998), p. 119.
7. Camps, 'Beginnings of pastoralism', pp. 618–19.
8. Le Quellec, *Art Rupestre et Préhistoire*, p. 119.
9. UNESCO, *General History of Africa*, Vol. I, p. 30.
10. Michael Brett and Elizabeth Fentress, *The Berbers* (Oxford, 1996), p. 15.
11. These Cretans should not be confused with the Greeks from Thera who founded the colony of Cyrene in 603 BC.
12. Lhote, *The Search for the Tassili Frescoes*, pp. 124–5.
13. Camps, 'Beginnings of pastoralism', p. 618.
14. *Ibid.*, pp. 620–1.
15. Oppian, *Cynegetica* I, 280–329, transl. A.W. Mair (Loeb Classical Library, London/Cambridge MA, 1928), p. 33.
16. Strabo, *The Geography*, 17.3.7, transl. H. L. Jones (Loeb Classical Library, London/Cambridge MA, 1932), Vol. VIII, p. 167.
17. *Ibid.*
18. Camps, 'Beginnings of pastoralism,' p. 622.
19. *Ibid.*, pp. 613–15.
20. *Ibid.*, p. 616.
21. *Ibid.*, p. 620.
22. Strabo, *Geography*, 17.3.19 (Vol. VIII, p. 197).
23. Aelian, *On the Characteristics of Animals*, III.2, transl. A. F. Scholfield (Loeb Classical Library, London/Cambridge MA, 1958), Vol. I, p. 161.
24. John Reader, *Africa: A Biography of the Continent* (London/New York, 1998), p. 266.
25. Lhote, *The Search for The Tassili Frescoes*, pp. 125–9.
26. Camps, 'Beginnings of pastoralism', p. 619.

CHAPTER 10 The Circulation of Horses in Historic Times

1. Edward Gibbon, *The History of the Decline and Fall of the Roman Empire* (Penguin edn, London/New York 1994), Vol. I, chapter 1, p. 43.
2. Polybius, *The Histories*, III, 117, transl. W. R. Paton (Loeb Classical Library, London/Cambridge MA, 1922), Vol. II, pp. 289–90.
3. Livy, XXI, XXII, transl. B. O. Foster (Loeb Classical Library, London/Cambridge MA, 1929), Vol. V, p. 63.
4. Plutarch, *Lives: Sertorius*, XII. 1–2, transl. B. Perrin (Loeb Classical Library, London/Cambridge MA, 1919), vol. VIII, p. 31.
5. Appian, *Roman History*, VIII, III, 13, transl. Horace White (Loeb Classical Library, London/Cambridge MA, 1912), Vol. I, p. 421.

6. Theodore Ayrault Dodge, *Hannibal* (New York, 1995), p. 150.
7. Polybius, *The Histories*, III, 33 (Vol. II, pp. 77–8).
8. *Ibid.*, III, 35 (pp. 83–4).
9. *Ibid.*, III, 43 (pp. 102–3).
10. *Ibid.*, III, 88 and 101 (pp. 215, 251).
11. Dodge, *Hannibal*, pp. 55–6.
12. *Ibid.*, p. 70.
13. Appian, *Roman History*, VI, X, 56 (Vol. I, p. 225).
14. Ibid., VI, X, 60 (Vol. I, pp. 231–2).
15. Ibid., VI, XII, 67 (Vol. I, p. 245).
16. Julius Caesar, *Civil Wars*, I, 38, transl. A. G. Peskett (Loeb Classical Library, London/Cambridge MA, 1914), pp. 58–9.
17. Julius Caesar, *The Gallic War*, VII, 55, trans. H. J. Edwards (Loeb Classical Library, London/ Cambridge MA, 1917), p. 459.
18. J. B. Bury, *The Invasion of Europe by the Barbarians* (London, 1928), p. 59.
19. R. C. Blockley, 'Warfare and diplomacy', pp. 411–36 in *The Cambridge Ancient History*, Vol. XIII (Cambridge, 1998), p. 424.
20. Norman Davies, *Europe: A History* (New York, 1996), p. 215.
21. Bernard F. Reilly, *The Medieval Spains* (Cambridge, 1993), p. 27.
22. Bury, *The Invasion of Europe by the Barbarians*, pp. 117–18.
23. Charles Oman, *A History of the Art of War in the Middle Ages*, 2 vols. (London, 1924), p. 21
24. E. Levi-Provençal, *Histoire de l'Espagne musulmane*, 3 vols. (Paris, 1999), Vol. I, p. 16.
25. Roger Collins, *Early Medieval Spain* (London/New York, 1995), p. 150.
26. Lévy-Provençal, *Histoire de l'Espagne musulmane*, Vol. I, p. 19.
27. Joseph F. O'Callaghan, *A History of Medieval Spain* (Cornell, 1983), pp. 95, 97, 100.
28. *Ibid.*, p. 118.
29. *Ibid.*, p. 119.
30. Reilly, *The Medieval Spains*, pp. 94, 99.
31. Hugh Kennedy, 'The Muslims in Europe', pp. 249–71 in *The New Cambridge Medieval History*, Vol. II (Cambridge, 1995), p. 267.

SOURCES OF ILLUSTRATIONS

The author and publishers wish to acknowledge the sources and thank the following for permission to reproduce the illustrations used in this book.

1.1, 3.1, 3.14, 3.16, 3.17, 3.19 Photographs by Jean Vertut, with kind permission of Mme Jean Vertut. 3.18 Reproduced from André Leroi-Gourhan, *Préhistoire de l'Art Occidental* (Paris, 1995), pl. 634, courtesy Mme Jean Vertut.

1.2, 1.6, 1.7 Reproduced from Baron Deisenberg, *L'Art de monter à cheval au description du ménage de sa perfection* (2 vols., Amsterdam and Leipzig, 1759).

1.5, 8.3, 8.5 Reproduced with permission from António Faustino de Carvalho, João Zilhão, Thierry Aubry, *Vale do Côa: Arte Rupestre e Pré-Historia* (Parque Arqueológico do Vale do Côa, Lisbon, 1996), p. 43.

1.8, 7.4, 7.13, 7.21 © Copyright The British Museum.

1.9, 1.10, 8.2, 8.7, 8.21, 8.22, 8.23 Collection of Arsênio Raposo Cordeiro, with kind permission.

1.11, 8.24 Photographs by VER Produções, reproduced from *O Cavalo e o Homem: Uma Relação Milenária*, The Rainer Daenhardt Collection at the Coudelaria de Alter (Coudelaria de Alter, Portugal, 2000), p. 22, no. 36, with permission of the Coudelaria de Alter.

2.8 Photograph and permission from the Institut für Ur- und Frühgeschichte und Archäologie des Mittelalters, University of Tübingen, Germany.

2.9, 2.10, 8.14, 9.9, 10.1 © Bob Langrish, with kind permission.

2.11 © Adrian Colston, with kind permission.

2.12, 2.15 Reprinted from Juan Antonio Garcia Castro, *Arte rupestre en España – Revista de Arqueologia* (Zugarto Ediciones s. a., Madrid, n. d.), pp. 99, 100.

2.13, 2.14, 10.4 © Coudelaria de Alter, Portugal. Serviço Nacional Coudélico, Ministério da Agricultura, Rural e das Pescas.

2.21 Horse statuettes, property of the author.

2.22, 7.2, 7.6, 7.9, 7.10, 7.11, 7.12, 7.14, 7.16, 7.17, 7.18, 7.19, 7.20, 7.22 From George Rawlinson, *The Five Great Monarchies of the Ancient Eastern* World, 4 vols. (London, 1862–5), Vols. II and III.

2.24 © Bruno Barbey/Magnum Photos.

3.3, 3.5, 3.11 Photo: French Ministry of Culture and Communication, Regional Direction for Cultural Affairs, Rhône-Alpes Region, Regional Department of Archaeology. We acknowledge their support in the preparation of this work.

3.4 Photo by the author.

3.12, 3.13, 8.1, 8.4 © Instituto Português de Arqueologia.

5.3 © Magnum Photos.

5.10 © Rijksmuseum van Oudheden (National Museum of Antiquities), Leiden, The Netherlands.

6.1, 8.6 Museo Arqueológico Nacional, Madrid. From Maria Luisa Cerdeño and Gerardo Vega, *La España de Altamira: Prehistoria en la penínsular Ibérica* (Historia de España 1, Ediciones Temas de Hoy s. a., Madrid, 1995), pp. 110, 139.

6.3 Photograph and permission from The National Museum of Denmark.

6.5, 7.15 Courtesy of the Oriental Institute of the University of Chicago.

7.1 Erich Lessing, The Arts & History Picture Library, akg-images London.

7.3 From Stuart Piggott, *Earliest Wheeled Transport* (Thames & Hudson, London, 1983), p. 25 illustration 5, with kind permission of Thames & Hudson.

7.24 Mike Andrews, The Ancient Art & Architecture Collection Ltd.

8.8, 8.12 From Ruy d'Andrade, *Alrededor del Caballo Español* (Lisbon, 1954), with kind permission of Snr Dna Maria Sommer d'Andrade.

8.9, 8.10 From Arsênio Raposo Cordeiro, *Cavalo Lusitano: O Filho do Vento* (Edições Inapa, Lisbon, 1989), with kind permission of the author.

8.11 From *O Cavalo Lusitano* (Interagro, Brazil, 1994).

8.15 Indiano XVIII, with kind permission of Lanys Kaye-Eddie, the Indiano Syndicate of the United States.

8.16, 8.18, 8.19, 8.25 Photographs by Pierre Rouillard, with kind permission, copyright La Caixa Fundacio, Barcelona. Published in AFAA, *Les Ibéres: catalogue d'exposition* (Paris, 1997).

8.17 From Richard J. Harrison, *Spain at the Dawn of History* (Thames & Hudson, 1988), p. 56, illustration 29, with kind permission of Thames & Hudson.

9.1, 9.2, 9.3, 9.4, 9.5, 9.6, 9.7, 9.8, 9.10, 9.11 Photographs by Maximilien Bruggman, with kind permission. Published in Henri J. Hugot and M. Bruggmann, *Sahara Art Rupestre* (Paris, 1999)

All maps drawn by Rodney Paull, based on maps appearing in the following works:

Figs. 3.2, 5.1, 5.5 *The Oxford Illustrated History of Prehistoric Europe* edited by Barry Cunliffe (Oxford University Press, Oxford, 1994); Figs. 2.17, 2.19 Miklos Jankovich, *They Rode into Europe* (London, 1971), pp. 45 and 41; Fig. 5.2 Katie Demakopoulou, Christiane Eluève, Jørgen Jensen, Albrecht Jockenhövel and Jean-Pierre Moher, *Gods and Heroes of the European Bronze Age* (Thames & Hudson, London, 1999), p. 114; Figs. 5.4, 5.8 Maria Luisa Cerdeño and Gerardo Vega, *La España de Altamira: Prehistoria en la península Ibérica* (Historia de España 1, Ediciones Temas de Hoy s. a., Madrid, 1995), p. 83; Fig. 5.6 Chris Scarre, *Exploring Prehistoric Europe* (Oxford University Press, Oxford/New York, 1998), p. 10; Figs. 5.7, 6.6, 7.8 William H. McNeill, *A World History* (New York, 1967), pp. 35, 54 and 45; Figs. 5.9, 6.7 J. P. Mallory, *In Search of the Indo-Europeans* (London, 1991), pp. 106, 105; Fig. 6.2 G. Camps, *La Préhistoire: A la Récherche du Paradis Perdu* (Paris, 1982), p. 366; Fig. 6.4

Stuart Piggott, *Ancient Europe* (Edinburgh, 1965), p. 101; Fig. 7.7 Stuart Piggott, *Earliest Wheeled Transport* (Thames & Hudson, London, 1983), p. 59 illustration 27; Fig. 8.20 Jaime Alvar, *De Argantonio a los Romanos* (Historia de España 2, Ediciones Temas de Hoy, Madrid, 1995), p. 15; Fig. 10.2 Arthur Ferril, *The Fall of the Roman Empire* (London, Thames & Hudson, 1986), p. 100; Fig. 10.3 Michael Grant, *The Fall of the Roman Empire* (London, Phoenix Giant, 1996), map 3.

Drawings by Rodney Paull based on photographs and illustrations appearing in the following works:

Fig. 1.3 *The Oxford Illustrated History of Prehistoric Europe* edited by Barry Cunliffe (Oxford University Press, Oxford, 1994); Fig. 1.4 H. Breuil, *Four Hundred Centuries of Cave Art* (Montignac, 1952); Fig. 2.1 Reed Wicander and James S. Munroe, *Historical Geology* (St Paul, Minnesota, 1989); Fig. 2.2 George Gaylord Simpson, *Horses* (New York, 1957), p. 114; Figs. 2.4, 2.16, 4.3, 4.4, 4.6, 8.13 Ruy d'Andrade, *Alrededor del Caballo Español* (Lisbon, 1954); Fig. 2.18 Zadneprovsky, from Sandor Bökönyi, 'Data on Iron Age horses of central and eastern Europe', Mecklenberg Collection, part I, *Bulletin of the American School of Prehistoric Research* 25 (1968), p. 45; Fig. 2.20 F. Hančar, *Das Pferd in prähistoischer Zeit* (Vienna, 1956); Fig. 2.23 S. I. Rudenko, *Nasedelnia Gorskaia Altaia* (1953); Figs. 3.6, 3.7, 3.8, 3.9, 3.1 0 André Leroi-Gourhan, *Préhistoire de l'Art Occidental* (Citadelles & Mazenod, Paris, 1995), pp. 597–9; Fig. 3.15 Peter J. Ucko and Andrée Rosenfeld, *Palaeolithic Cave Art* (London, 1967), pp. 154–5 after Leroi-Gourhan; Fig. 4.1 Obermaier & Wernert (1919); Figs. 4.2, 4.5 Camón Aznar, *Las Artes y los Pueblos de la España primitiva* (Madrid, 1954), figs. 352, 361; Fig. 7.5 J. G. Landels, *Engineering in the Ancient World* (University of California, 1978), p. 179.

Drawings by Maggie Raynor based on illustrations appearing in the following works:

Figs. 2.3, 2.5, 2.6, 2.7 Hermann Ebhardt, 'Ponies und Pferde im Röntgenbild nebst einigen stammesgeschichtlichen Bemerkungen dazu', *Säugetierkundliche Mitteilungen*, 10 JHg, BLV, Munich, as depicted in Hardy Oelke, *Born Survivors on the Eve of Destruction* (1997).

BIBLIOGRAPHY

Aelian. *On the Characteristics of Animals,* Vol. I, transl. A. F. Scholfield (Loeb Classical Library, London/Cambridge MA, 1958)

d'Andrade, Ruy. *Alrededor del Caballo Español* (Lisbon, 1954)

Appian. *Roman History,* Vol. I, transl. Horace White (Loeb Classical Library, London/Cambridge MA, 1912)

Arrian. *History of Alexander,* Vol. II, transl. P. A. Brunt (Loeb Classical Library, London/Cambridge MA, 1983)

Blázquez, José Mar'a. *Fen'cios, Griegos y Cartagineses en Occidente* (Madrid, 1992)

Blockley, R.C. 'Warfare and diplomacy', in *The Cambridge Ancient History,* Vol. XIII (Cambridge, 1998)

Bökönyi, Sandor. *The Przevalsky Horse* (London, 1974)

Bökönyi, Sandor. 'Data on Iron Age horses of central and eastern Europe', Mecklenberg Collection, part I, *Bulletin of the American School of Prehistoric Research* 25 (1968)

Braudel, Fernand. *The Mediterranean in the Ancient World* (London, 2001)

Brett, Michael and Elizabeth Fentress. *The Berbers* (Oxford, 1996)

Bury, J. B. *The Invasion of Europe by the Barbarians* (London, 1928)

Caesar, Julius. *Civil Wars,* transl. A. G. Peskett (Loeb Classical Library, London/Cambridge MA, 1914)

Caesar, Julius. *The Gallic War,* transl. H. J. Edwards (Loeb Classical Library, London/Cambridge MA, 1917)

Camps, G. 'Beginnings of pastoralism and cultivation in north-west Africa and the Sahara: origins of the Berbers', pp. 548–623 in *The Cambridge History of Africa*, Vol. I (Cambridge, 1982)

Camps, G. *La Préhistoire: A la Récherche du Paradis Perdu* (Paris, 1982)

Casson, Lionel. *The Ancient Mariners: Seafarers and Sea Fighters of the Mediterranean in Ancient Times* (Princeton, 1991)

Cavalli-Sforza, L. Luca. 'Genetic evidence supporting Marija Gimbutas' work on the origin of Indo-European People', in *From the Realm of the Ancestors: an Anthology in Honor of Marija Gimbutas*, ed. Joan Marler (Manchester CT, 1997)

Clabby, John. *The Natural History of the Horse* (London, 1976)

Cordeiro, Arsênio Raposo. *Cavalo Lusitano: O Filho do Vento* (Lisbon 1989)

Collins, Roger. *Early Medieval Spain: Unity in Diversity,* 400–1000 (London/New York, 1995)

Collins, Roger. 'Spain: the northern kingdoms and the Basques', pp. 272–89 in *The New Cambridge Medieval History,* Vol. II (Cambridge, 1995)

Collins, Roger. 'The Western kingdoms', pp. 112–34 in *The Cambridge Ancient History*, Vol. XIV (Cambridge, 2000)

Culican, W. 'Phoenicia and Phoenician colonization', pp. 461–546 in *The Cambridge Ancient History*, Vol. III.2 (Cambridge, 1991)

Cunliffe, Barry. *The Ancient Celts* (Oxford, 1997)

Davies, Norman. *Europe: A History* (London/New York, 1996)

Diaz-Andreu, Margarita and Simon Keay (eds.), *The Archaeology of Iberia: The Dynamics of Change* (London, 1997)

Diodorus Siculus. *Library of History,* Vol. VI, transl. C. H. Oldfather, and Vol. VIII, transl. C. Bradford Welles (Loeb Classical Library, London/Cambridge MA, 1954 and 1963)

Dodge, Theodore Ayrault. *Hannibal* (New York, 1995)

Drews, Robert. *The End of the Bronze Age* (Princeton, 1993)

Equine Research Publications. *Equine Genetics and Selection Procedures* (Texas, 1978)

Galán, Manuel Bendala. 'La civilización tartésica', pp. 595–642 in *História General de Espa–a y América,* Vol. I.1 (Madrid, 1985).

Gernet, Jacques. *A History of Chinese Civilization,* transl. J. R. Foster and Charles Hartman (2nd edn, Cambridge, 1996)

Gibbon, Edward. *The History of the Decline and Fall of the Roman Empire* (Penguin edn, London/New York 1994)

Grote, George. *A History of Greece,* 10 vols. (London, 1872)

Groves, Colin P. *Horses, Asses and Zebras in the Wild* (Newton Abbot, 1974)

Harding, Anthony. 'Reformation in Barbarian Europe 1300–1600 BC', pp. 304–35 in *The Oxford Illustrated History of Prehistoric Europe,* ed. Barry Cunliffe (Oxford, 1994)

Hedin, Sven. *The Silk Road* (London, 1938)

Herodotus. *The Histories,* transl. Robin Waterfield (Oxford/New York, 1998)

Homer. *The Iliad,* transl. Robert Fagles (New York, 1990).

Homer. *The Iliad,* Vol. II, transl. A. T. Murray (Loeb Classical Library, London/Cambridge MA, 1999)

Homer. *The Odyssey,* transl. Robert Fagles (New York, 1996).

Hucker, Charles O. *China's Imperial Past* (London, 1975)

Jankovich, Miklos. *They Rode into Europe* (London, 1971)

Keegan, John. *A History of Warfare* (London, 1993)

Kennedy, Hugh. 'The Muslims in Europe', pp. 249–71 in *The New Cambridge Medieval History,* Vol. II (Cambridge, 1995)

Kuhrt, Amélie. *The Ancient Near East,* Vol. I (London, 1995)

Le Quellec, Jean-Loïc. *Art Rupestre et Préhistoire du Sahara* (Paris, 1998)

Leroi-Gourhan, André. 'Histoire Universelle', in *Encyclopédie de la Pléiade* (Paris, 1956)

Leroi-Gourhan, André. *Préhistoire de l'Art Occidental* (Paris, 1995)

Levi-Provencal, E. *Histoire de l'Espagne musulmane,* 3 vols. (Paris, 1999)

Lhote, Henri. *The Search for the Tassili Frescoes* (New York, 1959)

Livy. Vol. V, transl. B. O. Foster (Loeb Classical Library, London/Cambridge MA, 1929)

McNeill, William H. *The Rise of the West* (Chicago, 1963)

Malbran-Labat, Florence. L'Armée et *L'Organisation Militaire de l'Assyrie* (Paris, 1982).

Mallory, J. P. *In Search of the Indo-Europeans* (London, 1991).

Mellars, Paul. 'The Upper Palaeolithic revolution', pp. 42–78 in *The Oxford Illustrated History of Prehistoric Europe*, ed. Barry Cunliffe (Oxford, 1994)

Mithen, Steven J. 'The Mesolithic Age', pp. 79–135 in *The Oxford Illustrated History of Prehistoric Europe*, ed. Barry Cunliffe (Oxford, 1994)

National Archaeological and Ethnological Museum of Lisbon. *Portugal das Origens à Época Romana,* ed. Francisco Alves (Lisbon, 1989)

O'Callaghan, Joseph F. *A History of Medieval Spain* (Cornell, 1983)

Oelke, Hardy. *Born Survivors on the Eve of Destruction* (1997)

Oman, Charles. *A History of the Art of War in the Middle Ages,* 2 vols. (London, 1924)

Oppian. *Cynegetica,* transl. A. W. Mair (Loeb Classical Library, London/Cambridge MA, 1928).

Piggott, Stuart. *Ancient Europe* (Edinburgh, 1965)

Piggott, Stuart. *Wagon, Chariot and Carriage: Symbol and Status in the History of Transport* (London/New York, 1992)

Plutarch. *Lives,* vol. VIII, transl. B. Perrin (Loeb Classical Library, London/Cambridge MA, 1919)

Polomé, Edgar. 'The impact of Marija Gimbutas on Indo-European Studies', pp. 102–7 in *From the Realm of the Ancestors: an Anthology in Honor of Marija Gimbutas*, ed. Joan Marler (Manchester CT, 1997)

Polybius. *The Histories,* vol. II, transl. W. R. Paton (Loeb Classical Library, London/Cambridge MA, 1922)

Rawlinson, George. *The Five Great Monarchies of the Ancient Eastern World,* 4 vols. (London, 1862–5)

Reader, John. *Africa: A Biography of the Continent* (London/New York, 1998)

Reilly, Bernard F. *The Medieval Spains* (Cambridge, 1993)

Renfrew, Colin. *Archaeology and Language: The Puzzle of Indo-European Origins* (London, 1987)

Rozoy, Jean-Georges. 'The Mesolithic way of life', in *L'Europe des Derniers Chasseurs,* ed. André Thévenin (Paris, 1999)

Rudgley, Richard. *The Lost Civilizations of the Stone Age* (London/New York, 1999)

Sandars, N. K. *Prehistoric Art in Europe* (Harmondsworth, 1985).

Scarre, Chris. *Exploring Prehistoric Europe* (Oxford/New York, 1998)

Schulten, Adolf. *Tartessos: Ein Beitrag zur ältesten Geschichte des Westens* (Hamburg, 1922); Spanish edn (Madrid 1972)

Sergent, Bernard. *Les Indo-Européens: histoire, langues, mythes* (Paris, 1995)

Shennan, Stephen. 'Ideology, change and the European Early Bronze Age', pp. 155–61 in *Symbolic and Structural Archaeology*, ed. I. Hodder (Cambridge, 1982)

Sherratt, Andrew. *Economy and Society in Prehistoric Europe: Changing Perspectives* (Edinburgh/Princeton, 1997)

Sherratt, Andrew. 'The emergence of élites: earlier Bronze Age Europe 2500–1300 BC', pp. 244–76 in *The Oxford Illustrated History of Prehistoric Europe*, ed. Barry Cunliffe (Oxford, 1994)

Simões de Abreu, Mila. 'O universo da arte rupestre: Arte paleol'tica', pp. 31–46 in *História da Arte Portuguesa*, Vol. I, ed. Paulo Pereira, 3 vols. (Lisbon, 1995)

Strabo. *The Geography*, Vols. II, III, V, and VIII, transl. H. L. Jones (Loeb Classical Library, London/Cambridge MA, 1923, 1924, 1928, and 1932).

Ucko, Peter J. and Andrée Rosenfeld, *Palaeolithic Cave Art* (London, 1967).

Uerpmann, H. P. *Die Domestikation des Pferdes im Chalkolithikum West und Mittleeuropas* (Madrider Mitteilungen, 1990).

UNESCO. *General History of Africa*, Vol. I, *Methodology and African Prehistory*, ed. J. Ki-Zerbo (Abridged Edition, London/Berkeley CA, 1990)

Walsh, Richard J. (ed.). *The Adventures of Marco Polo* (New York, 1948)

Xenephon. *Hellenica*, Vol. I, transl. Carleton L. Brownson (Loeb Classical Library, London/Cambridge MA, 1968)

INDEX

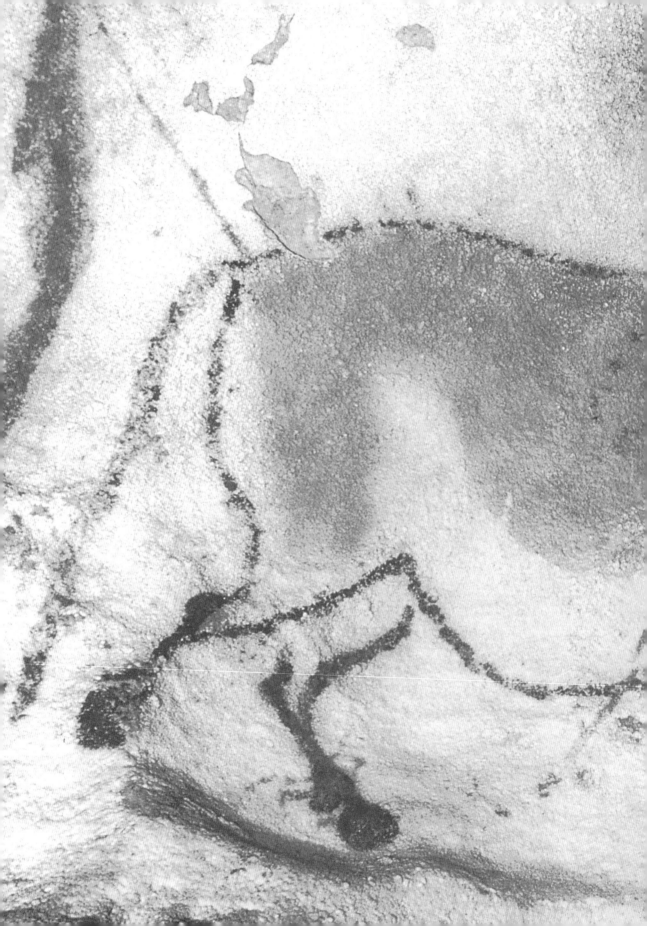